Diabetes
CREATE YOUR PLATE

MEAL
PREP
COOKBOOK

Diabetes
CREATE YOUR PLATE

MEAL PREP
COOKBOOK

100 Delicious Plate-Method Recipes

TOBY AMIDOR
MS, RD, CDN, FAND

Library and Archives Canada Cataloguing in Publication
Title: Diabetes create your plate meal prep cookbook : 100 delicious plate-method recipes /
  Toby Amidor MS, RD, CDN, FAND.
Other titles: Meal prep cookbook
Names: Amidor, Toby, author.
Description: Includes index.
Identifiers: Canadiana 20210350474 | ISBN 9780778807070 (softcover)
Subjects: LCSH: Diabetes—Diet therapy—Recipes. | LCGFT: Cookbooks.
Classification: LCC RC662 .A45 2022 | DDC 641.5/6314—dc23

Disclaimer

The recipes in this book have been carefully tested by our kitchen and our tasters. To the best of our knowledge, they are safe and nutritious for ordinary use and users. For those people with food or other allergies, or who have special food requirements or health issues, please read the suggested contents of each recipe carefully and determine whether or not they may create a problem for you. All recipes are used at the risk of the consumer.

We cannot be responsible for any hazards, loss or damage that may occur as a result of any recipe use.

For those with special needs, allergies, requirements or health problems, in the event of any doubt, please contact your medical adviser prior to the use of any recipe.

At the time of publication, all URLs referenced link to existing websites. Robert Rose Inc. is not responsible for maintaining, and does not endorse the content of, any website or content not created by Robert Rose Inc.

DESIGN AND PRODUCTION: Kevin Cockburn/PageWave Graphics Inc.
PHOTOGRAPHY, FOOD STYLING AND PROP STYLING: Ashley Lima
EDITOR: Kate Bolen
PROOFREADER: Karen Levy
INDEXER: Ken Della Penta
ADDITIONAL IMAGES: © Getty Images (pages 37, 56, 68, 82, 94, 110, 139, 169, 189, 205, 207, 267)

Published by Robert Rose Inc.
120 Eglinton Avenue East, Suite 800, Toronto, Ontario, Canada M4P 1E2
Tel: (416) 322-6552 Fax: (416) 322-6936
www.robertrose.ca

Printed and bound in China

1 2 3 4 5 6 7 8 9 CP 30 29 28 27 26 25 24 23 22

To my three amazing children,
Schoen, Ellena and Micah.
I love you.

CONTENTS

INTRODUCTION

Finding the time to get healthy meals on the table during the work and school week feels like an impossible task. As a working mother of three kids, I can absolutely relate. Trying to get my work completed, driving my kids to their evening activities, helping with homework, getting in some exercise and also getting a healthy meal on the table is no easy feat. As a person with diabetes, you have added challenges, including ensuring your plate is balanced for every meal and every snack. However, you can do it and this cookbook will help guide you! The main goal of meal prepping is to alleviate some of the stress that comes with preparing meals and snacks the day you eat them. Instead, by preparing and planning meals and snacks ahead of time, you'll help save about 45 minutes from your busy weeknight so you can spend time doing something else (even getting to bed earlier!).

One of the best ways to create new habits that stick is to start slowly — and this applies to meal prepping too. Instead of saying, "I am going to meal prep every single meal and snack this week," start with only two or three recipes. Then as you get comfortable cooking those dishes, work your way up to four, five or more. How slowly or quickly you go is up to you and your schedule. According to experts on behavioral changes, once you continue to do the task for at least six months it then becomes a habit. That is the goal with meal prepping — to make it a sustainable habit to help make your life easier and healthier. So how will you start?

This cookbook is divided into three parts, and it will guide you step-by-step. Starting in part 1, you will read about the concepts of successful meal prepping, specifically for a person with diabetes, in chapter 1. A person with diabetes is also at high risk for foodborne illness and that is why chapter 2 is so important to review. It's all about food safety practices that should be followed when meal prepping in order to ensure the food is safe to eat. Chapter 3 then reviews the Diabetes Plate Method, where you'll learn to just fill half your plate with non-starchy vegetables, one-quarter of your plate with carbohydrate foods (like grains, dairy, fruit or starchy vegetables) and one-quarter of your plate with lean protein. And this method translates seamlessly to meal prepping. This is great news because meal prepping can come in handy to get healthy, diabetes-friendly meals on the table in a flash — especially during those very busy workweeks.

Once you have read part 1, you can get into the kitchen and start cooking. Part 2 of the book, "Meal Prep Plans to Create Your Plate," has five meal plans for you to follow. The first meal plan starts with only three recipes and then you can work your way up once you are comfortable with that. If you have a job that provides your lunch, you may not need to meal prep all your meals — so Meal Plan 1 or 2 may be right for you. Use the meal plans however best suits your lifestyle.

Once you get the hang of meal prepping, you can swap in recipes or build your own meal plan based on the existing plans. That is where part 3 of the book comes in: the recipes. In this recipe section of the cookbook, you'll find recipes for breakfast, snacks, main soups and salads, lunch and dinner mains, grain and vegetable sides and then dressings, condiments and sauces that you can always mix and match as you wish.

Each recipe is a make-ahead meal designed for prepping in advance for the coming week. You will find packaging instructions, suggestions to complete your plate and storage information so that you can grab-and-go all week long. In every recipe you'll also find the nutrition information, and most recipes also have a "Toby's Tip" where I provide a cooking, shopping, substitution or other tip that may be useful to you.

Remember, meal prep at your own pace. Meal prepping takes time to learn and feel comfortable with, and I am confident that you can do it! Now get started on this wonderful journey of meal prepping and enjoy the delicious food you are about to make.

Happy, healthy meal prepping!

RECIPE LABELS

Each recipe will include any of the following eight labels.

 COMPLETE PLATE The recipe is a complete meal on its own and no other food or food groups are needed.

 FREEZER-FRIENDLY Recipes with this icon can be frozen for up to 2 months.

 ONE POT/PAN RECIPE The recipe is made using one pot or pan (or only a blender for a smoothie).

 30 MINUTES OR LESS The total time needed to make this recipe, including preparation and cooking time, is 30 minutes or less.

 VEGETARIAN The recipe includes only plant-based foods, like grains, fruits, vegetable, nuts, seeds and legumes; milk or other dairy products; or eggs.

 VEGAN Only plant-based foods are used in this recipe, like grains, fruits, vegetables, nuts, seeds and legumes. There are also no animal by-products, such as honey, used.

 DAIRY-FREE There are no milk or dairy foods in this recipe.

 GLUTEN-FREE There is no gluten in this recipe.

PART
1

HOW TO MEAL PREP FOR PEOPLE WITH DIABETES

CHAPTER 1

AN INTRODUCTION TO MEAL PREPPING

Meal prepping is the concept of preparing whole meals, several servings of a meal or snacks ahead of time. When it is time for a meal or snack, your food has already been portioned out and all you need to do is grab the container, heat (sometimes) and eat. An important thing to remember is that you do not need to prep every single dish for an entire week. Even preparing two or three dishes can help save you prepping and cooking time during a busy day. Meal prepping is individual to your schedule and how much time you want to spend in the kitchen on your meal prep day. Some weeks you may have more time to prepare more meals, while other weeks you may only be able to do a few meals. Either way, always feel great about whatever amount of meal prepping you do! This cookbook can help you, as a person with diabetes, perfect your meal prepping skills with meals that are suitable for your lifestyle.

In the pages ahead, we will take the concept of meal prepping and apply it to a diabetes-friendly eating plan, specifically in line with the Diabetes Plate Method. This chapter will provide you with an introduction to meal prepping.

THE BENEFITS OF MEAL PREPPING

Many folks ask me how I am able to get a healthy meal on the table during the busiest of workweeks — and meal prepping is the answer. There are numerous benefits to meal prepping.

- **SAVE MONEY AND REDUCE FOOD WASTE:** When you meal prep, you plan all your recipes in advance. This means you're gathering recipes and making shopping lists of the ingredients you need, which includes checking to see if you have ingredients on hand to avoid overbuying and wasting ingredients. Also, each recipe calls for specific portions, including for more expensive ingredients like meat, chicken and seafood. You can purchase exact amounts or come home and portion out the meat, chicken or seafood you need and freeze the rest for another week.

- **SAVE TIME DURING BUSY DAYS:** The last thing you want to do on a busy night is go to the store, pick up ingredients and then chop and cook. When you meal prep for the upcoming workweek on Sunday, this means all you need to do is heat and eat. This can save you at least 45 minutes, if not longer! Now you'll have be able to spend more time with your kids, significant other or just focus on much-needed "me time."

- **CREATE EASY, BALANCED, DIABETES-FRIENDLY PLATES:** When you meal prep using the Diabetes Plate Method, all your meals will be balanced. Your container will be filled so that half has low-carb vegetables; one-quarter has grains, starchy vegetables, yogurt or fruit; and one-quarter has lean protein. When you are ready to eat, you will have a diabetes-friendly, portion-controlled, balanced meal right at your fingertips. There is no carbohydrate counting or measuring that needs to be done.

- **CAN HELP BETTER CONTROL YOUR BLOOD SUGAR:** All recipes in this cookbook are appropriate for people with diabetes and have nutritional information available. In addition, by using the Diabetes Plate Method in your meal prepping, you will have a container with the appropriate amount of carbohydrates for a person with diabetes. Oftentimes when people are very busy and cannot cook dinner, they stop by the nearest fast-food joint and pick up whatever is available. This could potentially wreak havoc on your blood sugar. By meal prepping in advance, you will have balanced, healthy, diabetes-friendly meals ready to go, which can help keep your blood sugar under control, even on busy days.

- **HELP REDUCE WEEKDAY STRESS:** When it comes to dinner, many folks do not plan in advance, but scrambling at the last minute to cook something that is diabetes-friendly can be stressful. It can also be strenuous to worry if you are eating appropriately to manage your blood sugar. When you meal prep, this stress is alleviated because you have done some advance planning and already prepared well-portioned diabetes-friendly meals.

- **IMPROVE MULTITASKING SKILLS:** When meal prepping, there are a few tasks you will learn to do at the same time. For example, if you are baking a sheet-pan dinner, you have 10 or 15 minutes to whip up the dressing for the salad or chop the vegetables. Organizing your time in a way where you are multitasking is a skill that takes time to learn. It is important to start your meal prepping journey with only a few recipes and work your way up. The more you practice, the better you will get — and the more recipes you will feel comfortable preparing in one day.

10 DO'S AND DON'TS OF MEAL PREPPING

1 **DO BUILD YOUR WAY UP.** In the beginning, do not get intimidated by those Instagram meal preppers who showcase the ten recipes they just made. If you're a newbie, it is okay to start slow. Even if you have meal prepped before, you don't want to overdo it either. Start with as many recipes as you can handle, maybe two or three, and slowly build your way up to how much you are comfortable preparing.

2 **DON'T GO FOOD SHOPPING WITHOUT A SHOPPING LIST.** The last thing you want to do is go back and forth to the market because you forgot a few ingredients. Once you select your recipes, create a shopping list and start with the produce section. Having a set plan on how to food shop will minimize the chance of forgetting an ingredient, and it will help speed up your shopping experience.

3 **DO CHECK YOUR PANTRY BEFORE WRITING YOUR SHOPPING LIST.** Meal prepping is supposed to help you keep food costs under control. When creating your shopping list, do not rely on your memory to determine whether you have an ingredient. How many times have you thought you were out of onion powder, for example, only to realize you already have two containers and just bought a third? Always check your pantry, refrigerator and freezer before jotting down ingredients on your grocery list in order to prevent buying ingredients you already have.

4 **DON'T THINK YOU HAVE TO PREP ONLY ONE DAY A WEEK.** I find that on Sundays it is tough for me to spend an entire day in the kitchen because my kids have many activities. If you find that your Saturdays and Sundays are pretty booked, then you can prep two days a week. Take a few hours over the weekend and then again on a lighter weeknight (for me that is Wednesday). Meal prepping is supposed to make your life easier, so determine what works best for you.

5 **DO INDIVIDUALIZE RECIPES.** If, for example, you do not like the broccoli in a recipe, feel free to select another low-carb vegetable you enjoy instead. The same goes for the grain recommendations. If you want to swap out brown rice for quinoa, go for it! Just be mindful of filling half your container with low-carb vegetables; one-quarter with whole grains, starchy vegetables, yogurt or fruit; and one-quarter with lean protein.

6   **DON'T OVERPREP.** As much as you may want to impress your neighbors or social media followers, do not prepare more than you need for a week. Your freezer has limited storage space, and you may end up eating the extra food or, worse, tossing it! It will take a little practice, but prepare only what you need for the week ahead.

7   **DO USE YOUR FREEZER.** Some meals freeze well, like stews, chilis and soups. If you have enough space, make a double batch of a freezer-friendly dish and store half for a busy week when you have minimal time to meal prep.

8   **DON'T LEAVE EVERYTHING UNTIL THE LAST MINUTE.** One of the most important tasks of meal prepping is advance planning. Plan out your meals, time to go food shopping and time to prep, cook and pack food. Leaving everything for the last minute will sabotage your meal prepping efforts, as you will not have enough time to do everything.

9   **DO PORTION YOUR FOOD BEFORE STORING.** A big part of meal prepping is portioning out your food before storing it. This is especially important, because the balance of food in your meal prep container can help manage your blood sugar. If you portion your food as you eat it, you may end up giving yourself unequal portions and end up with not enough food. Divide your meals evenly before you store them.

10   **DON'T PREP WITHOUT ENOUGH CONTAINERS.** Before starting your meal prep journey, purchase enough meal prep containers for the week, and have additional containers for freezing extra food. If you don't prepare your containers in advance, you will end up not being able to pre-portion your food for the week. See page 20 for what to consider when purchasing meal prep storage containers.

SELECTING STORAGE CONTAINERS

Before beginning your meal prep journey, make sure you have enough containers to get started. Meal prep containers are single-serving containers large enough to store one meal, and it is also helpful to have tiny containers for dressings or toppings that get added right before eating on hand. Snack containers are smaller, and you should have enough of those as well. You will also need a few extra meal prep containers to store leftover portions, which you can freeze or serve to a friend or family member. Proper storage containers protect the flavor, texture and color of the food. They also reduce the exposure of the food to air (or oxygen), which helps maintain the quality of the food. If you have never purchased any single-serving meal prep containers before, I suggest trying out a few brands and reading the online reviews to see which will work best for you.

You also want to label your storage containers with the contents and use-by date. Masking tape and a Sharpie is the easiest way to get that done and will also work well on single-use plastic bags or reusable storage bags.

Here is what to consider when purchasing containers.

- **SINGLE COMPARTMENT OR MULTIPLE COMPARTMENTS:** Do you mind your food touching on your plate or do you prefer each food stay separated? Some meals may have multiple components, such as a piece of baked chicken breast, steamed broccoli and brown rice, while other meals may be an all-in-one combination, like One-Pot Ground Turkey with Vegetables and Pasta (page 206). This means you may want some containers with a single compartment and some with multiple compartments (especially if you don't like your foods touching). I like a combination of both, but it is a personal decision.

- **STACKABLE AND NESTABLE:** Your freezer, refrigerator and pantry have a limited amount of space. You can make the most out of that space by purchasing meal prep containers that easily stack over one another. You may also want to consider a meal prep container set that is nestable, so when you store them in your cabinet or pantry they take up less space.

- **MATERIAL:** Meal prep containers are made from a variety of materials, including glass, silicone, metal and plastic. Choose whatever is best suited for you and your lifestyle. If you ride on the train or take a bus to work, glass containers may seem heavy. A plastic container may be a sturdier and lighter choice. You may like the metal meal prep containers, but if you plan on reheating your meals in the microwave at work then it's probably not the right choice.

- **LEAKPROOF:** The last thing you want is to take the time to meal prep a delicious soup or saucy dish, and bring it to work only to find out that it spilled. Before you purchase your containers for solid food (like salads) and liquid food (like soups), be sure to carefully read the reviews for any issues with spillage. You may also want to test out your new meal prep containers. If you go to work on a bike, fill your container and take it for a ride and see how it does. If you drive in, see how it does when you have a filled container sitting in the car.

- **BPA-FREE:** No matter which type of container you choose, you want them to be BPA-free. Bisephenol A (BPA) is an industrial chemical that has been around since the 1960s. The Food and Drug Administration (FDA) concluded that BPA found in canned goods and storage containers is safe in small amounts. When it comes to meal prep containers, most manufacturers do label them BPA-free, so all you need to do is read the label. Avoid using plastic containers that contain the recycle codes 3 or 7, which indicate the items may contain BPA. Glass containers do not contain BPA.

- **OTHER QUALITIES:** If you plan on freezing some meals, you want to make sure the containers are freezer-safe. If you plan on reheating in the microwave or oven, then they should be microwave- or oven-safe. If you have a dishwasher and want to save time, many meal prep containers can be washed on the top rack, but check the label to see whether it is dishwasher-safe. All containers will have instructions on how to clean it, so give those a read too.

FAVORITE MEAL PREP CONTAINERS

There are many meal prep containers available, so do your research by checking online reviews and asking fellow meal preppers their favorite containers to use. Whatever you choose to purchase, you will want to test them out, so check the return policy before purchasing in case you decide to return them. The following are the five meal prep containers I like using, which you can use as a starting point.

- **BALL MASON JAR COMPANY GLASS JARS:** Glass mason jars make fabulous meal prep containers and come in all sorts of sizes. They are perfect for salads, soups, stews and other meals that can easily be placed in a jar. I prefer wide-mouth jars so the food is easy to scoop out. A canning funnel is also helpful for packing them. They are safe to place in the refrigerator, freezer and dishwasher.

- **PREP NATURALS GLASS MEAL PREP CONTAINERS:** These portion-controlled containers are airtight and come with and without compartments. They have locking lids that help prevent leaking. The containers are microwave-, oven- and freezer-safe, but the lids are not. The entire container, including the lid, is dishwasher safe. Lids, however, should be washed in the top rack only.

- **RUBBERMAID BRILLIANCE STORAGE SET:** This meal prep storage set comes as a 10-piece and up to 44-piece set. These plastic leakproof, airtight storage containers are BPA-free and help keep foods fresh and secure. The containers are clear like glass, so you can see inside. They are also odor and stain resistant, and have built-in vents under the latches that allow splatter-resistant microwave heating with the lid on. They are also stackable and safe in the dishwasher.

- **ENTHER MEAL PREP CONTAINERS:** These plastic meal prep bento boxes are available as single compartment and multi-compartment boxes, and they are microwave-safe and BPA-free. They are also dishwasher-safe and stackable for easy storage.

- **OXO GOOD GRIPS SMART SEAL LEAKPROOF FOOD STORAGE CONTAINER SET:** These airtight food storage containers have four locking tabs to secure the leakproof lids. The containers are made from BPA-free plastic and are microwave-, freezer- and dishwasher-safe.

CHAPTER 2

FOOD SAFETY WHEN MEAL PREPPING

When meal prepping, you are dealing with a large amount of food at once. You may usually shop for two or three recipes, but now you are shopping for more than that. This means there is an increased risk of mishandling the food, which can lead to food contamination and foodborne illness. Fortunately, the steps you need to take to ensure food safety are simple, easy to incorporate and hopefully most of the same ones you are currently taking at home.

When we talk about food safety, it is important to remember that people with diabetes are at a higher risk of foodborne illness. Diabetes affects various organs and systems within the body in ways that make them more susceptible to infections. For example, high glucose levels in the blood interfere with the ability of white blood cells to fight off infection, which increases the risk of contracting a foodborne illness. Also, diabetes may cause the stomach to produce low amounts of digestive acid, and the nerves in the stomach may not move food through your gastrointestinal tract as quickly. When food is in the stomach longer than necessary, bacteria can begin to multiply. If the levels of unhealthy bacteria in your stomach become too high, it can lead to foodborne illness. Lastly, if diabetes affects your kidney function, the kidneys may hold on to harmful microorganisms that can potentially make you sick. Luckily, if you follow these simple steps every time you handle food, from purchasing to cooking to storing, it can help minimize the risk of foodborne illness.

FOOD SAFETY DURING GROCERY SHOPPING

The market is the first place where you have control over the food you bring home. You want to carefully select, pack and transport food from the market to your home to keep it safe to eat. For a safe shopping experience, start by shopping the produce section, then the non-perishable items and finally select the refrigerated and frozen items last. Always read the dates on the labels to ensure quality and freshness of the food you are purchasing. Stop at the deli counter last and place the deli meats near the cold foods in your grocery cart. If you're picking up hot food, then place it away from the cold food. The fresh fruit and vegetables should be on top of other foods in your cart, which means you may need to shift them as you shop. This can help prevent heavier foods from damaging your fresh produce, and also prevent any raw meats from dripping onto your fresh produce. It is a good idea to put raw meat, poultry, fish and seafood in plastic bags before placing them in your cart.

When packing your food at the checkout counter, place raw meat, poultry and seafood in separate bags from foods that are ready-to-eat like fresh fruits and vegetables. Any chemicals, such as cleaning products, should be placed in bags separate from any food. If you use reusable grocery bags, make sure to wash them regularly.

If you plan on running errands for more than 30 minutes after going food shopping, then bring a cooler with ice packs for perishable foods. Perishable food must be refrigerated within 2 hours, and if the temperature is over 90°F (32°C), it must be refrigerated within 1 hour. The temperature of refrigerated foods can increase up to 10°F (6°C) on a typical drive home. In hot weather, keep perishable food in the air-conditioned car and not in the hot trunk. Once you get home, all perishable food should be refrigerated or frozen immediately.

STORING

Your refrigerator is a temporary way to keep food safe to eat. Although you can store food in your freezer for long periods of time, there are recommended storage times for your frozen food to help maintain the quality of the food. When storing your food, label it with the contents and use-by date so that you will know how long it can last. Below are storage guidelines for some common refrigerated and frozen foods.

COLD STORAGE FOR COMMON PERISHABLE FOODS

FOOD	REFRIGERATOR (40°F)	FREEZER (0°F)
Eggs, fresh in shell	3 to 5 weeks	Don't freeze
Deli or vacuum-packed salads: egg, chicken, ham, tuna and macaroni	3 to 5 days	Don't freeze well
Unopened luncheon meat	2 weeks	1 to 2 months
Opened luncheon meat	3 to 5 days	1 to 2 months
Bacon	7 days	1 month
Raw ground meat, including hamburger, beef, turkey, veal, pork, lamb and meat mixtures	1 to 2 days	3 to 4 months
FRESH BEEF, VEAL, LAMB AND PORK		
Steaks	3 to 5 days	6 to 12 months
Chops	3 to 5 days	4 to 6 months
Roasts	3 to 5 days	4 to 12 months
FRESH POULTRY		
Whole chicken or turkey	1 to 2 days	1 year
Pieces of chicken or turkey	1 to 2 days	9 months
SEAFOOD		
Lean fish (flounder, haddock, halibut, etc.)	1 to 2 days	6 to 8 months
Fatty fish (salmon, tuna, etc.)	1 to 2 days	2 to 3 months

Resource: https://www.fda.gov/media/74435/download

THAWING

Before you being to prep your meals, you may need to thaw frozen meat, poultry or fish. Never thaw food at room temperature, such as on your countertop. It is the perfect temperature for bacteria to grow, and the juices from the thawing item can contaminate your countertop and anything in the area. Instead, thaw food safely in the refrigerator, in the microwave or under cold running water. If you choose to use the microwave or cold water method to thaw your food, cook it immediately after.

PREPPING

There are two main concepts to keep in mind when prepping food: clean and separate. In order to clean, you want to wash your hands and surfaces regularly. Bacteria can spread throughout your kitchen and get onto countertops, cutting boards, utensils and food. Make sure to wash your hands with warm soapy water for at least 20 seconds (or sing the "Happy Birthday" song twice) before and after handling food and after using the restroom, your cell phone, changing diapers or handling pets. If you prepare raw meat, poultry or seafood, any used cutting boards, dishes, utensils and countertops should be washed with hot soapy water between products or if you are then going to handle a food product that will not be cooked (like fruits, vegetables or cheese). Synthetic cutting boards can be washed in the dishwasher. Alternatively, you can sanitize your cutting board and countertops by rinsing them in a solution made of 1 tablespoon (15 mL) of unscented liquid chlorine bleach to 1 gallon (3.75 L) of water.

A few other tips to remember to keep your kitchen clean include using paper towels to clean countertops and other kitchen surfaces. If you choose to use cloth towels, wash them often in the hot cycle in your washing machine. Rinse fruits and vegetables, and rub firm-skin fruit fruits and vegetables (like melon and avocados) under cool running tap water even if the skin or rind is not eaten. Lastly, do not forget to clean the lids of canned foods before opening.

The second thing to remember when preparing your food is to keep food separated. Cross-contamination happens when bacteria are transferred from one food or surface to another. This happens most often when handling raw meat, poultry, seafood and eggs. You want to keep the foods and juices away from foods that are ready-to-eat (like fresh fruit or yogurt).

Here are a few things to remember:

- Separate raw meat, poultry, seafood and eggs from other foods in your shopping cart, grocery bags and refrigerator.

- Do not place cooked food on a plate or bowl that previously held raw meat, poultry, seafood or eggs without washing it first with hot soapy water or running it through the dishwasher.

- Never reuse marinades from raw foods unless you boil the marinade first.

- Consider keeping two different cutting boards — one for raw foods like raw meat, poultry, fish and eggs and a second for ready-to-eat foods like fresh fruits and vegetables and cheese.

COOKING

Cooking is an important step for food safety, as cooking to the proper internal temperatures can destroy harmful bacteria that may be on your food. To make sure your food is cooked safely, use an instant-read food thermometer to measure the internal temperature of cooked foods. Looking at the color of the food is not a reliable indicator of doneness or the safety of the food. You can purchase an instant-read food thermometer online for $10 to $15. Digital thermometers with built-in temperatures for meat, poultry and fish are also available, but those can vary in price. When using a thermometer, check the internal temperature of the food in several places to make sure your meat, poultry, seafood or egg dish is cooked to safe minimum internal temperatures. Below is a chart of recommended safe minimum internal temperatures from the US FDA and the Canadian government.

SAFE MINIMUM INTERNAL COOKING TEMPERATURES

FOOD	TEMPERATURE
Beef, pork, veal, lamb, steaks, roasts and chops	145°F US (63°C Canada), after allowing roasts to rest for 3 minutes following removal from the heat source
Fish and seafood	145°F US (70°C Canada)
Ground beef, pork, veal and lamb	160°F US (71°C Canada)
Egg dishes	160°F US (74°C Canada)
Chicken, turkey and duck (whole, pieces or ground)	165°F US (82°C whole and 74°C pieces or ground, Canada)
Leftovers dishes	165°F US (74°C Canada)
Reheating sauces, soups and gravy	Bring to a boil

RESOURCES:
https://www.fda.gov/media/93628/download
https://www.canada.ca/en/health-canada/services/general-food-safety-tips/safe-internal-cooking-temperatures.html

STORING AND HEATING LEFTOVERS

Cooked foods containing meat, poultry, eggs, seafood and other perishable foods should be refrigerated or frozen within 2 hours of cooking. Cover the food properly to help maintain freshness and to prevent odors from spreading in your refrigerator. Larger amounts of food that you will be cooking for meal prepping should be divided into shallow containers for quicker cooling in the refrigerator and freezer. Most of your cooked foods can be stored for 3 to 4 days. If you have food you want to eat for 5 days, then consider freezing the last one or two servings in individual boxes. Below are guidelines for storing cooked foods in your refrigerator and freezer according to the US FDA and Canadian government.

When you are ready to eat your frozen meals, transfer the container to the refrigerator the night before to thaw. Reheat your microwave-safe or oven-safe container in the microwave or oven, or transfer the contents of the container into a pot or pan and reheat on the stove.

COLD STORAGE OF COOKED FOODS

FOOD	REFRIGERATOR (40°F US/4°C CANADA)	FREEZER (0°F US/-18°C CANADA)
Hard-cooked eggs	1 week	Don't freeze well
Cooked meat or poultry	3 to 4 days	2 to 6 months
Casseroles, quiche, omelets	3 to 4 days	2 months
Soups and stews	2 to 4 days	2 to 3 months
Gravy and meat broth	3 to 4 days	2 to 6 months
Fish and shellfish	1 to 4 days	2 to 4 months
Homemade salads: egg, chicken, ham, macaroni, tuna	3 to 5 days	Don't freeze well

RESOURCES:
https://www.foodsafety.gov/food-safety-charts/cold-food-storage-charts
https://www.fsis.usda.gov/wps/portal/fsis/topics/food-safety-education/get-answers/food-safety-fact-sheets/safe-food-handling/keep-food-safe-food-safety-basics/ct_index
https://www.canada.ca/en/health-canada/services/general-food-safety-tips/safe-food-storage.html

CHAPTER
3

MEAL PREP STEPS TO CREATE YOUR PLATE

It is important to remember that what you eat can impact your blood glucose levels, cholesterol, blood pressure and weight. Using the Diabetes Plate Method (also known as the plate method) is a simple and effective way to help manage your portions while balancing the food groups you eat. That is why this method is a useful tool for meal prepping — except instead of a plate, you are filling meal prep containers. It's straightforward and no special tools or counting are necessary! You can use your meal prep containers as visual guides to create balanced, diabetes-friendly meals.

With some planning and prepping, reaching for a healthy, diabetes-friendly meal is easy any day of the week. Balance out your meal prep containers using the Diabetes Plate Method, and you'll have complete grab-and-go meals and snacks stocked up for the week ahead. Below, the five steps to the Diabetes Plate Method have been adapted for your circular, square or rectangular meal prep containers, with or without divided compartments.

FIVE STEPS TO MEAL PREPPING USING THE DIABETES PLATE METHOD

Using the plate method for meal prepping is simple: include a larger portion of non-starchy vegetables, add a smaller portion of protein and another smaller portion of carbohydrate foods, such as grains, starchy vegetables, fruit or milk. The meal plans in part 2 of this book will get you started. Once you are comfortable with meal prepping, you can swap out different recipes from part 3 to balance your plate and create new meals.

Start with a meal prep container that can hold as much food as a 9-inch (23 cm) dinner plate. If you are someone who needs more calories than average, you can opt for large meal prep containers that can hold as much food as an 11- or 12-inch (28 or 30 cm) dinner plate. If you are someone who needs fewer calories than average, you can select meal prep containers that are slightly smaller and hold as much food as an 8-inch (20 cm) dinner plate.

Imagine your container is divided into three parts — one half and two quarters.

A WORD ON APPETIZERS AND DESSERTS

Pre-dinner bite-size munchies can take a toll on your blood sugar. If you know there will be appetizers, inquire as to what will be available so you can make the best choices to fill your plate — even though in this case the appetizers won't be on your main plate. Opt for low-carb vegetables whenever possible, because they have the lowest effect on your blood sugar. If you choose to have a carbohydrate option, like flatbread, swap it for carbohydrates during the main meal. If you would like to try several appetizers, choose small portions of two or three favorites and opt for protein, healthy fats or low-carb vegetables whenever possible.

You can work desserts into your meal plan by substituting a small portion of dessert for another carbohydrate food already in your meal. For example, if you would like a small slice of blueberry pie for dessert, skip the mashed potatoes or roll at dinner. It's all about making smart carbohydrate swaps and having a small portion.

If you do choose dessert, keep the following tips in mind:

- Decide ahead of time whether you will be having dessert, how much you will eat and which carbohydrate food you will swap for it.
- Share a serving of dessert with one or two people at the table.
- If you are attending a dinner party, offer to contribute a dessert so that you can bring a lighter version of your favorite sweet treat.

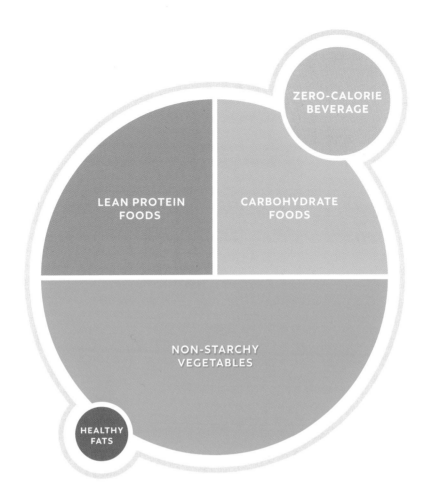

AT A GLANCE

Create your meal prep container:

STEP 1. Fill half of your meal prep container with non-starchy vegetables, such as broccoli, cauliflower, spinach, kale or another vegetable on page 37.

STEP 2. Fill one-quarter of your meal prep container with lean protein foods, such as lean meat, fish or seafood, eggs or plant-based protein.

STEP 3. Fill the final quarter of your meal prep container with carbohydrate foods, such as grains, starchy vegetables, fruit, milk or yogurt.

STEP 4. Choose a zero-calorie beverage like water or seltzer.

STEP 5. Use healthy fats (see page 46) in small amounts and add them to your meal prep container.

ZERO-CALORIE
BEVERAGE

LEAN
PROTEIN
FOODS

CARBOHYDRATE
FOODS

NON-STARCHY
VEGETABLES

1 // Fill half of your meal prep container with non-starchy vegetables.

There are two types of vegetables — starchy and non-starchy — and both are brimming with vitamins, minerals, fiber and phytochemicals, the natural plant compounds that help fight and prevent disease. Starchy vegetables are higher in carbohydrates, so they can cause a significant rise in blood glucose. They fall into the category of "carbohydrate foods," discussed in step 3. Non-starchy vegetables provide many health benefits for folks with diabetes, and they are also low in calories, fat and carbohydrates. These vegetables do not have a big effect on blood glucose levels, which means that you can enjoy more of them! With few calories and low in carbohydrates, non-starchy vegetables should take up the largest portion of your meal prep container.

COMMON NON-STARCHY VEGETABLES

Amaranth greens or Chinese spinach

Artichoke

Artichoke hearts

Asparagus

Baby corn

Bamboo shoots

Beans, such as green, wax and Italian

Bean sprouts

Beets

Broccoli

Brussels sprouts

Cabbage, such as green, bok choy and Chinese

Carrots

Cauliflower

Celery

Chayote

Coleslaw (packaged, no dressing)

Cucumber

Daikon

Eggplant

Greens, such as collard, kale, mustard and turnip

Heart of palm

Jicama

Kohlrabi

Leeks

Mushrooms

Okra

Onions

Pea pods

Peppers

Radishes

Rutabaga

Salad greens, such as chicory, endive, escarole, lettuce, romaine, spinach, arugula, radicchio and watercress

Sprouts

Squash, such as cushaw, summer, crookneck, spaghetti and zucchini

Sugar snap peas

Swiss chard

Tomatoes

Turnips

Water chestnuts

Yard-long beans

2 // Fill one-quarter of your meal prep container with lean protein.

Foods that are high in protein include fish and seafood, poultry, meats, eggs and cheese. There are also plant-based protein options such as beans, lentils, peas, nuts and soy. You may also hear this category referred to as "meat or meat substitutes." Protein is one of the three main nutrients in food (the other two are carbohydrates and fat). Proteins are used in the body for cell structure, to produce hormones like insulin and for other important functions. The biggest differences among foods in this group are how much fat they contain and, for the plant-based proteins, whether or not they contain carbohydrates.

FISH AND SEAFOOD

Try to incorporate fish or seafood into your eating plan at least twice a week, but limit fried seafood because it is high in fat and calories. Instead, opt for fish and seafood that is grilled, baked, steamed, microwaved, poached, broiled or pan seared.

AT A GLANCE

Include fish or other seafood in your eating plan twice a week. Look for:

- Fish high in omega-3 fatty acids, such as albacore tuna, herring, salmon, mackerel, rainbow trout and sardines
- Other fish, such as catfish, cod, flounder, haddock, halibut, orange roughy and tilapia
- Shellfish, such as clams, scallops, crab, imitation shellfish, lobster, shrimp and oysters

POULTRY

Poultry means more than just chicken! It also includes turkey, Cornish hen and duck. Choose poultry without the skin for less saturated fat and cholesterol, which have been associated with heart disease. Also, choose healthy cooking methods like baking, grilling, sautéing and stir-frying, and avoid cooking methods that are high in fat, like deep frying.

RED MEAT

There are many lean red meat and game options to select from. Red meat includes beef, pork, lamb and veal, while game includes venison (deer), ostrich and buffalo. The United States Department of Agriculture (USDA) and Food and Drug Administration (FDA) define lean as less than 10% fat by weight, or less than 10 grams of fat per 100 grams.

The Canadian government defines lean as containing 10% or less fat, and extra lean as containing 7.5% or less fat. Limit high-fat red meats, which are often higher in saturated fat, and processed red meats like sausage, bacon and hot dogs, which tend to be higher in saturated fat and sodium.

AT A GLANCE

When selecting red meat and game, look for these lean options:

- **BEEF:** Select or Choice grades trimmed of fat, including chuck, rib, rump roast, round, sirloin, cubed, flank, porterhouse, T-bone steak or tenderloin
- **GAME:** Buffalo, ostrich, rabbit, venison, dove, goose or pheasant (without the skin)
- **LAMB:** Chop, leg or roast
- **PORK:** Canadian bacon, center loin chop, ham or tenderloin
- **VEAL:** Loin chop or roast

EGGS AND CHEESE

You can also find protein in eggs and cheese. Select eggs that are large. As a general rule, use large eggs rather than medium, extra-large or jumbo to help keep portions under control. In addition, baking recipes typically require large eggs and might not work if you use other size eggs. When selecting cheese, low-fat and nonfat varieties have less saturated fat and cholesterol, but they may contain more sodium, so be sure to read the label.

PLANT-BASED PROTEIN

Whether you choose to avoid eating animal products (like meat and poultry) or would just like to incorporate some non-animal sources of protein into your eating plan, plant-based protein options are a healthy choice to include in your meal prep container. Unlike animal proteins, plant-based proteins provide fiber and can contain carbohydrates. Serving size varies for plant-based protein, so be sure to read the label. Below is a chart with examples of plant-based protein options arranged from highest to lowest of the carbohydrate content in one serving of the food.

PLANT-BASED PROTEINS

Bean products (such as baked beans and refried beans)

Beans (such as black, kidney or pinto)

Lentils (such as brown, green or yellow)

Peas (such as black-eyed or split)

Edamame

Hummus or falafel

Soy nuts

Nuts and nut spreads (such as almonds, almond butter, peanuts, peanut butter, cashews, cashew butter, walnuts or pistachios)

Products like meatless "chicken" nuggets, "beef" crumbles, "burgers," "meatballs," "bacon," "sausage" and "hot dogs" (carb content may vary — check nutrition facts panel)

Tempeh, tofu

Listed from highest to lowest carbohydrate content

3 // Fill one-quarter of your meal prep container with carbohydrate foods.

When you meal prep, carbohydrate foods should make up a smaller portion of your meal prep container because they can raise your blood glucose. Fill one-quarter of your meal prep container with any of the carbohydrate foods listed below:

- Grains and grain-based foods
- Starchy vegetables
- Beans and other legumes
- Fruit
- Milk and yogurt

GRAINS AND GRAIN-BASED FOODS

Whenever possible, select grain foods that are the most nutritious: whole intact grains. They are rich in vitamins, minerals, phytochemicals and fiber. Leave the processed, white flour–based products, especially the ones with added sugar, on the shelves or use them only for an occasional treat.

Most breads, cereals, crackers and rolls labeled as "made with" or "containing" whole grains do not have whole grains as the first ingredient. Terms like "multigrain" on the label can be tricky because

A WORD ABOUT WHOLE GRAINS

A whole grain is the entire grain, which includes the bran, germ and endosperm (starchy part). The most popular grain in the United States and Canada is wheat, so let's use that as an example. To make 100% whole wheat flour, the entire wheat grain is ground up. In 100% whole wheat flour there is more fiber and vitamins because the whole grain is used. Refined flours, like white and enriched wheat flour, include only part of the grain — the starchy part — and are not whole grain. They are missing many of the nutrients found in whole wheat flour. Flours and breads that do not use the whole grain tend to be enriched, meaning the nutrients lost are added back in. The list of whole-grain and whole wheat products is very long, but it includes whole wheat bread and pasta, tortillas and crackers that contain 100% whole wheat or 100% whole grains.

Finding whole-grain foods can sometimes be a challenge, but it gets easier once you know what you are looking for. Some foods only contain a small amount of whole grain, even if the front of the package says it contains whole grain. Always read the ingredients list and look for a source of whole grains as the first ingredient. The following are some common whole grains:

Barley	Farro	Rye
Brown rice	Millet	Sorghum
Buckwheat	Oats/oatmeal	Whole wheat flour
Bulgur (cracked wheat)	Popcorn, air-popped	Wild rice
Corn/cornmeal	Quinoa	

"multigrain" means that a product is made with more than one type of grain, but it could be referring to multiple whole grains or multiple refined grains. Always read labels carefully to find the most nutritious grain products available.

STARCHY VEGETABLES

Besides whole grains and grain products, starchy vegetables are also considered carbohydrate foods. Starchy vegetables are great sources of vitamins, minerals and fiber, and the best choices do not have added fats, sugar or sodium. While starchy vegetables can be part of a healthy meal prep container, they do raise blood glucose, so opt for smaller portions.

COMMON STARCHY VEGETABLES

Acorn squash	Corn	Parsnips	Potatoes
Butternut squash	Green peas	Plantains	Pumpkin

BEANS AND OTHER LEGUMES

Beans, peas and lentils contain both carbohydrates and protein. They also contain fiber, vitamins and minerals, making them a great addition to meal prep containers. Try to include these foods in some of your meal prep containers each week.

COMMON BEANS AND OTHER LEGUMES

Bean products, such as baked beans and refried beans (These products can be higher in fat and sugar, so read labels carefully before selecting.)

Beans, such as black, kidney and pinto

Edamame

Hummus and falafel

Lentils, such as brown, green and yellow

Nuts and nut spreads, such as almonds, almond butter, peanuts, peanut butter, cashews, cashew butter, walnuts and pistachios

Peas, such as black-eyed peas and split peas

Soy nuts

Tempeh and tofu

Some meatless products, such as "chicken" nuggets, "beef" crumbles, "burgers," "meatballs," "bacon," "sausage" and "hot dogs," are made with legumes or pulses. (Check the ingredients list of each product for more information.)

FRUITS

Fruits are loaded with vitamins, minerals and fiber, just like vegetables, but they do contain carbohydrates and can raise your blood glucose. That's why you should count fruit in the carbohydrate part of your meal plan. Depending on your personal meal plan and carb goals, you can enjoy a small piece of fruit as a snack between meals, or with breakfast or lunch. Having a fresh piece of fruit in your snack container, for example, is a fabulous way to satisfy your sweet tooth and get a nutrition boost.

The best choices of fruit are any that are fresh, frozen or canned without any added sugar. Choose canned fruit in juice or light or extra-light syrup. Frozen fruit should have one ingredient on the label — the fruit (and no added sugar).

COMMON FRUITS

Apples	Dried fruit, such as cherries, cranberries, dates, figs, prunes and raisins (Look for varieties with no added sugar and read labels, as portion sizes are much smaller.)	Fruit cocktail in water or 100% juice with no added sugar	Oranges
Applesauce		Grapefruit	Papaya
Apricots		Grapes	Peaches
Banana		Honeydew melon	Pears
Blackberries		Kiwi	Pineapple
Blueberries		Mango	Plums
Cantaloupe		Nectarines	Raspberries
Cherries			Strawberries
			Tangerines
			Watermelon

MILK AND DAIRY FOODS

Milk and dairy foods can fit into your meal prep meal plan and is a great way to get calcium and high-quality protein. Milk and dairy products, like yogurt, can raise blood glucose. When choosing milk and dairy foods, keep in mind that low-fat and nonfat milk and dairy have fewer overall calories and less saturated fat compared to full-fat milk and dairy foods. Depending on your health goals and the other foods you include in your meal plan, the lower-fat options may be right for you. Examples of low-fat and nonfat dairy products include nonfat milk (also called fat-free or skim milk), low fat (1%) milk, low-fat or nonfat yogurt or Greek yogurt, low-fat or nonfat cottage cheese and reduced-fat cheeses. If you're lactose intolerant or don't like milk, you may want to try lactose-free milk and dairy foods (such as lactose-free cheese, cottage cheese and yogurt) or fortified soy milk.

LOW-FAT AND NONFAT DAIRY PRODUCTS

Low-fat or nonfat cottage cheese	Nonfat milk (also called fat-free or skim milk), low fat (1%) milk
Low-fat or nonfat yogurt or Greek yogurt	Reduced-fat cheeses

4 // Choose water or another very low calorie or zero-calorie drink.

While food is often the focus of meal prepping for people with diabetes, remember that the beverages you drink can also affect your weight and blood glucose! Complete your meal prep meal with a very low calorie or zero-calorie drink.

Avoid sugary drinks like regular soda, fruit punch, fruit drinks, energy drinks, sports drinks and sweet tea. Juice, even 100% fruit or vegetable juice, can quickly raise blood glucose (more on that below).

ZERO-CALORIE DRINKS

Water is always the best beverage option, but there are other zero-calorie drinks to choose from. Sparkling water or unsweetened teas, either hot or cold, are great alternatives to plain water. You can also try making your own infused water at home. To make infused still or sparkling water, add flavorful fresh ingredients, such as cucumbers, strawberries, raspberries, lemon slices or fresh mint leaves, to a pitcher of still or sparkling water and refrigerate overnight or for up to 24 hours. Strain the produce or herbs before serving.

COFFEE AND TEA

Plain coffee and tea contain very few calories and grams of carbohydrates and can be part of your healthy meal prep containers. Hot or cold, black, green and herbal teas provide lots of flavor variety.

Keep in mind that ingredients added to coffee and tea, such as cream, sugar, other sweeteners and non-dairy creamer or beverage, can all add calories and carbohydrates. Using only a small amount of these ingredients or none at all will have the least impact on your blood glucose. Coffee drinks with flavors and syrups can contain excessive calories and carbohydrates, so be sure to read labels on prepackaged drinks or ask your barista for nutritional information at cafes, if available.

SUGAR-SUBSTITUTE DRINKS

Low-calorie sweeteners, also referred to as non-nutritive sweeteners, artificial sweeteners or sugar substitutes, have a long history of safe use in food and drinks. Common low-calorie sweeteners include aspartame, saccharine, sugar alcohols (like sucralose), stevia and stevia glycosides (purified stevia extract). They're commonly referred to as "intense" sweeteners because they are usually several hundred times the sweetness of regular table sugar. That means that a little goes a long way in coffee, tea, smoothies, batters and more. People with diabetes can substitute calorie-filled sweeteners like sugar with low-calorie sweeteners, which allows for greater flexibility with your health and dietary goals. Low-calorie sweeteners do not provide nutrition and should be used in small amounts when needed.

Most diet drinks sweetened with sugar substitutes (like diet soda or diet sweet tea) have 0 grams of carbohydrates per serving, so they will not raise blood glucose on their own. Replacing added sugars with low-calorie sweeteners may help reduce calorie and carbohydrate intake only if the beverages are used in place of other higher-calorie or higher-carbohydrate drinks.

There are other low-calorie drinks and drink mixes that also use sugar substitutes, so they may be a good alternative to added sugar–sweetened beverages like iced tea, lemonade and fruit punch.

MILK

To reduce calories and saturated fat, choose low-fat (1%) or nonfat milk. Some early research indicates that whole-milk dairy products may help reduce diabetes risk, but there is not strong enough evidence to recommend drinking it regularly for that purpose. One cup (250 mL) of nonfat milk provides about 12 grams of carbohydrates and 80 calories, plus calcium, vitamin D and eleven more essential nutrients. If you are lactose intolerant or do not like milk, other options include lactose-free milk or fortified soy milk. Remember, milk is considered a carbohydrate food, so be sure to consider which other carbohydrate foods you have packed in your meal prep container when including milk.

JUICE

Juice provides a lot of carbohydrates in a small portion and can be included in a diabetes-friendly diet in limited amounts. Typically about 4 fluid ounces (125 mL) or less of juice contain at least 15 grams of carbohydrates and 50 or more calories. If you choose to drink juice, be mindful of the portion and choose 100% juice with no added sugar. If you find yourself craving something sweet, consider packing a meal prep snack that includes a small portion of fruit rather than reaching for juice. Just be sure to work that fruit into your eating plan for the day.

5 // Use healthy fats in small amounts.

Fat is a macronutrient that our bodies need. More important than the total amount of fat consumed are the types of fat you eat. There are healthy fats and unhealthy fats.

Healthy fats include monounsaturated fats, polyunsaturated fats and omega-3 fatty acids. These can be added to any part of your meal prep container. Unhealthy fats include saturated fats and trans fats. In order to help lower your risk of heart disease, try to avoid eating unhealthy fats. See the Types of Fat table on page 47 for examples of unhealthy and healthy fats.

SATURATED FAT

Saturated fat is considered unhealthy because it raises blood cholesterol levels. High blood cholesterol is a risk factor for heart disease. People with diabetes are at high risk for heart disease, so limiting your saturated fat intake can help lower your risk of having a heart attack or stroke. The goal for people with and without diabetes is to eat less than 10% of calories from saturated fat. For most people, this is about 20 grams of saturated fat per day (based on a 2,000-calorie diet). That is not much when you consider that just 1 ounce (28 g) of cheese can have 8 grams of saturated fat. You can find more information on the saturated fat content of common foods in the table below. Many adults, especially women and sedentary men, may need less.

COMMON FOOD SOURCES AND QUANTITIES OF SATURATED FAT

FOOD	SERVING SIZE	SATURATED FAT
Butter	1 tablespoon (15 mL)	7.3 g
Heavy cream	1 tablespoon (15 mL)	3.5 g
Coconut oil	1 tablespoon (15 mL)	11.2 g
Palm oil	1 tablespoon (15 mL)	6.7 g
Bacon grease	1 tablespoon (15 mL)	5.1 g
Roasted chicken with skin	3 ounces (85 g)	3.2 g
Broiled hamburger (made with 80% lean/20% fat ground beef)	3 ounces (85 g)	5.7 g
Hot dog	1 dog	6 g

*Data from the USDA's website FoodData Central, available at https://fdc.nal.usda.gov.

TYPES OF FAT

FAT	EXAMPLES	
Saturated fat	• Butter • Chocolate • Coconut, coconut flakes and coconut oil • Cream sauces • Fatback and salt pork • Gravy made with meat drippings • High-fat dairy products like full-fat cheese, cream, whole milk, 2% milk and sour cream	• High-fat meats like regular ground beef, bologna, hot dogs, sausage, bacon and spareribs • Lard • Palm oil and palm kernel oil • Poultry (chicken and turkey) skin
Trans fat*	• Doughnuts • Fried foods • Some baked goods, including cakes, pie crusts, biscuits and cookies	• Some crackers • Some frozen pizzas • Some stick margarines and other spreads
Unsaturated fat (monounsaturated and polyunsaturated)	• Avocado • Canola oil • Corn oil • Cottonseed oil • Nuts like almonds, cashews, pecans and peanuts • Olive oil and olives • Peanut butter and peanut oil	• Pumpkin or sunflower seeds • Safflower oil • Salad dressings • Sesame seeds • Soybean oil • Sunflower oil • Walnuts
Omega-3 fatty acids (fish source)	• Albacore tuna • Herring • Mackerel • Rainbow trout	• Salmon • Sardines • Tuna
Omega-3 fatty acids (plant source)	• Canola oil • Flaxseed and flaxseed oil	• Tofu and other soybean products • Walnuts

*You can check whether a food contains trans fat by reading the ingredients list on the package and looking for the ingredient "partially hydrogenated oils."

To establish your specific daily saturated fat goal, speak with your registered dietitian nutritionist (RDN) or health care provider. Saturated fat grams are listed on the Nutrition Facts food label under total fat. As a general rule, compare labels to find options with less saturated fat.

TRANS FAT

Trans fat, like saturated fat, increases blood cholesterol levels. It's actually considered worse for you than saturated fat (though both are unhealthy!). This means that you want to eat as little trans fat as possible, especially if you are following a heart-healthy eating plan. All of the recipes in this cookbook contain minimal to no trans fat.

Trans fat is created by a process called hydrogenation, when liquid oil is made into solid fat. You can easily identify foods containing trans fat by reading the Nutrition Facts label. Stick margarines are a common source of trans fat; however, you can now readily find trans fat–free margarines, such as Smart Balance. When selecting margarine, read the label to make sure that it says "trans fat free."

HEALTHY FAT

Now that we've covered which fats to limit, let's talk about the ones you can incorporate into your healthy eating plan: unsaturated fats and omega-3 fatty acids. Unsaturated fats are divided into two groups known as monounsaturated fats and polyunsaturated fats. These are easy to incorporate into your meal prep containers.

HEALTHY FAT SWAPS FOR MEAL PREPPING

INSTEAD OF . . .	CHOOSE . . .
Butter in mashed potatoes	A drizzle of olive oil
Cream cheese in a sandwich	Almond butter, peanut butter or sunflower seed butter
Ground beef that is 80% lean/20% fat	Ground beef that is at least 90% lean/10% fat
Chicken with the skin	Chicken without the skin
Heavy cream to thicken soups	A combination of cornstarch or flour and low-sodium chicken or vegetable broth or water
Creamy dressings (such as ranch) for salads or dipping vegetables	Vinaigrette dressing, hummus or bean dip
An omelet made with 3 whole eggs	An omelet made with 1 whole egg and 3 egg whites
Coconut oil	Olive oil or canola oil

UNSATURATED FAT

Unsaturated fats are called "healthy" fat because they can lower your
bad (LDL) cholesterol. It is recommended for people with and without
diabetes to eat more unsaturated fat — both monounsaturated fats and
polyunsaturated fats — than saturated or trans fat. To include more
unsaturated fat, use plant-based oils when cooking, such as olive or canola,
rather than butter, margarine or shortening. Avocado is another healthy
fat choice. For salads, some healthy fat additions include nuts, seeds and
vinaigrettes, but be aware that like all fats, nuts, seeds and oils are high in
calories. If you are trying to lose weight or maintain your current weight,
keep in mind that the serving size of these foods is small. For example,
1 tablespoon (15 mL) of any oil has 120 calories.

OMEGA-3 FATTY ACIDS

Omega-3 fatty acids are a type of polyunsaturated fatty acid (also called
PUFA) that have many functions in your heart, blood vessels, lungs, immune
system and brain. There are three main types of omega-3 fatty acids: alpha-
linolenic acid (ALA), eicosapentaenoic acid (EPA) and docosahexaenoic acid
(DHA). ALA is found in land-based sources of omega-3s, such as chia seeds
and flaxseeds, whereas EPA and DHA come from marine-based sources,
like salmon, tuna, mackerel and some sea algae.

ALA is an essential type of omega-3 fatty acid, meaning the body cannot
make it on its own. However, the body is able to convert ALA to EPA and
DHA, but the rate of conversion is very low. Only about 1% to 5% of ALA
is converted to EPA and DHA, which makes the process inefficient. It is
best to get EPA and DHA directly from fatty fish, if possible. An easy way
to do this is to enjoy a non-fried serving of fatty fish two or three times a
week. (See the Types of Fat table on page 47 for examples of the sources
of omega-3 fatty acids.)

PART 2

MEAL PREP PLANS TO CREATE YOUR PLATE

MEAL PREP PLAN 1:
BEGINNER

Welcome to the world of meal prepping! This first menu is for those who are just starting to meal prep and for folks who plan to meal prep only a few meals and snacks a week. With this plan, each day you will have three containers available to you: one breakfast, one snack and one lunch or dinner.

You'll notice that some ingredients are used in multiple recipes, which helps minimize food waste. For example, the Carrot Cake Energy Bites (page 60) for the snack box use shredded carrots, and the Beef and Butternut Squash Stew (page 62) for the lunch or dinner box uses sliced carrots. That way you'll end up with fewer leftover carrots.

I've provided a sample meal plan for the week on page 55, but use this as a starting point and customize it to work with your needs and schedule. For instance, I've included the Carrot Cake Energy Bites as a morning snack, but you can eat it as an afternoon or evening snack. The Beef and Butternut Squash Stew is listed as dinner, but it can be eaten for lunch instead. You'll notice that I've only included the dishes prepared as part of the meal prep plan. To best manage your blood sugar, fill in the other meals and snacks at the beginning of the week. Easy snacks that you can purchase include peanut butter and fruit or nonfat Greek yogurt and nuts. Be sure to include plans for dining out, too.

Egg Muffins with Spinach and Feta 58

Carrot Cake Energy Bites 60

Beef and Butternut Squash Stew 62

WEEKLY MEAL PREP PLAN 1: BEGINNER

Below is a sample plan of when to eat meal prepped food during a work or school week. However, everyone has a different schedule, so customize this to fit your needs.

	BREAKFAST	AM SNACK	LUNCH	PM SNACK	DINNER
Monday	Egg Muffin Container	Carrot Cake Energy Bites Container			Beef and Butternut Squash Stew Container
Tuesday	Egg Muffin Container	Carrot Cake Energy Bites Container			Beef and Butternut Squash Stew Container
Wednesday	Egg Muffin Container	Carrot Cake Energy Bites Container			Beef and Butternut Squash Stew Container
Thursday	Egg Muffin Container	Carrot Cake Energy Bites Container			Beef and Butternut Squash Stew Container
Friday	Egg Muffin Container	Carrot Cake Energy Bites Container			Beef and Butternut Squash Stew Container

	CALORIES	FAT	SAT FAT	SODIUM	CARB	FIBER	PROTEIN

BREAKFAST: EGG MUFFIN CONTAINER

SERVE ON: Monday through Friday (5 days)

STORE: Portions 1 to 4 in the refrigerator and portion 5 of the egg muffin only in the freezer

	CALORIES	FAT	SAT FAT	SODIUM	CARB	FIBER	PROTEIN
Egg Muffins with Spinach and Feta	153.78	9.07 g	3.67 g	462.10 mg	4.27 g	0.53 g	13.24 g
1 whole wheat English muffin	120.0	1.0 g	0.0 g	190.0 mg	23.0 g	3.0 g	6.0 g
1 tbsp (15 mL) peanut butter	94.08	7.93 g	1.52	76.16 mg	3.84 g	0.91 g	3.51 g
Total Per Box	367.86	18.0 g	5.19 g	728.26 mg	31.11 g	4.44 g	22.75 g

SNACK: CARROT CAKE ENERGY BITES CONTAINER

SERVE ON: Monday through Friday (5 days)

STORE: All portions in the refrigerator and use the additional portion as a second snack during the week or serve to a friend

	CALORIES	FAT	SAT FAT	SODIUM	CARB	FIBER	PROTEIN
Carrot Cake Energy Bites	179.91	10.54 g	1.58 g	57.90 mg	18.94 g	3.45 g	4.39 g
Total Per Box	179.91	10.54 g	1.58 g	57.90 mg	18.94 g	3.45 g	4.39 g

LUNCH OR DINNER: BEEF AND BUTTERNUT SQUASH STEW CONTAINER

SERVE ON: Monday through Friday (5 days)

STORE: Portions 1 to 4 in the refrigerator and portions 5 and 6 in the freezer

	CALORIES	FAT	SAT FAT	SODIUM	CARB	FIBER	PROTEIN
Beef and Butternut Squash Stew	337.23	11.66 g	2.75 g	470.07 mg	23.49 g	5.09 g	36.67 g
1 cup (250 mL) steamed broccoli	19.88	0.25 g	0.04 g	19.17 mg	3.72 g	0.0 g	2.12 g
Total Per Box	357.11	11.91 g	2.79 g	489.24 mg	27.21 g	5.09 g	38.79 g

WEEKLY SHOPPING LIST

VEGETABLES

- broccoli: 1 cup (250 mL) florets
- butternut squash: ½
- carrots: 5
- celery: 2 stalks
- garlic: 2 cloves
- onion, yellow: 1 small, 1 medium
- spinach, baby: 3 cups (750 mL)

PANTRY

- apple cider vinegar
- black pepper, ground
- broth, low-sodium beef or vegetable: 2¾ cups (685 mL)
- canola oil
- cinnamon, ground
- coconut flakes, unsweetened: 2 tbsp (30 mL)
- cooking spray
- dates, pitted: ¼ cup (60 mL)

- English muffins, whole wheat: 6
- flour, unbleached all-purpose
- nutmeg, ground
- oil, olive
- parsley, dried flakes
- peanut butter
- raisins: ¼ cup (60 mL)
- rosemary, dried
- salt, sea
- salt, table
- thyme, dried
- tomatoes, no-salt-added diced: 14-oz can (398 mL)
- vanilla extract
- walnuts, raw or unsalted dry roasted: ⅓ cup (75 mL)

DAIRY AND EGGS

- eggs, large: 12
- feta cheese, crumbled: ½ cup (125 mL)
- milk, nonfat: ¾ cup (175 mL)

MEATS

- beef, top round: 1¾ lbs (875 g)

FROZEN

- green peas: 1¼ cups (300 mL)

EQUIPMENT

- blender (or food processor)
- box grater
- can opener
- cutting board
- knife
- measuring cups and spoons
- mixing bowls
- muffin pan, 12-cup
- sauté pan or pot, large, with cover
- skillet, medium
- whisk
- wooden spoons

STEP-BY-STEP MEAL PREP

1   Prepare the **Beef and Butternut Squash Stew** (page 62) through step 3.

2   While the stew is cooking, prepare the **Carrot Cake Energy Bites** (page 60) steps 1 through 5.

3   Continue preparing the **Beef and Butternut Squash Stew** (page 62) by following steps 4 and 5.

4   While the stew continues to cook, prepare the ingredients for the **Egg Muffins with Spinach and Feta** (page 58).

5   Preheat the oven to 350°F (180°C) and follow steps 1 through 4 for the **Egg Muffins with Spinach and Feta**.

6   While the egg muffins are cooking, let the stew cool.

7   Remove the egg muffins from the oven and let cool for at least 10 minutes.

8   Steam the broccoli.

9   Once cool, pack egg muffins according to the recipe and store two containers, covered, in the freezer. Store each of six English muffins and 1 tbsp (30 mL) peanut butter in the refrigerator until served.

10 Divide the stew as directed in step 6 and pack with 1 cup (250 mL) steamed broccoli in the same container or on the side. Store four containers in the refrigerator and two containers in the freezer.

EGG MUFFINS
WITH SPINACH AND FETA

SERVES	SERVING SIZE	TOTAL TIME	PREP TIME	COOK TIME
6	2 muffins	50 minutes	15 minutes	35 minutes

Eggs are a perfect protein because they contain all the essential amino acids needed for growth and your body's maintenance. But don't forget to eat the yolk! There is as much protein in an egg yolk as there is in the egg white. Each serving of two egg muffins contains a whole egg, which means you'll reap its full benefits.

2 tsp (10 mL) olive oil

1 small onion, chopped

3 cups (750 mL) baby spinach

6 large eggs

6 large egg whites

¾ cup (175 mL) nonfat milk

½ tsp (2 mL) salt

¼ tsp (1 mL) ground black pepper

½ cup (125 mL) crumbled feta cheese

Coat a 12-cup muffin pan with cooking spray
Preheat the oven to 350°F (180°C)

1 In a medium skillet over medium heat, heat the olive oil. When the oil is shimmering, add the onion and cook until softened, about 2 minutes. Add the spinach and cook until wilted, an additional 2 minutes. Remove the skillet from the heat and let cool slightly.

2 In a large bowl, whisk together the eggs, egg whites, milk, salt and pepper.

3 Divide the spinach mixture equally among the 12 prepared muffin cups. Pour the egg mixture over the spinach mixture and top each muffin with 2 tsp (10 mL) of the feta cheese.

4 Bake until the tops are golden brown, about 25 minutes. Let the muffins cool for 10 minutes before removing them from the pan.

5 TO STORE: In each of six containers, add two egg muffins. Cover and refrigerate for up to 4 days, or freeze for up to 2 months.

6 TO SERVE: If needed, thaw in the refrigerator overnight. To reheat, microwave uncovered on High for 45 seconds to 1 minute. Serve warm.

TOBY'S TIP | If you prefer, swap the spinach for 8 oz (225 g) of sliced cremini mushrooms. Cook for 5 to 7 minutes until the liquid is released.

PER SERVING				
	TOTAL CALORIES	TOTAL FAT	SATURATED FAT	TRANS FAT
	153.78	9.07 g	3.67 g	0 g
	SODIUM	CHOLESTEROL	TOTAL CARBOHYDRATES	FIBER
	462.10 mg	197.74 mg	4.27 g	0.53 g
	SUGARS	PROTEIN	POTASSIUM	PHOSPHORUS
	3.05 g	13.24 g	279.10 mg	187.74 mg

CARROT CAKE ENERGY BITES

SERVES	SERVING SIZE	TOTAL TIME	PREP TIME	COOK TIME
6	2 bites	20 minutes, plus 15 minutes refrigeration time	20 minutes	0 minutes

Bites or balls are easy to whip together, which makes them an ideal meal prep dish. They're perfect for making while another dish is cooking, especially since they do not require the use of the stove.

¼ cup (60 mL) pitted dates

¼ cup (60 mL) almond butter or walnut butter

½ cup (125 mL) gluten-free large-flake (old-fashioned) rolled oats

⅓ cup (75 mL) raw or unsalted roasted walnuts, coarsely chopped

2 carrots, grated

1 tbsp (15 mL) canola oil

1 tsp (5 mL) vanilla extract

½ tsp (2 mL) ground cinnamon

⅛ tsp (0.5 mL) ground nutmeg

⅛ tsp (0.5 mL) sea salt

¼ cup (60 mL) raisins

2 tbsp (30 mL) unsweetened coconut flakes

Food processor

1 Add the dates, nut butter, rolled oats, walnuts, carrots, oil, vanilla, cinnamon, nutmeg and salt to a food processor and purée until the mixture reaches a smooth consistency. Transfer the mixture to a medium bowl.

2 Add the raisins to the date mixture and fold to incorporate.

3 Spread the coconut flakes onto a large plate.

4 Using clean hands, form 2 tbsp (30 mL) of the mixture into a 1½-inch (4 cm) ball and gently roll the top into the coconut mixture. Repeat for the remaining mixture, making a total of 12 balls.

5 TO STORE: In six small containers, add two bites. Cover the containers and refrigerate to allow the bites to set for at least 15 minutes before eating. Store the bites for up to 5 days the refrigerator.

6 TO SERVE: Enjoy cold.

TOBY'S TIP | If you prefer, swap the raisins for chopped dried apricot halves or dried tart cherries.

	TOTAL CALORIES	TOTAL FAT	SATURATED FAT	TRANS FAT
PER SERVING	179.91	10.54 g	1.58 g	0 g
	SODIUM	CHOLESTEROL	TOTAL CARBOHYDRATES	FIBER
	57.90 mg	0 mg	18.94 g	3.45 g
	SUGARS	PROTEIN	POTASSIUM	PHOSPHORUS
	10.02 g	4.39 g	170.14 mg	18.79 mg

BEEF AND BUTTERNUT SQUASH STEW

SERVES	SERVING SIZE	TOTAL TIME	PREP TIME	COOK TIME
6	1½ cups (375 mL)	2 hours, 10 minutes	20 minutes	1 hour, 50 minutes

Nothing is better than knowing you have a warming bowl of delicious stew ready to heat and eat. This version combines the savory taste of beef with the sweet flavors of butternut squash — perfect for fall or winter. When it is not in season, swap the butternut squash for sweet potatoes.

2 tbsp (30 mL) unbleached all-purpose flour or whole wheat pastry flour

½ tsp (2 mL) dried parsley flakes

¼ tsp (1 mL) ground black pepper

¼ tsp (1 mL) dried thyme

¼ tsp (1 mL) dried rosemary

1¾ lbs (875 g) top round, cut into ¾-inch (2 cm) cubes

3 tbsp (45 mL) olive oil

2¾ cups (675 mL) low-sodium beef or vegetable broth, divided

1 medium onion, chopped

2 cloves garlic, minced

2 stalks celery, chopped

1. In a medium bowl, combine the flour, parsley, pepper, thyme and rosemary. Roll the beef cubes in the flour mixture, shaking off excess, and set aside.

2. Heat the olive oil in a large sauté pan or large pot over medium heat. When the oil is shimmering, add the dredged beef cubes in one layer and cook until they are browned on all sides, 8 minutes. Remove the beef cubes to a clean plate.

3. Using the same pan or pot, reduce the heat to medium-low and add ¼ cup (60 mL) of the broth. With a wooden spoon, scrape the browned pieces from the bottom of the pan and simmer for about 1 minute.

4. Add the onion and garlic and cook over medium heat until the onion softens and the garlic is fragrant, about 2 minutes. Add the celery and continue cooking until it softens, about 3 minutes. Return the beef to the pan or pot, add the remaining broth and diced tomatoes with juice and bring to a boil. Reduce the heat to low and simmer partially covered for 45 minutes, stirring occasionally.

5. Add the butternut squash, carrots and apple cider vinegar to the pan or pot and bring the mixture to a boil over high heat. Reduce the heat to low and simmer partially covered, stirring occasionally, for an additional 45 minutes. Add the green peas and stir to combine. Cover and cook for 5 minutes more.

	TOTAL CALORIES	TOTAL FAT	SATURATED FAT	TRANS FAT
PER SERVING	337.23	11.66 g	2.75 g	0 g
	SODIUM 470.07 mg	**CHOLESTEROL** 82.03 mg	**TOTAL CARBOHYDRATES** 23.49 g	**FIBER** 5.09 g
	SUGARS 10.49 g	**PROTEIN** 36.67 g	**POTASSIUM** 578.79 mg	**PHOSPHORUS** 310.70 mg

1 can (14 oz /398 mL) no-salt-added diced tomatoes, with juice

1/2 butternut squash, peeled with seeds removed, cut into bite-size chunks

3 carrots, cut into 1/2-inch (1 cm) rounds

1 tsp (5 mL) apple cider vinegar

1 1/4 cups (300 mL) frozen green peas, thawed

6 **TO STORE:** In each of six containers, add 1 1/2 cups (375 mL) of the stew. Cover and refrigerate for up to 4 days, or freeze for up to 2 months.

7 **TO SERVE:** If needed, thaw in the refrigerator overnight. To reheat, microwave uncovered on High for 2 to 2 1/2 minutes. Alternatively, reheat in a saucepan on the stove by bringing the stew to a boil and simmering over medium-low heat until heated through, about 10 minutes. Serve warm.

TOBY'S TIP | To avoid food waste, go to the meat counter of your local supermarket and ask the butcher to cut for you the exact amount you need. Alternatively, you can have them weigh the pieces available so you can get the amount closest to what you need.

MEAL PREP PLAN 2:

ADVANCED BEGINNER

This week is one step up in difficulty from Meal Prep Plan 1. Instead of three containers per day, it has four: one breakfast, one snack and two lunches or dinners. The Pesto Chicken Bake (page 76) contains chicken, and the rest of the dishes on the menu this week are plant-based and vegetarian-friendly.

Remember, cooked dishes will last for 4 days in the refrigerator, so freeze your meals for Friday and save extra servings in the freezer for another week. In the breakfast containers, be sure to only freeze the Cottage Cheese and Oat Pancakes (page 70). The remaining items for your breakfast — the hard-cooked egg and tomato — can be stored in the refrigerator until needed. The Cilantro-Lime Grilled Tofu (page 75) freezes well; however, store the salsa in the refrigerator in individual containers until you are ready to eat your meal this week. The second main meal, the Pesto Chicken Bake, also freezes well, as do the sides it's paired with.

Prepare the additional items for your Friday containers midweek, and make sure you add them to your boxes to complete the plate. On Friday, plan to enjoy a packaged snack, like whole grain crackers and low-fat cheese or a single-serving container of Greek yogurt topped with fruit or chopped nuts, or take a moment midweek to prepare an extra Red Pepper Hummus Snack Box (page 73).

Cottage Cheese and Oat Pancakes with Apple Butter 70

Red Pepper Hummus Snack Box 73

Cilantro-Lime Grilled Tofu 75

Pesto Chicken Bake 76

WEEKLY MEAL PREP PLAN 2: ADVANCED BEGINNER

Below is a sample plan of when to eat meal prepped food during a work or school week. However, everyone has a different schedule, so customize this to fit your needs.

	BREAKFAST	AM SNACK	LUNCH	PM SNACK	DINNER
Monday	Cottage Cheese and Oat Pancakes Container		Cilantro-Lime Grilled Tofu Container	Red Pepper Hummus Snack Box	Pesto Chicken Bake Container
Tuesday	Cottage Cheese and Oat Pancakes Container		Pesto Chicken Bake Container	Red Pepper Hummus Snack Box	Cilantro-Lime Grilled Tofu Container
Wednesday	Cottage Cheese and Oat Pancakes Container		Cilantro-Lime Grilled Tofu Container	Red Pepper Hummus Snack Box	Pesto Chicken Bake Container
Thursday	Cottage Cheese and Oat Pancakes Container		Pesto Chicken Bake Container	Red Pepper Hummus Snack Box	Cilantro-Lime Grilled Tofu Container
Friday	Cottage Cheese and Oat Pancakes Container		Cilantro-Lime Grilled Tofu Container		Pesto Chicken Bake Container

BREAKFAST: COTTAGE CHEESE AND OAT PANCAKES CONTAINER

SERVE ON: Monday through Friday (5 days)

STORE: Portions 1 to 4 in the refrigerator and portions 5 and 6 of only the pancakes with apple butter in the freezer

	CALORIES	FAT	SAT FAT	SODIUM	CARB	FIBER	PROTEIN
Cottage Cheese and Oat Pancakes with Apple Butter (page 70)	148.48	3.84 g	1.20 g	232.33 mg	17.85 g	2.27 g	10.78 g
1 large hard-cooked egg	77.50	5.30 g	1.63 g	62.00 mg	0.56 g	0.0 g	6.29 g
1 plum (Roma) tomato	11.16	0.12 g	0.02 g	3.10 mg	2.41 g	0.74 g	0.55 g
Total Per Box	237.14	9.26 g	2.85 g	297.43 mg	20.82 g	3.01 g	17.62 g

	CALORIES	FAT	SAT FAT	SODIUM	CARB	FIBER	PROTEIN
SNACK: RED PEPPER HUMMUS SNACK BOX							
SERVE ON: Monday through Thursday (4 days)							
STORE: All portions in the refrigerator							
Red Pepper Hummus Snack Box (page 73)	150.69	4.58 g	0.53 g	271.53 mg	23.92 g	5.55 g	5.45 g
Total Per Box	150.69	4.58 g	0.53 g	271.53 mg	23.92 g	5.55 g	5.45 g
LUNCH OR DINNER 1: CILANTRO-LIME GRILLED TOFU CONTAINER							
SERVE ON: Monday through Friday (5 days)							
STORE: Portions 1 to 4 in the refrigerator and portions 5 and 6 without the salsa in the freezer							
Cilantro-Lime Grilled Tofu (page 75) with Tomato Salsa (page 258)	146.86	10.89 g	0.91 g	288.89 mg	5.48 g	0.77 g	8.40 g
2 cups (500 mL) fresh spinach, sautéed	13.8	0.23 g	0.04 g	47.4 mg	2.18 g	1.32 g	1.72 g
1/3 cup (75 mL) dry or 3/4 cup (175 mL) cooked brown rice	162.34	1.32 g	0.26 g	7.31 mg	33.58 g	2.63 g	3.77 g
Total Per Box	323.00	12.44 g	1.21 g	343.60 mg	41.24 g	4.72 g	13.89 g
LUNCH OR DINNER 2: PESTO CHICKEN BAKE CONTAINER							
SERVE ON: Monday through Friday (5 days)							
STORE: Portions 1 to 4 in the refrigerator and portions 5 and 6 in the freezer							
Pesto Chicken Bake (page 76)	351.62	21.01 g	5.46 g	296.27 mg	1.97 g	0.50 g	37.18 g
2 fresh carrots or 1 cup (250 mL) sliced carrots, steamed	54.60	0.28 g	0.05 g	90.48 mg	12.82 g	4.68 g	1.19 g
1 3/4 oz (52 g) dry or 3/4 cup (175 mL) cooked whole wheat spaghetti	130.20	0.57 g	0.10 g	3.15 mg	27.87 g	4.72 g	5.60 g
Total Per Box	536.42	21.86 g	5.61 g	389.90 mg	42.66 g	9.90 g	43.97 g

WEEKLY SHOPPING LIST*

VEGETABLES

- carrots: 5 cups, sliced (1.25 L), or 10 carrots (2 lbs/1 kg)
- garlic: 2 cloves
- pepper, green bell: 1
- spinach: 12 cups (2 L)
- tomatoes, plum (Roma): 7 whole

FRUITS

- lemons: 1
- limes: 2

PANTRY

- black pepper, ground
- cayenne pepper
- chickpeas, canned low-sodium: 1¾ cups (425 mL)
- chili powder
- cinnamon, ground
- cooking spray
- maple syrup, sugar-free
- oats, large-flake (old-fashioned) rolled
- oil, extra virgin olive
- oil, olive
- peppers, roasted red: ¾ cup (175 mL)
- pita, whole wheat: 2
- rice, brown
- salt, table
- spaghetti, whole wheat
- tahini
- vanilla extract

DAIRY AND EGGS

- cheese, fresh mozzarella: 4 oz (125 g)
- cottage cheese, low-fat: 1 cup (250 mL)
- eggs, large: 9 whole eggs, 2 egg whites

MEATS/PROTEIN

- chicken breasts, thin sliced boneless skinless: six 5-oz (150 g) breasts
- tofu, extra-firm: 12 oz (375 g)

*SHOPPING NOTE

This week, there are three accompaniments. Buy a jar of each or add the following ingredients to your shopping list, as needed.

APPLE BUTTER

- apples (Cortland, Fuji, Braeburn or McIntosh): 1½ lbs (750 g)
- lemon: 1
- stevia brown sugar blend (such as Truvia or Splenda)

TOMATO SALSA

- tomatoes, plum (Roma): 1 lb (500 g)
- pepper, green bell: 1
- onion, red: ¼

- pepper, jalapeño: 1
- cilantro: ¼ cup (60 mL)
- limes: 2
- garlic: 1 clove

SIMPLE PESTO SAUCE

- basil, fresh: 1½ cups (375 mL)
- cheese, Parmesan, grated: ¼ cup (60 mL)
- pine nuts: ¼ cup (60 mL)
- garlic: 3 cloves

EQUIPMENT

- baking dish, glass: 13- by 9-inch (33 by 23 cm)
- blender (or food processor)
- can opener
- cutting board
- garlic press
- grill pan
- knife
- measuring cups and spoons
- mixing bowls
- saucepan, medium, with lid
- skillet, large
- spatula
- thermometer, instant-read
- tongs
- whisk
- wooden spoons

STEP-BY-STEP MEAL PREP

1 Prepare the **Cilantro-Lime Grilled Tofu** (page 75) through step 1. Cover the tofu and refrigerate for at least 30 minutes and up to 2 hours to marinate.

2 While the tofu is marinating, preheat the oven to 350°F (180°C). Prepare and pack the **Red Pepper Hummus Snack Box** (page 73).

3 Prepare the **Pesto Chicken Bake** (page 76) steps 1 through 4. While the chicken is baking, finish the tofu by following step 2 on page 75. Let the chicken cool for 10 minutes.

4 Prepare the **Cottage Cheese and Oat Pancakes** (page 70) steps 1 and 2.

5 Prepare the **Apple Butter** (page 72), then let it cool for 10 minutes.

6 To complete the boxes, prepare the following according to your favorite technique or package instructions: hard-cook four eggs, cook 1¾ cups (425 mL) dry brown rice, sauté 12 cups (3 L) fresh spinach, steam 6 cups (1.5 L) sliced carrots and boil 9 oz (275 g) dry whole wheat spaghetti. For the hard-cooked eggs, make at least four in advance for the week and cook up the remaining two as needed. For the carrots, spinach, pasta and brown rice, check the meal chart on page 67 for exact amounts to pack per serving.

7 Pack two pieces of the **Cilantro-Lime Grilled Tofu** with one-sixth of the sautéed spinach and ¾ cup (175 mL) cooked brown rice into each of six containers. Store four boxes in the refrigerator with the ¼ cup (60 mL) salsa and freeze two boxed without the salsa.

8 Pack one piece of the **Pesto Chicken Bake** with 1 cup (250 mL) of the steamed carrots and ¾ cup (175 mL) of the cooked whole wheat spaghetti into each of six containers. Store four boxes in the refrigerator and two in the freezer.

9 For the breakfast boxes, pack four containers with two **Cottage Cheese and Oat Pancakes**, 2 tbsp (30 mL) **Apple Butter**, one hard-cooked egg and one tomato, and store them in the refrigerator. Pack two containers with pancakes and apple butter only and store those in the freezer.

COTTAGE CHEESE AND OAT PANCAKES

WITH APPLE BUTTER

 · · ·

SERVES	SERVING SIZE	TOTAL TIME	PREP TIME	COOK TIME
6	2 pancakes, 2 tbsp (30 mL) apple butter	30 minutes	15 minutes	15 minutes

This is one breakfast my kids beg me to make repeatedly. The sweet-tart flavor of the apple butter balances the mild pancakes for a perfect breakfast combination! Make an extra batch of the apple butter to add to Greek yogurt, or top other breakfast goodies with 1 to 2 tbsp (15 to 30 mL).

1 cup (250 mL) gluten-free large-flake (old-fashioned) rolled oats

1 cup (250 mL) low-fat cottage cheese

3 eggs

2 egg whites

2 tbsp (30 mL) sugar-free maple syrup

1 tsp (5 mL) vanilla extract

½ tsp (2 mL) ground cinnamon

Cooking spray

¾ cup (175 mL) Apple Butter (page 72) or store-bought apple butter

Blender

1 In a blender, add the oats and blend until a flour-like consistency is achieved. Add the cottage cheese, eggs, egg whites, maple syrup, vanilla and cinnamon and blend until smooth.

2 Coat a large skillet or griddle with cooking spray and heat over medium heat. When the oil is shimmering, add 3 tbsp (45 mL) of the batter, leaving 1 inch (2.5 cm) between pancakes. Cook until bubbles form and the pancakes have browned on one side, 3 minutes. Flip the pancakes and cook for an additional 3 to 4 minutes. Repeat with the remaining batter for a total of 12 pancakes.

3 TO STORE: In each of six containers, add two pancakes and pack 2 tbsp (30 mL) of apple butter in a small container on the side. Cover and refrigerate for up to 4 days, or freeze the pancakes and apple butter for up to 2 months.

4 TO SERVE: If needed, thaw in the refrigerator overnight. Reheat the pancakes in a toaster oven or microwave on High for 30 seconds. Serve topped with the apple butter. Apple butter can also be reheated in the microwave on High for 15 to 20 seconds, if desired.

TOBY'S TIP | Use the remaining cottage cheese with fruit for a morning snack bowl.

	TOTAL CALORIES	TOTAL FAT	SATURATED FAT	TRANS FAT
PER SERVING	148.48	3.84 g	1.20 g	0.01 g
	SODIUM	CHOLESTEROL	TOTAL CARBOHYDRATES	FIBER
	232.33 mg	94.51 mg	17.85 g	2.27 g
	SUGARS	PROTEIN	POTASSIUM	PHOSPHORUS
	6.40 g	10.78 g	124.86 mg	105.67 mg

APPLE BUTTER

MAKES	SERVING SIZE	TOTAL TIME	PREP TIME	COOK TIME
2½ cups (625 mL)	2 tbsp (30 mL)	50 minutes	20 minutes	30 minutes

1½ lbs (750 g) apples, such as Cortland, Fuji, Braeburn or McIntosh, cored and coarsely chopped (about 4 whole apples)

½ cup (125 mL) water

Juice of 1 lemon

2 tbsp (30 mL) sugar-free maple syrup

2 tbsp (30 mL) stevia brown sugar blend (such as Truvia or Splenda)

¼ tsp (1 mL) ground cinnamon

⅛ tsp (0.5 mL) salt

Blender or immersion blender

1 In a medium saucepan, add the apples, water, lemon juice, maple syrup, brown sugar blend, cinnamon and salt and bring to a boil over high heat. Cover, reduce the heat to low and simmer until the mixture thickens, 30 minutes, stirring occasionally. Remove the saucepan from the heat and let cool for 10 minutes.

2 Transfer the mixture to a blender and purée until smooth. Alternatively, use an immersion blender in the saucepan and blend until smooth.

3 TO STORE: Transfer to an airtight sealable container and refrigerate for up to 1 week or label and freeze for up to 1 year. (The apple butter can be stored in individual portions or as a larger batch.)

TOBY'S TIP | Soft apples work best to make apple butter because they cook down faster. If you purchase apples at the local farmers' market, ask which other varieties not listed above work too.

	TOTAL CALORIES	TOTAL FAT	SATURATED FAT	TRANS FAT
PER SERVING	38.16	0.06 g	0.01 g	0.0 g
	SODIUM	CHOLESTEROL	TOTAL CARBOHYDRATES	FIBER
	17.65 mg	0.0 mg	6.33 g	0.84 g
	SUGARS	PROTEIN	POTASSIUM	PHOSPHORUS
	4.77 g	0.09 g	38.16 mg	3.88 mg

RED PEPPER HUMMUS SNACK BOX

 · · · ·

SERVES	SERVING SIZE	TOTAL TIME	PREP TIME	COOK TIME
4	3 tbsp (45 mL) hummus, 2 carrot sticks, $\frac{1}{2}$ cup (125 mL) cherry tomatoes, 3 slices whole wheat pita	15 minutes	15 minutes	0 minutes

This easy snack box can be tossed together in minutes. You can always whip up an extra one or two midweek so you can have them ready for the end of your week.

$\frac{3}{4}$ cup (175 mL) Roasted Red Pepper Hummus (page 74) or store-bought hummus

2 carrots, peeled and cut into sticks

2 cups (500 mL) cherry tomatoes

Two 6.5-oz (190 g) whole wheat pitas, cut into 6 pieces each

1 In each of four divided containers, place 3 tbsp (45 mL) hummus, 2 carrot sticks, $\frac{1}{2}$ cup (125 mL) cherry tomatoes and 3 slices pita.

2 **TO STORE:** Cover and refrigerate for up to 4 days.

3 **TO SERVE:** Enjoy cold.

TOBY'S TIP | If you prefer, swap whole wheat pita for pita chips.

TOTAL CALORIES 150.69	**TOTAL FAT** 4.58 g	**SATURATED FAT** 0.53 g	**TRANS FAT** 0.0 g
SODIUM 271.53 mg	**CHOLESTEROL** 0.0 mg	**TOTAL CARBOHYDRATES** 23.92 g	**FIBER** 5.55 g
SUGARS 5.42 g	**PROTEIN** 5.45 g	**POTASSIUM** 321.36 mg	**PHOSPHORUS** 57.63 mg

PER SERVING

ROASTED RED PEPPER HUMMUS

MAKES	SERVING SIZE	TOTAL TIME	PREP TIME	COOK TIME
2 cups (500 mL)	2 tbsp (30 mL)	15 minutes	15 minutes	0 minutes

1¾ cups (425 mL) canned low-sodium chickpeas, drained and rinsed

¾ cup (175 mL) roasted red peppers, drained from liquid

1 jalapeño pepper, seeded, ribs removed and coarsely chopped

1 clove garlic, minced

1 tbsp (15 mL) tahini

Juice of 1 lemon

¼ tsp (1 mL) ground black pepper

⅛ tsp (0.5 mL) salt

3 tbsp (45 mL) extra-virgin olive oil

Blender

1 Place the chickpeas, red peppers, jalapeño, garlic, tahini, lemon juice, black pepper, and salt in a blender and purée until smooth.

2 While the blender is running on Medium-Low, slowly drizzle in the olive oil until incorporated.

3 TO STORE: Transfer the hummus to a sealable container and refrigerate for up to 5 days.

TOBY TIP | Swap the roasted red peppers for red bell pepper for a different spin on this hummus.

	TOTAL CALORIES	TOTAL FAT	SATURATED FAT	TRANS FAT
PER SERVING	54.78	3.61 g	0.49 g	0.0 g
	SODIUM 91.76 mg	**CHOLESTEROL** 0.0 mg	**TOTAL CARBOHYDRATES** 4.60 g	**FIBER** 1.30 g
	SUGARS 1.02 g	**PROTEIN** 1.51 g	**POTASSIUM** 47.20 mg	**PHOSPHORUS** 29.08 mg

CILANTRO-LIME GRILLED TOFU

SERVES	SERVING SIZE	TOTAL TIME	PREP TIME	COOK TIME
6	2 pieces of tofu, ¼ cup (60 mL) tomato salsa	21 minutes, plus marinating time	15 minutes	6 minutes

The combination of cilantro and lime works beautifully in a variety of recipes that feature tofu, chicken or fish. If you love cilantro, don't be afraid to add more!

2 tbsp (30 mL) olive oil

Juice of 2 limes

¼ cup (60 mL) chopped cilantro

2 cloves garlic, minced

1 tsp (5 mL) chili powder

½ tsp (2 mL) salt

¼ tsp (1 mL) cayenne pepper

1¼ lbs (625 g) extra-firm tofu, drained and cut into 12 equal slices

Cooking spray

1½ cups (375 mL) Tomato Salsa (page 258) or store-bought tomato salsa

Grill pan

1   In a large bowl, whisk together the oil, lime juice, cilantro, garlic, chili powder, salt and cayenne pepper. Add the tofu and toss to evenly coat. Cover and place in the refrigerator for at least 30 minutes and up to 2 hours.

2   Heat a grill pan on high and coat with cooking spray. Grill the tofu slices until golden, 2 to 3 minutes on each side. Remove the tofu from the grill pan and set aside to cool.

3   TO STORE: In each of four containers, add two pieces of grilled tofu. In a separate compartment or a small separate container, add ¼ cup (60 mL) tomato salsa. Cover all containers and refrigerate for up to 4 days, or freeze only the tofu for up to 2 months.

4   TO SERVE: If needed, thaw in the refrigerator overnight. To reheat, microwave the tofu (without the salsa) uncovered on High for 45 to 60 seconds. Allow 2 minutes for the heat to distribute before removing the container from the microwave. Top with the salsa and serve warm.

TOBY'S TIP | Store extra tofu in a sealable container in the freezer for up to 2 months and use for another week of meal prepping.

	TOTAL CALORIES	TOTAL FAT	SATURATED FAT	TRANS FAT
PER SERVING	146.86	10.89 g	0.91 g	0.0 g
	SODIUM 288.89 mg	CHOLESTEROL 0.0 mg	TOTAL CARBOHYDRATES 5.48 g	FIBER 0.77 g
	SUGARS 1.22 g	PROTEIN 8.40 g	POTASSIUM 123.97 mg	PHOSPHORUS 14.71 mg

PESTO CHICKEN BAKE

SERVES	SERVING SIZE	TOTAL TIME	PREP TIME	COOK TIME
6	1 chicken breast	40 minutes	15 minutes	25 minutes

Add a burst of flavor to your chicken breast by using pesto sauce. This pesto adds healthy fats from the pine nuts and olive oil, which helps keep you feeling satisfied for longer.

6 (5-oz/150 g) thin sliced boneless skinless chicken breasts

¼ tsp (1 mL) salt

¼ tsp (1 mL) ground black pepper

6 tbsp (90 mL) Simple Pesto Sauce (page 264) or store-bought pesto sauce

4 oz (125 g) fresh mozzarella, cut into 6 slices

2 plum tomatoes, thinly sliced

13- by 9-inch (33 by 23 cm) glass baking dish coated with cooking spray

Preheat the oven to 350°F (180°C)

1 Sprinkle both sides of the chicken breasts with the salt and pepper.

2 Place the chicken breasts in a single layer in the prepared baking dish. Top each breast with 1 tbsp (15 mL) of the pesto sauce and spread it evenly using the back of a spoon. Top the pesto with one slice of mozzarella cheese and the tomato slices divided equally among the six breasts.

3 Bake until the cheese has melted and an instant-read thermometer inserted into the thickest part of the chicken registers 165°F (74°C), 25 minutes.

4 TO STORE: In each of six containers, add one chicken breast. Cover and refrigerate for up to 4 days or freeze for up to 2 months.

5 TO SERVE: If needed, thaw in the refrigerator overnight. To reheat, microwave uncovered on High for 1 minute. Allow 2 minutes for the heat to distribute before removing the container from the microwave. Serve warm.

TOBY'S TIP | Traditional pesto sauce includes pine nuts. If you are allergic to pine nuts, eliminate them from the recipe. When shopping for premade pesto sauce, look for varieties that are nut-free.

PER SERVING			
TOTAL CALORIES 351.62	TOTAL FAT 21.01 g	SATURATED FAT 5.46 g	TRANS FAT 0.01 g
SODIUM 296.27 mg	CHOLESTEROL 121.78 mg	TOTAL CARBOHYDRATES 1.97 g	FIBER 0.50 g
SUGARS 0.75 g	PROTEIN 37.18 g	POTASSIUM 569.42 mg	PHOSPHORUS 358.16 mg

MEAL PREP PLAN 3:

INTERMEDIATE

This week has three containers per day, but it is more advanced than Meal Prep Plan 2. This week you will be making one breakfast and three lunch or dinner main meals. One of the main meals is a salad that you can store in the refrigerator for a maximum of 4 days, so you'll need one more meal for the plan this week. You can use one of the frozen portions of the Three-Bean Beef Chili (page 88) and One-Pot Quinoa and Vegetables (page 89) from this week's menu for lunch and dinner on Friday, or if you've already made Meal Prep Plan 1 or 2, you can use one of your extra meals in the freezer for lunch on Friday for a little variety.

You'll notice there are no prepared snack recipes for this week, so be sure to plan for those. Good snack options include a trail mix, hummus and vegetables or a small apple with peanut butter. I've suggested an order for your weekly meal plan in the table on page 80, but the way you plan out your breakfasts, snacks, lunches and dinners depends on your schedule and preferences. Two of the recipes — Pecan Pie Muffins and Three-Bean Beef Chili — have other foods to finish the plate. They include one hard-cooked egg and two carrots per muffin and one medium whole wheat roll per serving of the chili.

WEEKLY MEAL PREP PLAN 3: INTERMEDIATE

Below is a sample plan of when to eat meal prepped food during a work or school week. However, everyone has a different schedule, so customize this to fit your needs.

	BREAKFAST	AM SNACK	LUNCH	PM SNACK	DINNER
Monday	Pecan Pie Muffin Container		Chicken and Soba Noodle Salad Container		Three-Bean Beef Chili Container
Tuesday	Pecan Pie Muffin Container		Chicken and Soba Noodle Salad Container		One-Pot Quinoa with Vegetables and Lima Beans Container
Wednesday	Pecan Pie Muffin Container		Chicken and Soba Noodle Salad Container		Three-Bean Beef Chili Container
Thursday	Pecan Pie Muffin Container		Chicken and Soba Noodle Salad Container		One-Pot Quinoa with Vegetables and Lima Beans Container
Friday	Pecan Pie Muffin Container		One-Pot Quinoa with Vegetables and Lima Beans Container		Three-Bean Beef Chili Container

BREAKFAST: PECAN PIE MUFFIN CONTAINER

SERVE ON: Monday through Friday (5 days)

STORE: Portions 1 to 5 in the refrigerator and the remaining muffins in the freezer

	CALORIES	FAT	SAT FAT	SODIUM	CARB	FIBER	PROTEIN
Pecan Pie Muffins (page 84)	204.21	9.29 g	2.10 g	244.91 mg	24.37 g	2.33 g	5.57 g
1 large hard-cooked egg	77.50	5.30 g	1.63 g	62.00 mg	0.56 g	0.0 g	6.29 g
2 carrots	50.0	0.29 g	0.05 g	84.18 mg	11.69 g	3.42 g	1.13 g
Total Per Box	331.71	14.88 g	3.78 g	391.09 mg	36.63 g	5.75 g	12.99 g

	CALORIES	FAT	SAT FAT	SODIUM	CARB	FIBER	PROTEIN

LUNCH OR DINNER 1: CHICKEN AND SOBA NOODLE SALAD CONTAINER

SERVE ON: Monday through Thursday (4 days)

STORE: All portions in the refrigerator

	CALORIES	FAT	SAT FAT	SODIUM	CARB	FIBER	PROTEIN
Chicken and Soba Noodle Salad (page 86) with Spicy Peanut Dressing (page 266)	391.26	12.85 g	2.42 g	472.07 mg	33.86 g	3.80 g	36.60 g
Total Per Box	391.26	12.85 g	2.42 g	472.07 mg	33.86 g	3.80 g	36.60 g

LUNCH OR DINNER 2: THREE-BEAN BEEF CHILI CONTAINER

SERVE ON: Monday, Wednesday and Friday (3 days)

STORE: Portions 1 and 2 in the refrigerator and portions 3 to 6 in the freezer

	CALORIES	FAT	SAT FAT	SODIUM	CARB	FIBER	PROTEIN
Three-Bean Beef Chili (page 88)	336.70	7.81 g	1.95 g	357.70 mg	41.75 g	16.11 g	22.17 g
1 medium whole wheat roll (2.5-inch/6 cm diameter)	95.76	1.69 g	0.3 g	187.56 mg	18.40 g	2.70 g	3.13 g
Total Per Box	432.46	9.50 g	2.25 g	545.26 mg	60.15 g	18.81 g	25.3 g

LUNCH OR DINNER 3: ONE-POT QUINOA WITH VEGETABLES AND LIMA BEANS CONTAINER

SERVE ON: Tuesday, Thursday and Friday (3 days)

STORE: Portions 1 and 2 in the refrigerator and portions 3 to 6 in the freezer (use one this week and store three for another week)

	CALORIES	FAT	SAT FAT	SODIUM	CARB	FIBER	PROTEIN
One-Pot Quinoa with Vegetables and Lima Beans (page 89)	254.13	4.16 g	0.55 g	294.35 mg	43.94 g	7.12 g	9.37 g
Total Per Box	254.13	4.16 g	0.55 g	294.35 mg	43.94 g	7.12 g	9.37 g

WEEKLY SHOPPING LIST

VEGETABLES

- carrots: 12
- cilantro: ¼ cup (60 mL)
- cucumber, English: ½
- garlic: 6 cloves
- onion, yellow: 2
- pepper, red bell: 1

FRUITS

- limes: 2

PANTRY

- baking powder
- baking soda
- beans, canned no-salt-added black: 1¾ cups (425 mL)
- beans, canned no-salt-added kidney: 1¾ cups (425 mL)
- beans, canned no-salt-added pinto: 1¾ cups (425 mL)
- black pepper, ground
- broth, low-sodium beef
- broth, low-sodium vegetable
- chiles, canned green, chopped: ½ cup (125 mL)
- chili powder
- cinnamon, ground
- cumin, ground
- flour, all-purpose
- flour, 100% whole wheat
- ginger, ground
- oil, canola
- oil, olive
- oregano, dried
- paprika
- parsley, dried flakes
- peanut butter, creamy
- pecans, raw: ½ cup (125 mL)
- quinoa
- roll, whole wheat: 6
- salt, table
- soba (buckwheat) noodles
- soy sauce, reduced-sodium
- stevia brown sugar blend (such as Truvia or Splenda)
- Thai chile sauce (such as Sriracha)
- tomatoes, canned no-salt-added crushed: 3¼ cups (300 mL)
- tomatoes, canned no-salt-added diced: 3½ cups (875 mL)
- vanilla extract
- vinegar, unseasoned rice
- wheat germ, toasted

DAIRY AND EGGS

- butter, unsalted
- eggs, large: 5
- milk, nonfat
- yogurt, nonfat plain Greek: ½ cup (125 mL)

MEATS/PROTEIN

- beef, at least 90% lean ground: 8 oz (250 g)
- chicken breasts, boneless skinless: 1 lb (500 g)

FROZEN

- edamame, shelled
- lima beans: 1 cup (250 mL)
- vegetables, mixed: 3 cups (750 mL)

EQUIPMENT

- box grater
- can opener
- colander
- cutting board
- garlic press
- grill pan or large skillet
- knife
- measuring cups and spoons
- mixing bowls
- muffin pan, 12-cup
- saucepan, large
- sauté pan, large
- spatula
- thermometer, instant-read
- vegetable peeler
- whisk
- wooden spoons

STEP-BY-STEP MEAL PREP

1 Prepare the **Pecan Pie Muffins** (page 84) through step 7.

2 While the muffins are baking, prepare the **Chicken and Soba Noodle Salad** (page 86) through step 2.

3 Remove the muffins from the oven and let cool for 2 to 3 minutes before removing from the muffin pan.

4 Continue preparing the salad by making the **Spicy Peanut Dressing** (page 266) and follow the **Chicken and Soba Noodle Salad** (page 86) recipe through step 4. Pack the salad into containers and refrigerate.

5 Prepare the **Three-Bean Beef Chili** (page 88) through step 2. While the chili is cooking, prepare the ingredients for the **One-Pot Quinoa with Vegetables and Lima Beans** (page 89).

6 Allow the chili to cool for 15 minutes before packing into six boxes. Cover the boxes and pack one medium whole wheat roll alongside each box. Refrigerate two boxes and store the remaining four in the freezer.

7 Cook the **One-Pot Quinoa with Vegetables and Lima Beans** (page 89) through step 3. Let cool for 10 minutes.

8 Hard-cook the eggs and let cool in an ice bath. Pack five muffins into five boxes with one hard-cooked egg and two carrots in each box. Store in the refrigerator. Pack the remaining seven muffins into individual sealable freezer-friendly bags or containers and freeze for up to 2 months.

9 Pack the **One-Pot Quinoa with Vegetables and Lima Beans** into six boxes. Store two boxes in the refrigerator and four boxes in the freezer.

PECAN PIE MUFFINS

SERVES	SERVING SIZE	TOTAL TIME	PREP TIME	COOK TIME
12	1 muffin	35 minutes	15 minutes	20 minutes

Your entire home will be smell so delicious when you're baking these muffins. It's the cinnamon and nutmeg that will have your neighbors knocking on your door.

1¼ cups (300 mL) unbleached all-purpose flour

1 cup (250 mL) 100% whole wheat flour

¼ cup (60 mL) toasted wheat germ

2 tsp (10 mL) baking powder

1 tsp (5 mL) ground cinnamon

½ tsp (2 mL) baking soda

½ tsp (2 mL) salt

⅛ tsp (0.5 mL) ground nutmeg

½ cup (125 mL) nonfat plain Greek yogurt

½ cup (125 mL) nonfat milk

½ cup (125 mL) water

¼ cup (60 mL) stevia brown sugar blend (such as Truvia or Splenda)

3 tbsp (45 mL) canola oil

2 tbsp (30 mL) unsalted butter, melted

12-cup muffin pan coated with cooking spray
Preheat the oven to 350°F (180°C)

1 TO MAKE THE MUFFINS: In a medium bowl, sift together the all-purpose flour, whole wheat flour, wheat germ, baking powder, cinnamon, baking soda, salt and nutmeg.

2 In a separate medium bowl, whisk together the yogurt, milk, water, brown sugar blend, oil, butter, egg and vanilla.

3 Gently fold the dry mixture into the wet mixture. Mix together with as few strokes as possible until the dry ingredients are moistened. Do not overmix. Add the pecans and fold until just combined.

4 TO MAKE THE TOPPING: In a small bowl, combine the brown sugar blend and cinnamon.

5 TO BAKE: Divide the batter evenly among the 12 prepared muffin cups. Tap the muffin tin on the counter several times to get rid of any air bubbles. Evenly sprinkle the topping mixture over the batter.

6 Bake in the center of the oven until a tester inserted into one or two muffins comes out clean, 18 to 20 minutes. Remove from the oven and let cool in the pan for 2 to 3 minutes. Remove the muffins to a wire rack and let cool completely.

7 TO STORE: Place one muffin into each of twelve sealable freezer-friendly bags or containers. Store five at room temperature or in the refrigerator and freeze the remaining muffins for up to 2 months.

PER SERVING			
TOTAL CALORIES 204.21	**TOTAL FAT** 9.29 g	**SATURATED FAT** 2.10 g	**TRANS FAT** 0 g
SODIUM 244.91 mg	**CHOLESTEROL** 21.18 mg	**TOTAL CARBOHYDRATES** 24.37 g	**FIBER** 2.33 g
SUGARS 5.66 g	**PROTEIN** 5.57 g	**POTASSIUM** 126.30 mg	**PHOSPHORUS** 119.74 mg

1 large egg, beaten

1 tsp (5 mL) vanilla extract

½ cup (125 mL) raw pecans, coarsely chopped

TOPPING

1 tbsp (15 mL) stevia brown sugar blend (such as Truvia or Splenda)

½ tsp (2 mL) ground cinnamon

8 TO SERVE: If needed, thaw at room temperature overnight. Enjoy at room temperature or warm in the microwave on High for 20 to 30 seconds.

TOBY'S TIP | To make sure the muffins don't stick to the inside of the muffin pan, thoroughly coat inside the wells with the cooking spray.

CHICKEN AND SOBA NOODLE SALAD

SERVES	SERVING SIZE	TOTAL TIME	PREP TIME	COOK TIME
4	2 cups (500 mL)	37 minutes	20 minutes	17 minutes

Chicken, colorful veggies and soba noodles are drizzled with Spicy Peanut Dressing for a one-dish meal that will be a regular in your weekly rotation.

1 lb (500 g) boneless skinless chicken breast, cut into 1-inch (2.5 cm) pieces

¼ tsp (1 mL) ground black pepper

1 tbsp (15 mL) olive oil or canola oil

4 oz (125 g) soba (buckwheat) noodles

1 cup (250 mL) shelled edamame

2 carrots, peeled and grated

1 red bell pepper, cut into 1-inch (2.5 cm) strips

½ English cucumber (7½ oz/ 230 g), sliced lengthwise and cut into half-moons

¼ cup (60 mL) chopped cilantro

6 tbsp (90 mL) Spicy Peanut Dressing (page 266)

Grill pan or large skillet

1 Sprinkle the chicken with the black pepper.

2 In a grill pan or large skillet, heat the oil over medium heat. When the oil is shimmering, add the chicken and cook, turning on all sides, until an instant-read thermometer registers 165°F (74°C) when inserted into the chicken, 8 minutes. Remove the pan from the heat and let cool for 10 minutes.

3 Fill a large saucepan three-quarters with water and bring to a boil over high heat. Add the soba noodles and return to a boil. Reduce the heat to medium and simmer for 5 minutes, then stir in the edamame. Return to a boil over high heat. Reduce the heat to medium and simmer until the soba noodles are cooked, 4 minutes. Drain and rinse the noodles and edamame with cold water. Set aside to cool for 10 minutes.

4 In a large bowl, add the cooled chicken, soba noodles and edamame, carrots, bell pepper, cucumber and cilantro. Toss to combine. Drizzle with the dressing and toss to evenly coat.

5 TO STORE: In each of four containers, add 2 cups (500 mL) of the salad. Cover and refrigerate for up to 4 days.

6 TO SERVE: Enjoy cold.

TOBY'S TIP | To make this dish vegetarian, swap the chicken for the same amount of extra-firm tofu.

PER SERVING	TOTAL CALORIES	TOTAL FAT	SATURATED FAT	TRANS FAT
	391.26	12.85 g	2.42 g	0.01 g
	SODIUM	**CHOLESTEROL**	**TOTAL CARBOHYDRATES**	**FIBER**
	472.07 mg	82.78 mg	33.86 g	3.80 g
	SUGARS	**PROTEIN**	**POTASSIUM**	**PHOSPHORUS**
	6.69 g	36.60 g	626.74 mg	334.87 mg

THREE-BEAN BEEF CHILI

 · · · ·

SERVES	SERVING SIZE	TOTAL TIME	PREP TIME	COOK TIME
6	About 1½ cups (375 mL)	1 hour	15 minutes	45 minutes

There's nothing more warming than a bowl of chili, especially when it's bursting with three different kinds of beans! Make a double batch and freeze individual containers for a week without time to meal prep.

1 tbsp (15 mL) olive oil

1 yellow onion, chopped

2 cloves garlic, minced

8 oz (250 g) at least 90% lean ground beef

1 can (28 oz/796 mL) no-salt-added crushed tomatoes

1¾ cups (425 mL) canned no-salt-added black beans

1¾ cups (425 mL) canned no-salt-added pinto beans

1¾ cups (425 mL) canned no-salt-added kidney beans

1 cup (250 mL) low-sodium beef broth or water

½ cup (125 mL) canned chopped green chiles, with juice

2 tbsp (30 mL) chili powder

1 tbsp (15 mL) ground cumin

1 tsp (5 mL) paprika

½ tsp (2 mL) salt

1 In a large sauté pan, heat the olive oil over medium heat. When the oil is shimmering, add the onion and garlic and cook until the onion is translucent and the garlic is fragrant, 3 minutes. Add the ground beef and brown on all sides, breaking up the pieces with the back of a spoon, 8 minutes.

2 Add the crushed tomatoes, black beans, pinto beans, kidney beans, broth, green chiles, chili powder, cumin, paprika and salt and stir to combine. Bring the mixture to a boil over high heat. Reduce the heat to medium-low and simmer, covered, stirring occasionally, until the flavors combine, 30 minutes. Remove the pan from the heat and allow the chili to cool for at least 15 minutes.

3 TO STORE: Divide the chili among six containers, about 1½ cups (375 mL) in each. Cover and refrigerate for up to 4 days or freeze for up to 2 months.

4 TO SERVE: If needed, thaw in the refrigerator overnight. To reheat, microwave uncovered on High for 90 seconds. Allow 2 minutes for the heat to distribute before removing the container from the microwave. Alternatively, reheat in a small saucepan and bring to a boil over high heat. Reduce the heat to medium and cook until heated through, 10 minutes. Serve warm.

TOBY'S TIP | If you prefer, swap the ground beef for ground lamb or ground pork.

TOTAL CALORIES 336.70	**TOTAL FAT** 7.81 g	**SATURATED FAT** 1.95 g	**TRANS FAT** 0.24 g
SODIUM 357.70 mg	**CHOLESTEROL** 24.56 mg	**TOTAL CARBOHYDRATES** 41.75 g	**FIBER** 16.11 g
SUGARS 6.15 g	**PROTEIN** 22.17 g	**POTASSIUM** 1,135.15 mg	**PHOSPHORUS** 397.30 mg

PER SERVING

ONE-POT QUINOA
WITH VEGETABLES AND LIMA BEANS

SERVES	SERVING SIZE	TOTAL TIME	PREP TIME	COOK TIME
6	1¾ cups (425 mL)	40 minutes	15 minutes	25 minutes

This meatless lunch or dinner is a snap to make using frozen vegetables and frozen beans. There is minimal chopping, and frozen veggies can be stored in your freezer for several months. It's a win-win.

1 tbsp (15 mL) olive oil or canola oil

1 yellow onion, chopped

2 cloves garlic, minced

3 cups (750 mL) frozen mixed vegetables, thawed

1 cup (250 mL) frozen lima beans, thawed

2½ cups (625 mL) low-sodium vegetable broth

1 cup (250 mL) quinoa

3½ cups (300 mL) canned no-salt-added diced tomatoes, with juice

1 tsp (5 mL) dried parsley flakes

1 tsp (5 mL) dried oregano

½ tsp (2 mL) ground cumin

½ tsp (2 mL) salt

¼ tsp (1 mL) ground black pepper

1 In a large sauté pan, heat the olive oil over medium heat. When the oil is shimmering, add the onion and garlic and cook until the onion is translucent and the garlic is fragrant, 3 minutes.

2 Add the mixed vegetables, lima beans, broth, quinoa, diced tomatoes with juice, parsley, oregano, cumin, salt and pepper and bring to a boil over high heat. Reduce the heat to low, cover and simmer until the flavors combine, the quinoa is cooked through and much of the liquid is absorbed, 15 minutes. Remove the pan from the heat and allow the dish to cool for at least 15 minutes.

3 TO STORE: In each of six containers, add 1¾ cups (425 mL) of the quinoa and vegetables. Cover and refrigerate for up to 4 days or freeze for up to 2 months.

4 TO SERVE: If needed, thaw in the refrigerator overnight. To reheat, microwave uncovered on High for 60 to 90 seconds. Allow 2 minutes for the heat to distribute before removing the container from the microwave. Serve warm.

TOBY'S TIP | If you prefer, swap the lima beans for the same amount of canned no-salt-added cannellini beans.

	TOTAL CALORIES	TOTAL FAT	SATURATED FAT	TRANS FAT
PER SERVING	254.13	4.16 g	0.55 g	0.0 g
	SODIUM	CHOLESTEROL	TOTAL CARBOHYDRATES	FIBER
	294.35 mg	0.0 mg	43.94 g	7.12 g
	SUGARS	PROTEIN	POTASSIUM	PHOSPHORUS
	8.43 g	9.37 g	321.32 mg	165.20 mg

<table>
<tr>
<td>

CHAPTER

7

</td>
<td>

MEAL PREP PLAN 4:

ADVANCED INTERMEDIATE

</td>
</tr>
</table>

This week is a little more advanced because there are five main recipes, which means nearly all of your meals and snacks are covered for the week! You will be making one breakfast, one snack and three main lunches or dinners, and you will have four meal or snack boxes prepared per day.

Just like in Meal Prep Plan 3, one of the mains is a salad that can be stored in the refrigerator for a maximum of 4 days. For lunch and dinner on Friday, you can have one of the frozen servings of Lemon-Basil Chicken with Cauliflower Rice (page 101) or Roasted Salmon in Barbecue Sauce (page 102), or if you have made any of the previous three meal plans, you can incorporate one or more of the containers that you stashed in the freezer. For the roasted salmon, don't forget to add 1 cup (250 mL) steamed broccoli and ¾ cup (175 mL) cooked quinoa to each box. When you thaw a frozen serving of the Lemon-Basil Chicken, be sure to add an orange to complete your plate.

There is one prepared snack recipe for this week, so be sure to plan for additional snacks you may need. Good snack options include one cheese stick and a piece of fruit, guacamole with cut-up vegetables or Greek yogurt topped with granola.

Peanut Butter–Blueberry Yogurt Bowls 96

Spinach Salad with Hard-Cooked Egg 98

Turkey and Cheese Roll-Ups 100

Lemon-Basil Chicken with Cauliflower Rice 101

Roasted Salmon in Barbecue Sauce 102

WEEKLY MEAL PREP PLAN 4: ADVANCED INTERMEDIATE

Below is a sample plan of when to eat meal prepped food during a work or school week. However, everyone has a different schedule, so customize this to fit your needs.

	BREAKFAST	AM SNACK	LUNCH	PM SNACK	DINNER
Monday	Yogurt Bowl	Roll-Ups Container	Spinach Salad Container		Roasted Salmon Container
Tuesday	Yogurt Bowl	Roll-Ups Container	Spinach Salad Container		Lemon-Basil Chicken Container
Wednesday	Yogurt Bowl	Roll-Ups Container	Spinach Salad Container		Roasted Salmon Container
Thursday	Yogurt Bowl	Roll-Ups Container	Spinach Salad Container		Lemon-Basil Chicken Container
Friday	Yogurt Bowl	Roll-Ups Container	Lemon-Basil Chicken Container		Roasted Salmon Container

BREAKFAST: PEANUT BUTTER–BLUEBERRY YOGURT BOWL

SERVE ON: Monday through Friday (5 days)

STORE: All portions in the refrigerator

	CALORIES	FAT	SAT FAT	SODIUM	CARB	FIBER	PROTEIN
Peanut Butter–Blueberry Yogurt Bowls (page 96)	175.77	6.28 g	0.85 g	86.04 mg	19.05 g	2.85 g	14.48 g
Total Per Box	175.77	6.28 g	0.85 g	86.04 mg	19.05 g	2.85 g	14.48 g

SNACK: TURKEY AND CHEESE ROLL-UPS CONTAINER

SERVE ON: Monday through Friday (5 days)

STORE: All portions in the refrigerator

	CALORIES	FAT	SAT FAT	SODIUM	CARB	FIBER	PROTEIN
Turkey and Cheese Roll-Ups (page 100)	84.56	2.0 g	0.93 g	249.50 mg	2.27 g	0.41 g	14.75 g
Total Per Box	84.56	2.0 g	0.93 g	249.50 mg	2.27 g	0.41 g	14.75 g

	CALORIES	FAT	SAT FAT	SODIUM	CARB	FIBER	PROTEIN

LUNCH OR DINNER 1: SPINACH SALAD CONTAINER

SERVE ON: Monday through Thursday (4 days)

STORE: All portions in the refrigerator

	CALORIES	FAT	SAT FAT	SODIUM	CARB	FIBER	PROTEIN
Spinach Salad with Hard-Cooked Egg (page 98) and Lighter Parmesan Dressing (page 254)	216.23	14.10 g	3.50 g	459.45 mg	9.21 g	2.66 g	13.75 g
1 medium whole wheat roll (2.5 inch/5 cm diameter)	95.76	1.69 g	0.3 g	187.56 mg	18.40 g	2.70 g	3.13 g
Total Per Box	311.99	15.79 g	3.53	647.01 mg	27.61 g	5,36 g	16.77 g

LUNCH OR DINNER 2: ROASTED SALMON IN BARBECUE SAUCE CONTAINER

SERVE ON: Monday, Wednesday and Friday (3 days)

STORE: Portions 1 and 2 in the refrigerator and portions 3 and 4 in the freezer (use one this week and the other for another week)

	CALORIES	FAT	SAT FAT	SODIUM	CARB	FIBER	PROTEIN
Roasted Salmon in Barbecue Sauce (page 102)	243.97	9.06 g	1.39 g	137.83 mg	10.16 g	0.16 g	28.22 g
1 cup (250 mL) steamed broccoli	54.60	0.64 g	0.12 g	63.96 g	11.20 g	5.15 g	3.71 g
¼ cup (60 mL) dry or ¾ cup (175 mL) cooked quinoa	166.50	2.66 g	0.32 g	9.71 mg	29.55 g	3.88 g	6.11 g
Total Per Box	465.07	12.36 g	1.83 g	211.50 mg	50.91 g	9.19 g	38.04 g

LUNCH OR DINNER 3: LEMON-BASIL CHICKEN CONTAINER

SERVE ON: Tuesday, Thursday and Friday (3 days)

STORE: Portions 1 and 2 in the refrigerator and portions 3 and 4 without the orange in the freezer (use one this week and store one for another week)

	CALORIES	FAT	SAT FAT	SODIUM	CARB	FIBER	PROTEIN
Lemon-Basil Chicken with Cauliflower Rice (page 101)	332.24	11.60 g	1.95 g	460.17 mg	12.19 g	3.48 g	42.30 g
1 orange	61.57	0.16 g	0.02 g	0.00 mg	15.39 g	3.14 g	1.23 g
Total Per Box	393.81	11.76 g	1.97 g	460.17 mg	27.58 g	6.62 g	43.53 g

WEEKLY SHOPPING LIST

VEGETABLES

- basil: 1 cup (250 mL)
- broccoli, florets: 4 cups (1 L)
- cucumbers, Kirby: 1
- garlic: 6 cloves
- kale, Lacinato, chopped: 3 cups (750 mL)
- onion, yellow: 1
- spinach, baby: 4 cups (1 L)
- tomatoes, cherry: 1 cup (250 mL)

FRUITS

- blueberries: 2½ cups (625 mL)
- lemon: 1
- oranges: 5

PANTRY

- almonds, unsalted roasted: 5 tbsp (75 mL)
- black pepper
- broth, low-sodium vegetable: 1 cup (250 mL)
- cinnamon, ground
- cooking spray
- ketchup, no added salt
- oil, olive
- maple syrup, sugar-free
- mayonnaise, light
- paprika, smoked
- parsley, dried flakes
- peanut butter, smooth
- quinoa, dry
- roll, whole wheat (medium): 4
- salt, table
- stevia brown sugar blend (such as Truvia or Splenda)
- sunflower seeds, unsalted: ¼ cup (60 mL)
- vinegar, apple cider
- vinegar, white wine
- Worcestershire sauce

DAIRY AND EGGS

- buttermilk, low-fat: ½ cup (125 mL)
- cheese, Parmesan grated: 1½ tbsp (22 mL)
- eggs, large: 4
- yogurt, nonfat plain Greek: 2¾ cups (675 mL)

MEATS/PROTEIN

- bacon, turkey: 2 oz (60 g)
- chicken breasts, boneless skinless: 1½ lbs (750 g)
- salmon fillet: 1¼ lbs (625 g)

FROZEN

- cauliflower rice: 12 oz (375 g)

EQUIPMENT

- baking dish, glass: 11- by 7-inch (28 by 18 cm)
- blender
- colander
- cutting board
- garlic press
- glass jars: 4
- knife
- measuring cups and spoons
- mixing bowls
- pot, large with lid
- sauté pan, large
- skillet, medium
- thermometer, instant-read
- toothpicks
- whisk
- wooden spoons

STEP-BY-STEP MEAL PREP

1. Prepare the **Spinach Salad with Hard-Cooked Egg** (page 98) through step 1 and let the eggs cool.

2. While the eggs are cooking, prepare the **Peanut Butter–Blueberry Yogurt Bowls** (page 96) through step 3. Pack according to the recipe and refrigerate.

3. Prepare the **Easy Barbecue Sauce** (page 263) through step 1, then complete step 1 of the **Roasted Salmon in Barbecue Sauce** (page 102).

4. While the salmon is marinating, continue preparing the **Spinach Salad with Hard-Cooked Egg** (page 98) through step 3. Pack the salad into containers according to the recipe. Add 1 medium whole wheat roll to each container, or store on the side, and refrigerate.

5. Prepare the **Turkey and Cheese Roll-Ups** (page 100) through step 2. Pack the roll-ups into containers according to the recipe and refrigerate.

6. Continue preparing the **Roasted Salmon in Barbecue Sauce** (page 102) through step 3.

7. While the salmon is roasting, cook 1 cup (250 mL) dry quinoa according to package instructions and steam 4 cups (1 L) of broccoli.

8. Let the salmon cool while you prepare the **Lemon-Basil Chicken with Cauliflower Rice** (page 101) through step 3.

9. While the **Lemon-Basil Chicken with Cauliflower Rice** cools, pack the salmon into containers and add 1 cup (250 mL) of steamed broccoli and ¾ cup (175 mL) of cooked quinoa to each. Refrigerate two boxes and freeze the remaining two boxes.

10. Pack the chicken into four containers. Store two boxes with one orange each in the refrigerator and freeze the remaining two boxes without oranges.

PEANUT BUTTER–BLUEBERRY YOGURT BOWLS

SERVES	SERVING SIZE	TOTAL TIME	PREP TIME	COOK TIME
5	½ cup (125 mL) yogurt mixture, ½ cup (125 mL) blueberries, 1 tbsp (15 mL) almonds	20 minutes	20 minutes	0 minutes

Start your day with protein and calcium–filled Greek yogurt paired with peanut butter, nuts, and fruit. The creamy Greek yogurt is complemented with crunchy nuts and tart blueberries.

2 tbsp (30 mL) smooth peanut butter

2½ cups (625 mL) nonfat plain Greek yogurt

2 tbsp (30 mL) sugar-free maple syrup

⅛ tsp (0.5 mL) ground cinnamon

2½ cups (625 mL) fresh blueberries

5 tbsp (75 mL) chopped unsalted roasted almonds

1 In a microwave-safe bowl, add the peanut butter and microwave on High for 30 seconds to soften. Let cool for 5 minutes.

2 In a medium bowl, whisk together the peanut butter, yogurt, maple syrup and cinnamon.

3 TO STORE: In each of five divided containers, add ½ cup (125 mL) of the yogurt mixture. In two separate compartments in each container, add ½ cup (125 mL) of blueberries and 1 tbsp (15 mL) of almonds. Cover and refrigerate for up to 5 days.

4 TO SERVE: Top the yogurt with the blueberries and almonds. Enjoy cold.

TOBY TIP | If you prefer, swap the blueberries for strawberries, raspberries or blackberries and the peanut butter for almond butter.

	TOTAL CALORIES	TOTAL FAT	SATURATED FAT	TRANS FAT
PER SERVING	175.77	6.28 g	0.85 g	0.0 g
	SODIUM 86.04 mg	**CHOLESTEROL** 0.0 mg	**TOTAL CARBOHYDRATES** 19.05 g	**FIBER** 2.85 g
	SUGARS 12.41 g	**PROTEIN** 14.48 g	**POTASSIUM** 309.69 mg	**PHOSPHORUS** 208.78 mg

SPINACH SALAD
WITH HARD-COOKED EGG

SERVES	SERVING SIZE	TOTAL TIME	PREP TIME	COOK TIME
4	1 cup (250 mL) spinach, $\frac{1}{4}$ cup (60 mL) tomatoes, $\frac{1}{4}$ Kirby cucumber, 1 egg, 2 tbsp (30 mL) turkey bacon, 1 tbsp (15 mL) sunflower seeds, $1\frac{1}{2}$ tbsp (22 mL) dressing	31 minutes	20 minutes	11 minutes

This is the ultimate grab-and-go salad that will make all your coworkers drool! Pile the vegetables in a mason jar and top with a hard-cooked egg, pieces of bacon and a sprinkle of sunflower seeds. It's a lunch that will be the talk of the office. If you prefer, swap the dressing for Balsamic Vinaigrette (page 252) or Simple Lemon-Herb Vinaigrette (page 253).

4 large eggs

Cooking spray

2 slices (2 oz/60 g) turkey bacon

4 cups (1 L) baby spinach

1 cup (250 mL) cherry tomatoes

1 Kirby cucumber, thinly sliced

$\frac{1}{4}$ cup (60 mL) unsalted sunflower seeds

6 tbsp (90 mL) Lighter Parmesan Dressing (page 254)

1 In a large pot, cover the eggs with cold water and bring to a boil. After 3 minutes, remove the pot from the heat, cover and let stand for 15 minutes. Drain and place the eggs in a bowl filled with water and ice to completely cool, about 10 minutes.

2 Coat a medium skillet with cooking spray and heat over medium heat. When the oil is shimmering, add the turkey bacon and cook, flipping several times, until crispy, 8 minutes. Transfer to a cutting board and let cool for 10 minutes, and then coarsely chop.

3 Once the hard-cooked eggs have cooled, peel and quarter them, then set aside. When the bacon has cooled, coarsely chop and set aside.

4 TO STORE: In each of four 16-oz (500 mL) lidded glass jars, place 1 cup (250 mL) spinach, $\frac{1}{4}$ cup (60 mL) cherry tomatoes, one-quarter of the cucumber slices, 1 quartered egg and about 2 tbsp (30 mL) of the turkey bacon. Sprinkle with 1 tbsp (15 mL) of the sunflower seeds. In small separate containers, add $1\frac{1}{2}$ tbsp (22 mL) of the dressing. Cover all containers and refrigerate for up to 4 days.

5 TO SERVE: Drizzle the salad with the dressing immediately before eating. Enjoy cold.

PER SERVING			
TOTAL CALORIES 216.23	**TOTAL FAT** 14.10 g	**SATURATED FAT** 3.50 g	**TRANS FAT** 0.03 g
SODIUM 459.45 mg	**CHOLESTEROL** 205.85 mg	**TOTAL CARBOHYDRATES** 9.21 g	**FIBER** 2.66 g
SUGARS 3.80 g	**PROTEIN** 13.75 g	**POTASSIUM** 316.36 mg	**PHOSPHORUS** 210.70 mg

TURKEY AND CHEESE ROLL-UPS

SERVES	SERVING SIZE	TOTAL TIME	PREP TIME	COOK TIME
5	2 roll-ups	15 minutes	15 minutes	0 minutes

Snacks don't have to be complicated, but a little creativity goes a long way. This no-cook, three-ingredient snack is easy to put together and fun to eat. Try swapping the low-carb veggie on top. Zucchini, summer squash, cucumber or bell pepper are all great options!

10 cherry tomatoes

10 (1/2 oz/150 g) slices low-sodium turkey breast

10 (1/2 oz/150 g) slices reduced-fat Swiss cheese

1 On each of 10 toothpicks skewer a cherry tomato.

2 On a cutting board, lay out one slice of turkey breast and top with a slice of cheese. Roll together and secure in the center with a tomato-skewered toothpick. Repeat with the remaining cheese and turkey for a total of 10 roll-ups.

3 **TO STORE:** In each of five containers, add two rolls-up. Cover and refrigerate for up to 5 days.

4 **TO SERVE:** Enjoy cold.

TOBY'S TIP | For a variation on this snack, swap the turkey breast for low-sodium ham.

	TOTAL CALORIES	TOTAL FAT	SATURATED FAT	TRANS FAT
PER SERVING	84.56	2.0 g	0.93 g	0.0 g
	SODIUM	**CHOLESTEROL**	**TOTAL CARBOHYDRATES**	**FIBER**
	249.50 mg	19.80 mg	2.27 g	0.41 g
	SUGARS	**PROTEIN**	**POTASSIUM**	**PHOSPHORUS**
	1.27 g	14.75 g	111.66 mg	177.56 mg

LEMON-BASIL CHICKEN
WITH CAULIFLOWER RICE

SERVES	SERVING SIZE	TOTAL TIME	PREP TIME	COOK TIME
4	1¾ cups (425 mL)	40 minutes	20 minutes	20 minutes

Make your own low-carb cauliflower rice by finely chopping cauliflower florets in a blender or food processor, or find it in the freezer aisle. Paired here with flavorful chicken and hearty kale, this one-pot meal will be a regular in your meal prep rotation.

1½ lbs (750 g) boneless skinless chicken breasts, cut into 1-inch (2.5 cm) pieces

½ tsp (2 mL) salt, divided

½ tsp (2 mL) ground black pepper, divided

2 tbsp (30 mL) olive oil

1 yellow onion, chopped

2 cloves garlic, minced

12 oz (375 g) frozen cauliflower rice, thawed

1 cup (250 mL) low-sodium chicken broth

Juice of 1 lemon

3 cups (750 mL) chopped Lacinato kale, stems removed

1 cup (250 mL) basil, sliced into ribbons

1 Sprinkle both sides of the chicken with ¼ tsp (1 mL) of the salt and ¼ tsp (1 mL) of the pepper.

2 In a large sauté pan, heat the oil over medium heat. When the oil is shimmering, add the onion and garlic and cook until the onion is translucent and the garlic is fragrant, 3 minutes. Add the chicken and cook on all sides until browned, 8 minutes. Transfer the chicken and vegetables to a clean plate.

3 In the same sauté pan, add the cauliflower rice and broth and bring to a boil over high heat. Reduce the heat to low and simmer for 5 minutes. Add the lemon juice, cooked chicken and vegetables, and remaining ¼ tsp (1 mL) salt and ¼ tsp (1 mL) pepper. Toss to evenly coat. Add the kale and basil and continue cooking over medium heat, stirring occasionally, until the kale is wilted, 4 minutes.

4 TO STORE: In each of four containers, add 1¾ cups (425 mL) of the chicken and cauliflower rice mixture. Cover and refrigerate for up to 4 days or freeze for up to 2 months.

5 TO SERVE: If needed, thaw in the refrigerator overnight. To reheat, microwave uncovered on High for 60 to 90 seconds. Allow 2 minutes for the heat to distribute before removing from the microwave. Serve warm.

TOBY'S TIP | Try swapping the kale for spinach.

PER SERVING	TOTAL CALORIES	TOTAL FAT	SATURATED FAT	TRANS FAT
	332.24	11.60 g	1.95 g	0.01 g
	SODIUM	CHOLESTEROL	TOTAL CARBOHYDRATES	FIBER
	460.17 mg	124.17 mg	12.19 g	3.48 g
	SUGARS	PROTEIN	POTASSIUM	PHOSPHORUS
	3.39 g	42.30 g	866.11 mg	407.71 mg

ROASTED SALMON IN BARBECUE SAUCE

	SERVES	SERVING SIZE	TOTAL TIME	PREP TIME	COOK TIME
	4	1 (5-oz/150 g) fillet	28 minutes (plus 30 minutes to 4 hours to marinate)	10 minutes	18 minutes

Roasted salmon makes a great go-to dish. It's delicious plain, and it's also super easy to give it a quick marinade and cook it up within 15 to 20 minutes. Cooked salmon freezes nicely, so you can stash two servings in the refrigerator and the other two in the freezer for later in the week. To save time, swap the homemade barbecue sauce for store-bought low-sugar barbecue sauce.

1¼ lbs (300 mL) salmon fillet

½ cup (125 mL) Easy Barbecue Sauce (page 263)

Cooking spray

1 In a large container, add the salmon and pour the barbecue sauce over the top. Turn to evenly coat. Cover and marinate in the refrigerator for at least 30 minutes and up to 4 hours.

2 Preheat the oven to 400°F (200°C) and coat an 11- by 7-inch (28 by 18 cm) glass baking dish with cooking spray.

3 Remove the salmon from the marinade, letting the excess drip off, and place the salmon skin-side down in the prepared baking dish. Discard the excess marinade. Roast the salmon until it is opaque and an instant-read thermometer registers 145°F (63°C), 15 to 18 minutes. Set the salmon aside to cool for 10 minutes and cut into four equal pieces.

4 TO STORE: In each of four containers, add one (5-oz/150 g) piece of the roasted salmon. Cover and refrigerate for up to 4 days or freeze for up to 2 months.

5 TO SERVE: If needed, thaw in the refrigerator overnight. To reheat, microwave uncovered on High for 45 seconds to 1 minute. Allow 2 minutes for the heat to distribute before removing from the microwave. Serve warm.

TOBY'S TIP | Instead of roasting, try grilling the salmon for 6 to 8 minutes on each side, using the doneness cues in step 3.

	TOTAL CALORIES	TOTAL FAT	SATURATED FAT	TRANS FAT
PER SERVING	243.97	9.06 g	1.39 g	0.0 g
	SODIUM	**CHOLESTEROL**	**TOTAL CARBOHYDRATES**	**FIBER**
	137.83 mg	77.92 mg	10.16 g	0.16 g
	SUGARS	**PROTEIN**	**POTASSIUM**	**PHOSPHORUS**
	8.07 g	28.22 g	706.78 mg	284.19 mg

MEAL PREP PLAN 5:

ADVANCED

This week's meal plan has all of your meals (and most of your snacks) covered for the week. The six main recipes include one breakfast, two snacks and three main lunches or dinners. This plan sets you up with five meal and snack boxes per day until Friday, when you'll need to add in two additional snacks.

As in the last two meal plans, one of the main meals — Baked Falafel Bowls (page 118) — can only be refrigerated for up to 4 days. For lunch and dinner on Friday, you can use one of the frozen portions of the Deconstructed Skillet Lasagna (page 120) or Teriyaki Pork Tenderloin (page 117) from this week's menu, or you can incorporate frozen containers stashed from meal plans in previous weeks.

The two prepared snack recipes for this week will provide you with two snacks per day for four days. Be sure to plan for Friday snacks, as well as any additional snacks you may need throughout the week. Good snack options include Greek yogurt and chopped nuts, cheese and whole-grain crackers or a small apple with peanut butter.

WEEKLY MEAL PREP PLAN 5: ADVANCED

Below is a sample plan of when to eat meal prepped food during a work or school week. However, everyone has a different schedule, so customize this to fit your needs.

	BREAKFAST	AM SNACK	LUNCH	PM SNACK	DINNER
Monday	Eggs with Spinach and Beans Container	Whipped Cottage Cheese Container	Baked Falafel Bowls	Kiwi-Melon Fruit Salad Container	Teriyaki Pork Tenderloin Container
Tuesday	Eggs with Spinach and Beans Container	Whipped Cottage Cheese Container	Baked Falafel Bowls	Kiwi-Melon Fruit Salad Container	Decon-structed Skillet Lasagna Container
Wednesday	Eggs with Spinach and Beans Container	Whipped Cottage Cheese Container	Baked Falafel Bowls	Kiwi-Melon Fruit Salad Container	Teriyaki Pork Tenderloin Container
Thursday	Eggs with Spinach and Beans Container	Whipped Cottage Cheese Container	Baked Falafel Bowls	Kiwi-Melon Fruit Salad Container	Decon-structed Skillet Lasagna Container
Friday	Eggs with Spinach and Beans Container		Decon-structed Skillet Lasagna Container		Teriyaki Pork Tenderloin Container

	CALORIES	FAT	SAT FAT	SODIUM	CARB	FIBER	PROTEIN

BREAKFAST: EGGS WITH SPINACH AND BEANS CONTAINER

SERVE ON: Monday through Friday (5 days)

STORE: Portions 1 to 4 in the refrigerator and portion 5 in the freezer

	CALORIES	FAT	SAT FAT	SODIUM	CARB	FIBER	PROTEIN
Egg with Spinach and Beans (page 112)	205.40	10.84 g	2.31 g	381.17 mg	16.28 g	5.01 g	11.22 g
Total Per Box	205.40	10.84 g	2.31 g	381.17 mg	16.28 g	5.01 g	11.22 g

SNACK 1: WHIPPED COTTAGE CHEESE CONTAINER

SERVE ON: Monday through Thursday (4 days)

STORE: All portions in the refrigerator

	CALORIES	FAT	SAT FAT	SODIUM	CARB	FIBER	PROTEIN
Whipped Cottage Cheese with Berries and Pistachios (page 114)	203.25	8.37 g	1.56 g	28.21 mg	15.99 g	5.34 g	18.23 g
Total Per Box	203.25	8.37 g	1.56 g	28.21 mg	15.99 g	5.34 g	18.23 g

SNACK 2: KIWI-MELON FRUIT SALAD CONTAINER

SERVE ON: Monday through Thursday (4 days)

STORE: All portions in the refrigerator

	CALORIES	FAT	SAT FAT	SODIUM	CARB	FIBER	PROTEIN
Kiwi-Melon Fruit Salad with Almonds (page 116)	133.00	9.5 g	0.73 g	16.00 mg	11.25 g	1.97 g	2.64 g
Total Per Box	133.00	9.5 g	0.73 g	16.00 mg	11.25 g	1.97 g	2.64 g

LUNCH OR DINNER 1: BAKED FALAFEL BOWLS

SERVE ON: Monday through Thursday (4 days)

STORE: All portions in the refrigerator

	CALORIES	FAT	SAT FAT	SODIUM	CARB	FIBER	PROTEIN
Baked Falafel Bowls (page 118) with Lemon-Tahini Sauce (page 261) and Easy Herbed Quinoa (page 230)	378.98	20.14 g	2.63 g	322.25 mg	39.71 g	8.79 g	11.50 g
Total Per Box	378.98	20.14 g	2.63 g	322.25 mg	39.71 g	8.79 g	11.50 g

	CALORIES	FAT	SAT FAT	SODIUM	CARB	FIBER	PROTEIN

LUNCH OR DINNER 2: DECONSTRUCTED SKILLET LASAGNA CONTAINER

SERVE ON: Tuesday, Thursday and Friday (3 days)

STORE: Portions 1 and 2 in the refrigerator and portions 3 to 6 in the freezer (use one this week and store three for another week)

	CALORIES	FAT	SAT FAT	SODIUM	CARB	FIBER	PROTEIN
Deconstructed Skillet Lasagna (page 120)	329.85	13.26 g	4.78 g	276.73 mg	39.71 g	8.79 g	20.91 g
Total Per Box	329.85	13.26 g	4.78 g	276.73 mg	39.71 g	8.79 g	20.91 g

LUNCH OR DINNER 3: TERIYAKI PORK TENDERLOIN CONTAINER

SERVE ON: Monday, Wednesday and Friday (3 days)

STORE: Portions 1 and 2 in the refrigerator and portions 3 to 6 in the freezer (use one this week and store three for another week)

	CALORIES	FAT	SAT FAT	SODIUM	CARB	FIBER	PROTEIN
Teriyaki Pork Tenderloin (page 117)	110.12	1.98 g	0.64 g	336.69 mg	1.82 g	0.03 g	19.69 g
1/3 cup (75 L) dry or 3/4 cup cooked soba (buckwheat) noodles	84.64	0.09 g	0.02 g	51.30 mg	18.33 g	0.0 g	4.33 g
2 carrots or 1 cup (250 mL) sliced steamed carrots	50.0	0.29 g	0.05 g	84.18 mg	11.69 g	3.42 g	1.13 g
Total Per Box	244.76	2.36 g	0.71 g	472.17 mg	31.84 g	3.45 g	25.15 g

WEEKLY SHOPPING LIST

VEGETABLES

- carrots: 13
- cilantro: ½ cup (125 mL)
- cucumbers, Kirby: 4
- garlic: 3 cloves
- mushrooms, cremini: 8 oz (250 g)
- onion, yellow: 1
- parsley, fresh: ½ cup (125 mL)
- shallots: 2
- spinach, baby: 6 cups (1.5 L)
- tomatoes, cherry: 2 cups (500 mL)
- zucchini: 1

FRUITS

- blackberries: 2 cups (500 mL)
- kiwi: 1
- lemon: 2
- lime: 1
- melon, cantaloupe, diced: about 8¼ oz (257 g)
- melon, honeydew, diced: 9 oz (275 g)

PANTRY

- almonds, unsalted roasted: ¼ cup (60 mL)
- baking powder
- basil, dried
- beans, canned no-salt-added cannellini: 1¾ cups (425 mL)
- black pepper, ground
- broth, low-sodium vegetable: 1¾ cups (425 mL)
- cooking spray
- cumin, ground
- garlic powder
- hot pepper flakes
- oil, canola
- oil, olive
- onion powder
- oregano, dried
- parsley, dried flakes
- pasta, lasagna sheets
- pistachios, unsalted shelled: ½ cup (125 mL)
- quinoa
- salt, table
- soba (buckwheat) noodles, dry
- stevia brown sugar blend (such as Truvia or Splenda)
- tahini
- thyme, dried
- tomatoes, no-salt-added crushed: 28 oz (796 mL) can
- vinegar, white wine

DAIRY AND EGGS

- cheese, Parmesan grated: 6 tbsp (90 mL)
- cheese, ricotta: ¾ cup (175 mL)
- cottage cheese, low-fat: 2 cups (500 mL)
- eggs, large: 5

MEATS/PROTEIN

- beef, at least 90% lean ground: 12 oz (375 g)
- pork tenderloin: 1¼ lbs (625 g)

EQUIPMENT

- baking dish, glass: 11- by 7-inch (28 by 18 cm)
- baking sheet
- blender or food processor
- brush (for basting)
- colander
- cutting board
- garlic press
- knife
- measuring cups and spoons
- microplane grater
- mixing bowls
- saucepan, medium with lid
- sauté pan, large with lid
- thermometer, instant-read
- whisk
- wooden spoons

STEP-BY-STEP MEAL PREP

1   Prepare the **Teriyaki Marinade** (page 259).

2   Follow step 1 for **Teriyaki Pork Tenderloin** (page 117).

3   While the pork is marinating, prepare the **Kiwi-Melon Fruit Salad with Almonds** (page 116) and pack into containers according to the recipe.

4   Preheat the oven to 400°F (200°C) and continue preparing the **Teriyaki Pork Tenderloin** through step 3.

5   While the pork is cooking, prepare the **Eggs with Spinach and Beans** (page 112) through step 2. Allow the mixture to cool for 10 minutes and then pack into containers according to step 3 and store four boxes in the refrigerator and one box in the freezer.

6   Prepare the falafel balls for the **Baked Falafel Bowls** (page 118) through step 2.

7   Let the pork tenderloin cool for 10 minutes, then cut into six equal pieces. Turn the oven down to 375°F (190°C).

8   Bake the falafel balls according to step 3 (page 118).

9   Prepare the **Lemon-Tahini Sauce** (page 261) for the **Baked Falafel Bowls**.

10   Prepare the **Easy Herbed Quinoa** (page 230) for the **Baked Falafel Bowls.**

11   Pack the **Baked Falafel Bowls** (page 118) according to step 4 and store in the refrigerator.

12   Prepare the **Deconstructed Skillet Lasagna** (page 120) through step 5.

13   While the lasagna is cooking, prepare steamed carrots and the soba noodles according to the package instructions to complete the plate for the **Teriyaki Pork Tenderloin** containers.

14   Allow the lasagna to cool.

15   Prepare the **Whipped Cottage Cheese with Berries and Pistachios** (page 114), pack according to step 2 and refrigerate.

16   Pack the pork tenderloin into six containers along with ¾ cup (175 mL) of soba (buckwheat) noodles and 1 cup (250 mL) of steamed carrots. Store two containers in the refrigerator and four containers in the freezer.

17   Pack the lasagna into six containers. Store two containers in the refrigerator and four containers in the freezer.

EGGS WITH SPINACH AND BEANS

SERVES	SERVING SIZE	TOTAL TIME	PREP TIME	COOK TIME
5	About 1 cup (250 mL) spinach-bean mixture, 1 egg	35 minutes	15 minutes	20 minutes

Spinach for breakfast? Absolutely! Breakfast is a perfect time to add low-carb vegetables and plant-based proteins to your meal plan. The spinach and beans provide fiber, which helps keep you feeling satisfied during your busy morning.

2 tbsp (30 mL) olive oil

2 shallots, chopped

6 cups (1.5 L) baby or chopped spinach

1¾ cups (425 mL) canned no-salt-added cannellini beans, drained and rinsed

½ tsp (2 mL) salt

¼ tsp (1 mL) ground black pepper

5 large eggs

1 Heat the oil in a large sauté pan over medium heat. When the oil is shimmering, add the shallots and cook until softened, 2 minutes. Add the spinach and cook until wilted, 3 minutes. Add the beans, salt and pepper and toss to combine.

2 Using the back of a mixing spoon, create five wells in the spinach mixture. Gently crack an egg into each well. Cover the sauté pan and cook until the eggs are cooked through, 8 minutes.

3 TO STORE: In each of five containers, add about 1 cup (250 mL) of the spinach-bean mixture with 1 egg. Cover and refrigerate for up to 4 days or freeze for up to 2 months.

4 TO SERVE: If needed, thaw in the refrigerator overnight. To reheat, microwave uncovered on High for 1 minute. Allow 2 minutes for the heat to distribute before removing the container from the microwave. Serve warm.

TOBY'S TIPS | Enjoy with Tomato Salsa (page 258).

	TOTAL CALORIES	TOTAL FAT	SATURATED FAT	TRANS FAT
PER SERVING	205.40	10.84 g	2.31 g	0.02 g
	SODIUM 381.17 mg	**CHOLESTEROL** 186.0 mg	**TOTAL CARBOHYDRATES** 16.28 g	**FIBER** 5.01 g
	SUGARS 1.15 g	**PROTEIN** 11.22 g	**POTASSIUM** 264.83 mg	**PHOSPHORUS** 171.40 mg

WHIPPED COTTAGE CHEESE
WITH BERRIES AND PISTACHIOS

SERVES	SERVING SIZE	TOTAL TIME	PREP TIME	COOK TIME
4	1/2 cup (125 mL) blended cottage cheese, 1/2 cup (125 mL) blackberries, 2 tbsp (30 mL) chopped pistachios	15 minutes	15 minutes	0 minutes

Not a fan of the texture of cottage cheese? No problem! Toss it in the blender and the result is smooth, creamy and filled with protein and calcium. I've also used this cottage cheese hack for dips, pancakes and other dishes.

2 cups (500 mL) low-fat no-salt-added cottage cheese

2 tbsp (30 mL) sugar-free maple syrup

2 cups (500 mL) fresh blackberries

1/2 cup (125 mL) unsalted shelled pistachios, coarsely chopped

Food processor or blender

1 Add the cottage cheese and sugar-free maple syrup to the food processor or blender. Process or blend on High until the mixture becomes smooth, 1 minute.

2 TO STORE: In each of four containers, add 1/2 cup (125 mL) of the blended cottage cheese and top with 1/2 cup (125 mL) of the blackberries and 2 tbsp (30 mL) of the chopped pistachios. Cover and refrigerate for up to 4 days.

3 TO SERVE: Enjoy cold.

TOBY'S TIP | If you prefer, swap the blackberries for blueberries, raspberries, strawberries or a combination of berries. You can also swap the cottage cheese for nonfat plain Greek yogurt—just skip step 1.

	TOTAL CALORIES	TOTAL FAT	SATURATED FAT	TRANS FAT
PER SERVING	203.25	8.37 g	1.56 g	0.0 g
	SODIUM	**CHOLESTEROL**	**TOTAL CARBOHYDRATES**	**FIBER**
	28.21 mg	4.52 mg	15.99 g	5.34 g
	SUGARS	**PROTEIN**	**POTASSIUM**	**PHOSPHORUS**
	7.75 g	18.23 g	368.65 mg	239.37 mg

KIWI-MELON FRUIT SALAD
WITH ALMONDS

 · · ·

SERVES	SERVING SIZE	TOTAL TIME	PREP TIME	COOK TIME
6	½ cup (125 mL) fruit salad, 2 tbsp (30 mL) chopped almonds	20 minutes	20 minutes	0 minutes

Fruit salad is the perfect snack to help curb your sweet tooth. The tart flavor of lime juice complements the sweet flavor of the melon. Top it with almonds for some healthy fat and to help slow down the absorption of the natural sugar found in fruit.

2 tbsp (30 mL) canola oil

Juice and zest of 1 lime

1 tsp (5 mL) stevia brown sugar blend (such as Truvia or Splenda)

1 kiwi, peeled and diced

1½ cups (375 mL) diced cantaloupe

1½ cups (375 mL) diced honeydew melon

6 tbsp (90 mL) raw almonds, coarsely chopped

1 In a medium bowl, whisk together the canola oil, lime juice, lime zest and brown sugar blend. Add the kiwi, cantaloupe and honeydew and toss to evenly coat.

2 TO STORE: In each of four containers, add ½ cup (125 mL) of the fruit salad with the juice. In four small resealable bags or containers, add 2 tbsp (30 mL) of the almonds. Cover or seal and store the containers in the refrigerator for up to 4 days.

3 TO SERVE: Sprinkle the fruit salad with the nuts before eating and enjoy cold.

TOBY'S TIP | If you prefer, swap in watermelon for some or all of the melon.

	TOTAL CALORIES	TOTAL FAT	SATURATED FAT	TRANS FAT
PER SERVING	133.0	9.5 g	0.73 g	0.02 g
	SODIUM 16.0 mg	**CHOLESTEROL** 0.0 mg	**TOTAL CARBOHYDRATES** 11.25 g	**FIBER** 1.97 g
	SUGARS 8.67 g	**PROTEIN** 2.64 g	**POTASSIUM** 298.67 mg	**PHOSPHORUS** 58.25 mg

TERIYAKI PORK TENDERLOIN

	SERVES	SERVING SIZE	TOTAL TIME	PREP TIME	COOK TIME
	6	3 oz (90 g)	1 hour, plus marinating (30 minutes to 8 hours)	15 minutes	45 minutes

Pork tenderloin is a lean, delicately flavored meat. Marinades work well with this cut, and it can be cooked quickly on the grill or in stir-fries. It takes a bit longer to roast, but for best results, keep your eye on the clock and don't overcook it.

1¼ lbs (625 g) pork tenderloin

6 tbsp (90 mL) Teriyaki Marinade (page 259), divided

11- by 7-inch (28 by 18 cm) glass baking dish coated with cooking spray

1   In a large container, add the pork tenderloin and pour ¼ cup (60 mL) of the marinade over the top. Turn to evenly coat. Reserve the remaining 2 tbsp (30 mL) of the marinade. Cover the container and place the pork in the refrigerator for at least 30 minutes and up to 8 hours.

2   Preheat the oven to 400°F (200°C). Remove the pork from the marinade, shaking off the excess, and place it into the prepared baking dish. Discard the remaining marinade from the container.

3   Roast, basting with the reserved marinade every 15 minutes, until an instant-read thermometer registers 145°F (63°C) when inserted into the thickest part, about 45 minutes. Let the pork rest for 10 minutes before slicing against the grain into ¼-inch (0.5 cm) thick medallions.

4   TO STORE: In each of four containers, place about 3 oz (90 g) of the pork. Cover and refrigerate for up to 4 days or freeze for up to 2 months.

5   TO SERVE: If needed, thaw in the refrigerator overnight. To reheat, microwave uncovered on High for 1 minute. Allow 2 minutes for the heat to distribute before removing the container from the microwave. Serve warm.

TOBY'S TIP | To change up the flavor, swap the marinade for Soy-Garlic Marinade (page 260) or Simple Pesto Sauce (page 264).

	TOTAL CALORIES	TOTAL FAT	SATURATED FAT	TRANS FAT
PER SERVING	110.12	1.98 g	0.64 g	0.02 g
	SODIUM	CHOLESTEROL	TOTAL CARBOHYDRATES	FIBER
	336.69 mg	45.36 mg	1.82 g	0.03 g
	SUGARS	PROTEIN	POTASSIUM	PHOSPHORUS
	1.65 g	19.69 g	499.93 mg	274.67 mg

BAKED FALAFEL BOWLS

SERVES	SERVING SIZE	TOTAL TIME	PREP TIME	COOK TIME
4	4 falafel balls, ¼ cup (60 mL) Easy Herbed Quinoa, ½ cup (60 mL) cherry tomatoes, 1 Kirby cucumber, 1 tbsp (15 mL) Lemon-Tahini Sauce	45 minutes	20 minutes	25 minutes

Falafel balls are made from blended chickpeas, herbs and spices, and traditionally they are deep fried. You can still get the delicious flavor by baking them.

FALAFEL BALLS

1¾ cups (425 mL) canned no-salt-added chickpeas, drained and rinsed

½ cup (125 mL) parsley, chopped

½ cup (125 mL) cilantro, chopped

2 tbsp (30 mL) olive oil

1 tbsp (15 mL) lemon juice

1 tsp (5 mL) ground cumin

1 tsp (5 mL) onion powder

1 tsp (5 mL) garlic powder

½ tsp (2 mL) baking powder

¼ tsp (1 mL) ground black pepper

⅛ tsp (0.5 mL) salt

Food processor or blender
Baking sheet coated with cooking spray
Preheat the oven to 375°F (190°C)

1 In a food processor or blender, add the chickpeas, parsley, cilantro, olive oil, lemon juice, ground cumin, onion powder, garlic powder, baking powder, pepper and salt. Pulse until just combined.

2 Spoon 1 tbsp (15 mL) of the chickpea mixture and using clean hands roll into a ball. Place on the prepared baking sheet and, using your palm, press down gently. Repeat for the remaining chickpea mixture to make a total of 16 falafel balls.

3 Bake the falafel balls, flipping halfway through, until they are browned and crisp, 12 minutes on each side.

4 TO STORE: In each of four containers, place 4 falafel balls with ¼ cup (60 mL) of the Easy Herbed Quinoa, ½ cup (60 mL) of the cherry tomatoes, and 1 sliced cucumber. Place 1 tbsp (15 mL) of the tahini sauce in a separate small container. Cover all containers and refrigerate for up to 4 days.

5 TO SERVE: Enjoy cold with the tahini sauce drizzled over the top.

PER SERVING			
TOTAL CALORIES 378.98	**TOTAL FAT** 20.14 g	**SATURATED FAT** 2.63 g	**TRANS FAT** 0.0 g
SODIUM 322.25 mg	**CHOLESTEROL** 0.0 mg	**TOTAL CARBOHYDRATES** 39.71 g	**FIBER** 8.79 g
SUGARS 5.20 g	**PROTEIN** 11.50 g	**POTASSIUM** 802.07 mg	**PHOSPHORUS** 262.44 mg

BOWLS

¼ cup (60 mL) Lemon-Tahini
Sauce (page 261) or store-bought
tahini

1 cup (250 mL) Easy Herbed
Quinoa (page 230)

2 cups (500 mL) cherry tomatoes

4 Kirby cucumbers, thinly sliced

TOBY'S TIP | Swap the fresh herbs to include
what you have available in your fridge or garden,
such as mint or dill.

DECONSTRUCTED SKILLET LASAGNA

SERVES	SERVING SIZE	TOTAL TIME	PREP TIME	COOK TIME
6	1$\frac{1}{3}$ cups (325 mL)	55 minutes	20 minutes	35 minutes

Enjoy this speedier and lighter version of lasagna that tastes just like the real deal!

6 dry whole wheat lasagna sheets, broken into pieces

$\frac{3}{4}$ cup (175 mL) part-skim ricotta cheese

1 tsp (5 mL) dried parsley flakes

1 tsp (5 mL) dried basil leaves

1 tsp (5 mL) dried oregano leaves

2 tbsp (30 mL) olive oil

1 yellow onion, chopped

2 cloves garlic, minced

12 oz (375 g) at least 90% lean ground beef

8 oz (250 g) cremini mushrooms, chopped

1 carrot, grated

1 zucchini, grated

3$\frac{1}{4}$ cups (810 g) canned no-salt-added crushed tomatoes, with juice

$\frac{1}{4}$ tsp (1 mL) salt

$\frac{1}{4}$ tsp (1 mL) ground black pepper

$\frac{1}{8}$ tsp (0.5 mL) hot pepper flakes

6 tbsp (90 mL) grated Parmesan cheese

1 Fill a medium saucepan three-quarters with water and bring to a boil over medium heat. Add the broken lasagna noodles and cook until al dente, 10 minutes. Drain and set aside.

2 In a small bowl, mix together the ricotta, parsley, basil and oregano.

3 In a large sauté pan, heat the olive oil over medium heat. When the oil is shimmering, add the onion and garlic and cook until the onion is translucent and the garlic is fragrant, 3 minutes. Add the ground beef and cook until browned on all sides, breaking up large pieces with the back of a spoon, 6 minutes.

4 Add the mushrooms, carrot and zucchini and cook until the vegetables are softened, 5 minutes. Add the cooked lasagna noodles, crushed tomatoes with juice, salt, black pepper and hot pepper flakes and mix to combine. Bring the mixture to a boil over high heat, reduce the heat to medium-low, cover and simmer until the flavors combine, about 10 minutes.

5 Uncover and stir in the ricotta cheese mixture. Sprinkle with the Parmesan cheese.

6 TO STORE: In each of six containers, place 1$\frac{1}{3}$ cups (325 mL) of the lasagna. Cover and refrigerate for up to 4 days or freeze for up to 2 months.

7 TO SERVE: If needed, thaw in the refrigerator overnight. To reheat, microwave uncovered on High for 90 seconds. Allow 2 minutes for the heat to distribute before removing the container from the microwave. Serve warm.

PER SERVING			
TOTAL CALORIES 329.85	TOTAL FAT 13.26 g	SATURATED FAT 4.78 g	TRANS FAT 0.24 g
SODIUM 276.73 mg	CHOLESTEROL 45.56 mg	TOTAL CARBOHYDRATES 31.10 g	FIBER 6.98 g
SUGARS 9.14 g	PROTEIN 20.91 g	POTASSIUM 917.32 mg	PHOSPHORUS 313.63 mg

PART 3

RECIPES

CHAPTER 9

BREAKFASTS

ALMOND CHERRY SMOOTHIE PACKS

 · · · · ·

SERVES	SERVING SIZE	TOTAL TIME	PREP TIME	COOK TIME
5	1½ cups (375 mL)	15 minutes	15 minutes	0 minutes

The trick to meal prepping smoothies is to make freezer packs. Just transfer the contents of your freezer pack right in your blender, add a little liquid and purée. Your morning smoothie is ready to go in less than 5 minutes.

5 cups (1.25 L) frozen pitted sweet cherries

15 ice cubes

10 tbsp (155 mL) raw almonds, coarsely chopped

1¼ tsp (6 mL) zero-calorie stevia sweetener (such as Truvia or Splenda)

½ tsp (2 mL) plus ⅛ tsp (0.5 mL) ground cinnamon

5 cups (1.25 L) unsweetened almond milk, divided

Blender

1 In each of five zip-top plastic bags, add 1 cup (250 mL) of the cherries, 3 of the ice cubes, 2 tbsp (30 mL) of the almonds, ¼ tsp (1 mL) of the sweetener and ⅛ tsp (0.5 mL) of the cinnamon.

2 **TO STORE:** Seal, label and date the bags. Freeze for up to 2 months.

3 **TO SERVE:** Remove a bag from the freezer and pour the contents into the blender. Add 1 cup (250 mL) of the almond milk and blend until smooth. Pour into a tall glass and enjoy.

TOBY'S TIP | Don't forget to chop the nuts before freezing. Once you take them out of the freezer they will be tough to chop and some blenders may not be able to handle them whole.

COMPLETE YOUR PLATE

1 hard-cooked egg and 1 cup (250 mL) sliced cucumbers and tomato

	TOTAL CALORIES	TOTAL FAT	SATURATED FAT	TRANS FAT
PER SERVING	200.4	9.30 g	0.68 g	0 g
	SODIUM	**CHOLESTEROL**	**TOTAL CARBOHYDRATES**	**FIBER**
	22.71 mg	0 mg	26.56 g	5.51 g
	SUGARS	**PROTEIN**	**POTASSIUM**	**PHOSPHORUS**
	18.96 g	4.92 g	156.00 mg	91.16 mg

CRUNCHY PEACH PARFAITS

SERVES	SERVING SIZE	TOTAL TIME	PREP TIME	COOK TIME
5 (Makes 2 cups/ 500 mL granola)	$1/_4$ cup (60 mL) yogurt, $1/_4$ cup (60 mL) peaches with juice, $1/_4$ cup (60 mL) granola	55 minutes	20 minutes	35 minutes

Parfaits are layers of yogurt, fruit and granola or nuts — a variety of flavors and textures in every bite. Fresh or canned peaches work beautifully in this recipe.

HOMEMADE GRANOLA

$3/_4$ cup (175 mL) gluten-free large-flake (old-fashioned) rolled oats

$1/_4$ cup (60 mL) raw or unsalted roasted cashews, coarsely chopped

3 tbsp (45 mL) unsalted sunflower seeds

2 tbsp (30 mL) unsweetened shredded coconut

2 tbsp (30 mL) sugar-free maple syrup

1 tbsp (15 mL) canola oil

$1/_4$ tsp (1 mL) vanilla extract

$1/_4$ tsp (1 mL) ground cinnamon

$1/_8$ tsp (0.5 mL) kosher salt

1 large egg white

2 tbsp (30 mL) dried tart cherries

Rimmed baking sheet lined with parchment paper
Preheat the oven to 300°F (150°C)

1 TO MAKE THE HOMEMADE GRANOLA: In a medium bowl, mix together the oats, cashews, sunflower seeds, coconut, maple syrup, oil, vanilla, cinnamon and salt.

2 In a small bowl, whisk the egg white until frothy. Gently fold the egg white into the oats mixture, distributing it evenly.

3 Spread the granola in a single layer on the prepared baking sheet. Bake, using a spatula to turn sections of the granola over and breaking up larger pieces halfway through, until the granola is slightly browned and dried, 30 to 35 minutes.

4 Transfer the baking sheet to a cooling rack and let cool completely. Once cool, use a spatula to break up any larger pieces of the granola. Sprinkle in the tart cherries and gently toss to distribute.

5 TO ASSEMBLE THE PARFAITS: In each of four jars, add $1/_4$ cup (60 mL) of the yogurt. Top with $1/_4$ cup (60 mL) of the canned peaches with juice and about $1/_4$ cup (60 mL) of the granola. Repeat the layers one more time, ending with the granola. Assemble the fifth parfait 1 or 2 days before eating.

6 TO STORE: Cover the assembled parfaits and refrigerate for up to 4 days. Store the granola in a sealable container or plastic bag at room temperature for up to 2 weeks.

PER SERVING	TOTAL CALORIES	TOTAL FAT	SATURATED FAT	TRANS FAT
	244	10.78 g	2.4 g	0 g
	SODIUM	CHOLESTEROL	TOTAL CARBOHYDRATES	FIBER
	117.19 mg	5.67 mg	22.20 g	2.97 g
	SUGARS	PROTEIN	POTASSIUM	PHOSPHORUS
	8.83 g	16.16 g	293.77 mg	217.71 mg

PARFAITS

2½ cups (625 mL) nonfat plain Greek yogurt

2 cups (500 mL) Homemade Granola

2½ cups (625 mL) no-sugar-added canned peaches, with juice

COMPLETE YOUR PLATE

1 cup (250 mL) sliced cucumber or bell pepper

TOBY'S TIPS | If you prefer, swap the cashews for your favorite nut, like almonds, pistachios or walnuts.

Oats are naturally gluten-free, but some brands process their oats in a facility that also processes products with gluten. Check the label of your oats to make sure it was manufactured in a facility that is gluten-free.

GREEK YOGURT
WITH HOMEMADE MUESLI

SERVES	SERVING SIZE	TOTAL TIME	PREP TIME	COOK TIME
5 (Makes 2 cups/ 500 mL muesli)	½ cup (125 mL) yogurt with syrup, 6 tbsp (90 mL) muesli	25 minutes	15 minutes	10 minutes

Muesli is popular in Germany and Switzerland and is made of a combination of oats, nuts, seeds and dried fruit. Typically it is mixed with milk or yogurt for breakfast.

MUESLI

1 cup (250 mL) large-flake (old-fashioned) rolled oats

6 tbsp (90 mL) raw cashews, chopped

¼ cup (60 mL) unsalted shelled sunflower seeds

3 tbsp (45 mL) dried cranberries

3 tbsp (45 mL) seedless raisins

2 tbsp (30 mL) toasted wheat bran

YOGURT

2½ cups (625 mL) nonfat plain Greek yogurt

2 tbsp (30 mL) sugar-free maple syrup

Rimmed baking sheet lined with parchment paper
Preheat the oven to 350°F (180°C)

1 TO MAKE THE MUESLI: Pour the oats onto the prepared baking sheet and toast in the oven, tossing halfway through, until golden brown, about 10 minutes.

2 Remove the oats from the oven and let cool for at least 10 minutes.

3 In a medium bowl, add the toasted oats, cashews, sunflower seeds, cranberries, raisins and wheat bran. Toss to combine.

4 TO MAKE THE YOGURT: In a small bowl, add the yogurt and maple syrup and stir to combine.

5 TO ASSEMBLE: In each of four jars, add ½ cup (125 mL) of the yogurt mixture and top with 6 tbsp (90 mL) of the muesli. Stir to combine. Assemble the fifth jar 1 to 2 days before eating.

6 TO STORE: Cover the assembled yogurt and muesli jars and refrigerate for up to 4 days. Store the muesli in a sealable container or plastic bag at room temperature for up to 2 weeks.

COMPLETE YOUR PLATE

1 cup (250 mL) sliced cucumbers or carrots

	TOTAL CALORIES	TOTAL FAT	SATURATED FAT	TRANS FAT
PER SERVING	258.77	9.62 g	1.57 g	0 g
	SODIUM	CHOLESTEROL	TOTAL CARBOHYDRATES	FIBER
	53.80 mg	5.67 mg	26.39 g	3.73 g
	SUGARS	PROTEIN	POTASSIUM	PHOSPHORUS
	12.06 g	16.98 g	327.44 mg	263.43 mg

CRUSTLESS EGG QUICHE
WITH SPINACH, MUSHROOMS AND FETA

SERVES	SERVING SIZE	TOTAL TIME	PREP TIME	COOK TIME
5	1 slice	1 hour	15 minutes	45 minutes

Quiche is a versatile dish. Try swapping the mushrooms and spinach for other non-starchy vegetables like peppers and onions and the feta for reduced-fat Cheddar cheese.

1 tbsp (15 mL) olive oil

1 yellow onion, chopped

1 clove garlic, minced

1 lb (500 g) cremini mushrooms, thinly sliced

4 cups (1 L) baby spinach

5 large eggs, beaten

4 large egg whites, beaten

1/2 cup (125 mL) low-fat milk

1/4 tsp (1 mL) salt

1/8 tsp (0.5 mL) ground black pepper

1/3 cup (75 mL) crumbled feta cheese

COMPLETE YOUR PLATE

1 slice 100% whole wheat bread with 1 tsp (5 mL) light butter spread

8-inch (20 cm) pie dish coated with cooking spray
Preheat the oven to 425°F (220°C)

1 In a medium skillet, heat the oil over medium heat. When the oil is shimmering, add the onion and garlic and cook until the onion is translucent and the garlic is fragrant, 2 minutes. Add the mushrooms and cook until softened, about 5 minutes. Add the spinach and cook, stirring occasionally, until wilted, 3 minutes more. Remove the skillet from the heat and let cool for 10 minutes.

2 In a medium bowl, whisk together the eggs, egg whites, milk, salt and pepper.

3 Spread the spinach and mushroom mixture on the bottom of the prepared pie dish. Pour the egg mixture over the top and sprinkle evenly with the cheese.

4 Bake until the top is browned and a knife inserted about 1 inch (2.5 cm) from the edge comes out clean, 30 to 35 minutes. Remove from the oven and let cool for 10 minutes. Cut the quiche into five equal slices.

5 TO STORE: In each of five containers, add one slice of quiche. Cover and refrigerate for up to 5 days or freeze for up to 2 months.

6 TO SERVE: If frozen, thaw in the refrigerator overnight. Serve warm, cold or at room temperature. To reheat, microwave uncovered on High for 45 to 60 seconds.

	TOTAL CALORIES	TOTAL FAT	SATURATED FAT	TRANS FAT
PER SERVING	196.73	11.05 g	4.36 g	0 g
	SODIUM	**CHOLESTEROL**	**TOTAL CARBOHYDRATES**	**FIBER**
	418.35 mg	200.57 mg	10.63 g	1.86 g
	SUGARS	**PROTEIN**	**POTASSIUM**	**PHOSPHORUS**
	4.75 g	15.12 g	599.64 mg	292.94 mg

SHAKSHUKA
WITH CHICKPEAS AND SPINACH

 · · · ·

SERVES	SERVING SIZE	TOTAL TIME	PREP TIME	COOK TIME
5	1¼ cups (300 mL) shakshuka with 1 egg, ½ pita	40 minutes	15 minutes	25 minutes

Shakshuka is a Mediterranean dish that cooks eggs in a tomato, pepper and onion sauce. This version adds more vegetables and legumes to make it even more nutritious.

1 tbsp (15 mL) olive oil

1 large yellow onion, cut into ½-inch (1 cm) strips

2 red bell peppers, cut into 1-inch (2.5 cm) strips

1 clove garlic, minced

1 can (28 oz/796 mL) no-salt-added crushed tomatoes, with juice

1¾ cups (425 mL) low-sodium canned chickpeas, drained and rinsed

2 tbsp (30 mL) chopped fresh cilantro, or 1 tsp (5 mL) dried cilantro

¼ tsp (1 mL) salt

¼ tsp (1 mL) ground black pepper

1 tsp (5 mL) Thai chile sauce (such as Sriracha)

1. In a large sauté pan, heat the oil over medium heat. When the oil is shimmering, add the onion and bell peppers and sauté until softened, about 5 minutes. Add the garlic and cook until fragrant, about 1 minute.

2. Stir in the crushed tomatoes with juice, chickpeas, cilantro, salt, black pepper and Thai chile sauce. Increase the heat to medium-high and bring the mixture to a boil, then reduce the heat to medium-low. Add the spinach and stir to combine. Cover the pan and simmer, stirring occasionally, for about 10 minutes to let the flavors blend.

3. Using a wooden spoon, create a well in the tomato mixture along the outer edge of the pan. Break 1 egg into a small bowl or glass and gently pour into the well. Repeat with the remaining 4 eggs to form a circle along the outer edge of the pan. Reduce the heat to low, cover and cook until the eggs are set, about 6 minutes.

4. TO STORE: In each of five containers, add 1¼ cups (300 mL) of the shakshuka (including 1 egg). Wrap the pita halves individually in plastic wrap or aluminum foil and store on the side. Cover the containers and refrigerate for up to 4 days or freeze for up to 2 months.

	TOTAL CALORIES	TOTAL FAT	SATURATED FAT	TRANS FAT
PER SERVING	327.68	10.18 g	2.02 g	0 g
	SODIUM	**CHOLESTEROL**	**TOTAL CARBOHYDRATES**	**FIBER**
	590.07 mg	186.00 mg	44.89 g	11.23 g
	SUGARS	**PROTEIN**	**POTASSIUM**	**PHOSPHORUS**
	13.68 g	17.59 g	682.94 mg	171.99 mg

3 cups (750 mL) baby spinach

5 large eggs

2½ large (8-inch/20 cm) whole wheat pitas, halved (5 pieces)

5 **TO SERVE:** If frozen, thaw in the refrigerator overnight. To reheat the shakshuka with the egg, microwave uncovered on High for 60 to 90 seconds. Allow 2 minutes for the heat to distribute before removing the container from the microwave. Serve warm with a pita half.

TOBY'S TIP | If you prefer, swap the chickpeas for low-sodium white cannellini or red kidney beans. Both work beautifully in this recipe.

SCRAMBLED EGG BREAKFAST BOWLS
WITH SPINACH, PEPPERS AND TURKEY

SERVES	SERVING SIZE	TOTAL TIME	PREP TIME	COOK TIME
5	1 cup (250 mL) turkey mixture, $\frac{1}{3}$ cup (75 mL) eggs, 2 tbsp (30 mL) cheese, 1 tortilla	35 minutes	15 minutes	20 minutes

This filling breakfast bowl is a great way to set yourself up for success on a busy day. With lean protein, lots of non-starchy vegetables and Mexican-inspired flavors, this bowl provides plenty of nutrition and sustained energy starting first thing in the morning.

3 tbsp (45 mL) olive oil, divided

1 medium onion, halved and thinly sliced

8 oz (250 g) at least 90% lean ground turkey

2 red bell peppers, cut into 1-inch (2.5 cm) strips

1$\frac{3}{4}$ cups (425 mL) no-salt-added canned black beans, drained and rinsed

$\frac{1}{2}$ tsp (2 mL) chili powder

$\frac{1}{4}$ tsp (1 mL) paprika

$\frac{1}{4}$ tsp (1 mL) salt, divided

1 cup (250 mL) low-sodium tomato sauce

3 cups (750 mL) baby spinach

1 In a large sauté pan, heat 2 tbsp (30 mL) of the oil over medium heat. When the oil is shimmering, add the onion and cook until softened, 2 minutes. Add the ground turkey. Using a wooden spoon to break up any large pieces, cook until browned, about 3 minutes. Using a slotted spoon, remove the turkey and onion and place on a clean plate.

2 In the same sauté pan, heat the remaining 1 tbsp (15 mL) oil over medium heat. When the oil is shimmering, add the peppers and cook until slightly softened, 4 minutes. Add the beans, chili powder, paprika and $\frac{1}{8}$ tsp (0.5 mL) of the salt and toss to combine. Add the tomato sauce and spinach, return the turkey to the pan, then stir to combine and cook for 2 minutes. Reduce the heat to medium-low, cover and cook, stirring occasionally, until the flavors combine, 5 minutes. Remove the pan from the heat and let cool for 10 minutes. Wipe the pan clean using a paper towel.

3 In a medium bowl, whisk together the eggs, milk, coriander, black pepper and remaining $\frac{1}{8}$ tsp (0.5 mL) salt.

4 Coat the same sauté pan with cooking spray and place over medium heat. When the oil is shimmering, pour the egg mixture into the pan. Using a spatula, move the eggs toward the center of the pan until they are cooked through, 4 to 5 minutes.

	TOTAL CALORIES	TOTAL FAT	SATURATED FAT	TRANS FAT
PER SERVING	421.57	21.11 g	5.77 g	0.07 g
	SODIUM	**CHOLESTEROL**	**TOTAL CARBOHYDRATES**	**FIBER**
	370.43 mg	228.99 mg	31.25 g	7.63 g
	SUGARS	**PROTEIN**	**POTASSIUM**	**PHOSPHORUS**
	6.82 g	27.20 g	554.89 mg	406.58 mg

5 large eggs

¼ cup (60 mL) nonfat milk

¼ tsp (1 mL) ground coriander

¼ tsp (1 mL) ground black pepper

Cooking spray

10 tbsp (155 mL) shredded reduced-fat Monterey Jack cheese

Five 6-inch (15 cm) corn tortillas

5 **TO STORE:** In each of five containers, add 1 cup (250 mL) of the turkey mixture and top with ⅓ cup (75 mL) of the eggs. Sprinkle with 2 tbsp (30 mL) of the cheese. Wrap the tortillas individually and store with the breakfast bowls. Cover the containers and refrigerate for up to 4 days or freeze without the tortillas for up to 2 months.

6 **TO SERVE:** If frozen, thaw in the refrigerator overnight. To reheat, microwave uncovered on High for 45 to 60 seconds. Allow 2 minutes for the heat to evenly distribute before removing the container from the microwave. Serve warm with a tortilla.

TOBY'S TIP | If you want to add more heat to the dish, increase the chili powder by ¼ tsp (1 mL).

HASH BROWN, HAM AND EGG CASSEROLE

SERVES	SERVING SIZE	TOTAL TIME	PREP TIME	COOK TIME
8	1 piece	1 hour, 15 minutes	20 minutes	55 minutes

Casseroles are ideal for make-ahead meals because they have lots of servings and tend to freeze well. Freeze half of the servings in this casserole so you can have breakfast for next week too!

HASH BROWNS

2 russet potatoes (unpeeled), shredded (2¼ cups/560 mL)

2 tbsp (30 mL) olive oil

¼ tsp (1 mL) salt

¼ tsp (1 mL) ground black pepper

CASSEROLE

Cooking spray

6 oz (175 g) low-sodium ham, diced into ½-inch (1 cm) cubes

1 green bell pepper, diced

1 red bell pepper, diced

2 cups (500 mL) broccoli florets, in bite-size pieces

1 **TO MAKE THE HASH BROWNS:** Add the shredded potatoes to a colander. Drain and discard the excess liquid.

2 In a medium skillet, heat the oil over medium heat. When the oil is shimmering, add the potatoes, salt and black pepper and stir to combine. Using a spatula to flip frequently, brown the potatoes on both sides, about 10 minutes. Transfer the hash browns to a paper towel–lined plate and let cool for 10 minutes.

3 **TO MAKE THE CASSEROLE:** Preheat the oven to 350°F (180°C). Coat an 11- by 7-inch (28 by 18 cm) glass baking dish with cooking spray.

4 Spread the hash browns evenly over the bottom of the baking dish. Top with the ham, green bell pepper, red bell pepper and broccoli.

5 In a medium bowl, whisk together the eggs, milk, mustard, onion powder, garlic powder and black pepper.

6 Pour the egg mixture over the hash browns and vegetables. Sprinkle the cheese on top. Bake until the top is browned and a tester inserted into the casserole comes out clean, about 45 minutes.

PER SERVING			
TOTAL CALORIES 180.56	**TOTAL FAT** 8.40 g	**SATURATED FAT** 2.54 g	**TRANS FAT** 0 g
SODIUM 439.03 mg	**CHOLESTEROL** 160.84 mg	**TOTAL CARBOHYDRATES** 11.59 g	**FIBER** 1.23 g
SUGARS 2.18 g	**PROTEIN** 14.51 g	**POTASSIUM** 397.33 mg	**PHOSPHORUS** 227.61 mg

8 large eggs

1 cup (250 mL) low-fat (1%) milk

1 tsp (5 mL) Dijon mustard

$\frac{1}{2}$ tsp (2 mL) onion powder

$\frac{1}{2}$ tsp (2 mL) garlic powder

$\frac{1}{4}$ tsp (1 mL) ground black pepper

$1\frac{1}{2}$ cups (375 mL) shredded low-fat Cheddar cheese

COMPLETE YOUR PLATE

A fruit (apple, pear or 2 clementine oranges)

7 Let cool for 10 minutes before cutting into eight equal pieces.

8 **TO STORE:** In each of eight containers, add one piece of casserole. Cover and refrigerate for up to 4 days or freeze for up to 2 months.

9 **TO SERVE:** If frozen, thaw in the refrigerator overnight. To reheat, microwave uncovered on High for 45 to 60 seconds. Allow 2 minutes for the heat to distribute before removing the container from the microwave. Serve warm.

TOBY'S TIP | For a different take, swap the russet potato for sweet potato.

STRAWBERRY OAT PANCAKES

SERVES	SERVING SIZE	TOTAL TIME	PREP TIME	COOK TIME
5	2 pancakes, 1/4 cup (60 mL) yogurt	30 minutes	15 minutes	15 minutes

Pancakes are delicious topped with fresh berries, but when you mix them right into the batter, you get that sweet-tart flavor in every bite.

PANCAKES

1 cup (250 mL) unbleached all-purpose flour

1/2 cup (125 mL) 100% whole wheat flour

1/2 cup (125 mL) large-flake (old-fashioned) rolled oats

1 tbsp (15 mL) stevia brown sugar blend (such as Truvia or Splenda)

1 1/2 tsp (7 mL) baking powder

1/2 tsp (2 mL) baking soda

1/2 tsp (2 mL) salt

1 cup (250 mL) nonfat milk

1/2 cup (125 mL) nonfat plain Greek yogurt

2 tbsp (30 mL) canola oil

2 large eggs, beaten

1/2 tsp (2 mL) vanilla extract

1 1/2 cups (375 mL) sliced strawberries

Cooking spray

Griddle or large skillet

1 **TO MAKE THE PANCAKES:** In a medium bowl, mix together the all-purpose flour, whole wheat flour, oats, brown sugar blend, baking powder, baking soda and salt.

2 In a separate medium bowl, whisk together the milk, yogurt, oil, eggs and vanilla.

3 Pour the flour mixture into the wet mixture and stir gently until just combined. Do not overmix. Gently fold in the strawberries.

4 Coat a griddle or large skillet with cooking spray and heat over medium heat.

5 Using a 1/3 cup (75 mL) scoop, add batter to the griddle or skillet, leaving room between cakes. Cook until the top is bubbly and the edges are set, 3 to 4 minutes, then flip over and cook for another 2 to 3 minutes until golden brown. Remove to a clean plate and repeat with the remaining batter to make a total of 10 pancakes.

6 **TO MAKE THE TOPPING:** In a small bowl, stir together the yogurt and syrup.

7 **TO STORE:** In each of five containers, add 2 pancakes. In five small separate containers or in a separate compartment, add 1/4 cup (60 mL) of the yogurt. Cover and refrigerate for up to 4 days. Freeze the pancakes only for up to 2 months.

PER SERVING	TOTAL CALORIES	TOTAL FAT	SATURATED FAT	TRANS FAT
	334.26	9.00 g	1.34 g	0.03 g
	SODIUM	**CHOLESTEROL**	**TOTAL CARBOHYDRATES**	**FIBER**
	590.47 mg	797.35 mg	45.63 g	3.75 g
	SUGARS	**PROTEIN**	**POTASSIUM**	**PHOSPHORUS**
	10.35 g	17.75 g	363.16 mg	278.07 mg

TOPPING

1¼ cups (300 mL) nonfat plain Greek yogurt

2 tbsp (30 mL) sugar-free maple syrup

COMPLETE YOUR PLATE

1 sliced non-starchy vegetable, like tomato or cucumber

8 **TO SERVE:** If frozen, thaw in the refrigerator overnight. Microwave the pancakes only uncovered on High for 30 to 45 seconds. Allow 2 minutes for the heat to distribute before removing the container from the microwave.

TOBY'S TIP | If you prefer, swap the strawberries for the same amount of blueberries or raspberries.

PINEAPPLE-COCONUT OVERNIGHT OATS

	SERVES	SERVING SIZE	TOTAL TIME	PREP TIME	COOK TIME
	5	1 jar	15 minutes, plus overnight refrigeration	15 minutes	0 minutes

Overnight oats are a simple, no-cook way to ensure that you have breakfast ready to go all week long. The tropical flavors in this dish are perfect for summer, or for a little bit of sunshine any time of the year.

2$\frac{1}{2}$ cups (625 mL) gluten-free large-flake (old-fashioned) rolled oats

3$\frac{1}{3}$ cups (825 mL) nonfat milk

5 tsp (25 mL) sugar-free maple syrup

5 tbsp (75 mL) unsweetened shredded coconut

1$\frac{1}{4}$ cups (300 mL) fresh or frozen and thawed pineapple chunks

10 tbsp (150 mL) sliced almonds

Five 16-oz (500 g) glass jars with lids

1 In a large bowl, combine the oats, milk, maple syrup and coconut flakes.

2 TO STORE: Among five jars, divide the oats mixture. In each of five small sealable containers or zip-top plastic bags, add $\frac{1}{4}$ cup (60 mL) of the pineapple. In five additional small sealable containers or zip-top plastic bags, add 2 tbsp (30 mL) of the almonds. Cover or seal and refrigerate overnight and up to 5 days.

3 TO SERVE: Add the pineapple and almonds to the oatmeal and stir to combine. Enjoy cold or warm the oatmeal without the toppings in the microwave uncovered on High for 1$\frac{1}{2}$ to 2 minutes. Top with the pineapple and almonds after reheating.

TOBY'S TIP | If you prefer, swap the same amount of pineapple for fresh or frozen mango.

PER SERVING				
	TOTAL CALORIES 328.94	**TOTAL FAT** 11.92 g	**SATURATED FAT** 3.69 g	**TRANS FAT** 0 g
	SODIUM 77.39 mg	**CHOLESTEROL** 3.26 mg	**TOTAL CARBOHYDRATES** 45.32 g	**FIBER** 7.02 g
	SUGARS 14.18 g	**PROTEIN** 13.49 g	**POTASSIUM** 421.14 mg	**PHOSPHORUS** 223.42 mg

FRUIT AND NUT BREAKFAST COOKIES

SERVES	SERVING SIZE	TOTAL TIME	PREP TIME	COOK TIME
9	1 cookie	33 minutes	15 minutes	18 minutes

You can enjoy diabetes-friendly cookies for breakfast! The trick is using whole grains, nuts and fruit in the batter so you have a medley of nutritious ingredients.

¾ cup (175 mL) unbleached all-purpose flour

¾ cup (175 mL) 100% whole wheat flour

½ cup (125 mL) large-flake (old-fashioned) rolled oats

1 tsp (5 mL) ground cinnamon

1 tsp (5 mL) baking soda

¼ tsp (1 mL) ground nutmeg

¼ tsp (1 mL) salt

1 medium ripe banana, mashed

¼ cup (60 mL) stevia brown sugar blend (such as Truvia or Splenda)

¼ cup (60 mL) canola oil

2 tbsp (30 mL) sugar-free maple syrup

2 large eggs, beaten

1 tsp (5 mL) vanilla extract

¼ cup (60 mL) shelled unsalted pistachios, coarsely chopped

2 baking sheets lined with parchment paper and coated with cooking spray

Preheat the oven to 350°F (180°C)

1   In a medium bowl, mix together the all-purpose flour, whole wheat flour, oats, cinnamon, baking soda, nutmeg and salt.

2   In a large bowl, whisk together the mashed banana, brown sugar blend, oil, maple syrup, eggs, and vanilla until the mixture is smooth and creamy.

3   Gently fold the dry ingredients into the wet ingredients and stir until just combined. Fold in the pistachios, walnuts, cherries and apricots, making sure to evenly distribute them throughout the batter.

4   Using clean hands, roll 3 tbsp (45 mL) of dough into a ball and place on a prepared baking sheet. Repeat with the remaining dough, leaving about 2 inches (5 cm) between cookies. Gently press down on the top of each cookie to flatten slightly.

5   Bake until the cookies are soft and golden brown and a tester inserted into the center of one or two cookies comes out clean, 15 to 18 minutes. Transfer the cookies to a wire rack and let cool for 5 minutes.

6   TO STORE: Place cookies in individual zip-top plastic bags and store them on the counter for up to 1 week. Extra cookies can be stored in individual zip-top plastic bags in the freezer for up to 2 months.

	TOTAL CALORIES	TOTAL FAT	SATURATED FAT	TRANS FAT
PER SERVING	201.07	9.84 g	1.13 g	0 g
	SODIUM	**CHOLESTEROL**	**TOTAL CARBOHYDRATES**	**FIBER**
	202.97 mg	37.20 mg	24.44 g	2.67 g
	SUGARS	**PROTEIN**	**POTASSIUM**	**PHOSPHORUS**
	4.57 g	5.19 g	159.08 mg	87.03 mg

3 tbsp (45 mL) raw walnuts, coarsely chopped

¼ cup (60 mL) dried tart cherries

3 tbsp (45 mL) dried apricots, chopped

COMPLETE YOUR PLATE

Celery or carrot sticks with 1 tbsp (15 mL) peanut butter or almond butter

7 **TO SERVE:** If frozen, thaw on the counter overnight. Serve at room temperature or warm. To reheat, place the cookie on a baking sheet in an oven preheated to 350°F (180°C) for about 5 minutes or until warmed through.

TOBY'S TIP | Rinse your hands in cool water before rolling the dough. The dough will be easier to roll and won't stick as much to your hands.

WHOLE WHEAT WAFFLES
WITH PEANUT BUTTER YOGURT TOPPING

SERVES	SERVING SIZE	TOTAL TIME	PREP TIME	COOK TIME
6	$\frac{1}{2}$ waffle, $\frac{1}{4}$ cup (60 mL) topping	33 minutes	15 minutes	18 minutes

Instead of frozen toasted waffles, make your own better-for-you version that can be whipped up in about 30 minutes. Dress up your waffle with a mouthwatering, protein-filled peanut butter and yogurt topping that'll have you running to the table in the morning.

WAFFLES

1 cup (250 mL) unbleached all-purpose flour

1 cup (250 mL) 100% whole wheat flour

$\frac{1}{3}$ cup (75 mL) toasted wheat germ

2 tsp (10 mL) baking powder

$\frac{1}{2}$ tsp (2 mL) salt

$1\frac{1}{2}$ cups (375 mL) nonfat milk

$\frac{1}{3}$ cup (75 mL) canola oil

2 tbsp (30 mL) stevia brown sugar blend (such as Truvia or Splenda)

1 large egg, beaten

Cooking spray

8-inch (20 cm) waffle iron

1 **TO MAKE THE WAFFLES:** Preheat the waffle iron.

2 In a medium bowl, sift together the all-purpose flour, whole wheat flour, wheat germ, baking powder and salt.

3 In a large bowl, whisk together the milk, oil, brown sugar blend and egg. Add the dry mixture to the wet mixture and stir gently to combine.

4 Coat the preheated waffle iron with cooking spray. Add $1\frac{1}{4}$ cups (300 mL) of batter and, using the back of a spoon, spread the batter evenly. Cook for 3 minutes or according to the manufacturer's instructions, until the waffle is set and golden brown. Transfer to a clean plate and repeat with the remaining batter to make a total of three 8-inch (20 cm) waffles.

5 **TO MAKE THE TOPPING:** In a small bowl, stir together the yogurt, peanut butter, syrup and vanilla.

6 **TO STORE:** In each of six containers, place $\frac{1}{2}$ of a waffle. In each of six small containers or in a separate compartment, add $\frac{1}{4}$ cup (60 mL) of the topping. Cover and refrigerate for up to 4 days or freeze the waffle only for up to 2 months.

	TOTAL CALORIES	TOTAL FAT	SATURATED FAT	TRANS FAT
PER SERVING	414.84	20.40 g	2.46 g	0 g
	SODIUM	**CHOLESTEROL**	**TOTAL CARBOHYDRATES**	**FIBER**
	x mg	34.11 mg	44.72 g	4.32 g
	SUGARS	**PROTEIN**	**POTASSIUM**	**PHOSPHORUS**
	10.02 g	16.25 g	315.00 mg	295.25 mg

TOPPING

1 cup (250 mL) nonfat plain Greek yogurt

¼ cup (60 mL) creamy peanut butter

1 tbsp (15 mL) sugar-free maple syrup

¼ tsp (1 mL) vanilla extract

COMPLETE YOUR PLATE

1 non-starchy vegetable, like sliced tomato or cucumber

7 **TO SERVE:** If frozen, thaw in the refrigerator overnight. Toast the waffle in a toaster oven until slightly browned, or warm it uncovered in the microwave on High for 30 seconds. Allow 2 minutes for the heat to distribute before removing the container from the microwave. Serve warm with the yogurt topping.

TOBY'S TIP | Swap the peanut butter for the same amount of almond butter, sunflower seed butter or other nut or seed butter of your choice.

CHAPTER

10

SNACKS

HOMEMADE HUMMUS
WITH VEGETABLES

 · · · ·

SERVES	SERVING SIZE	TOTAL TIME	PREP TIME	COOK TIME
6	¼ cup (60 mL) hummus, 4 baby carrots, 3 celery sticks, 3 cherry tomatoes	20 minutes	20 minutes	0 minutes

Hummus is a fantastic dip to include in your snack rotation. It's easy to make, too! Just add a few ingredients to your blender, and blend until smooth. Soon, you'll be a hummus-making expert.

1¾ cups (425 mL) low-sodium canned chickpeas, drained and rinsed

1 clove garlic, minced

1 tbsp (15 mL) tahini

Juice of 1 lemon

¼ tsp (1 mL) salt

¼ tsp (1 mL) ground black pepper

3 tbsp (45 mL) extra virgin olive oil

24 baby carrots

6 stalks celery, cut into thirds

18 cherry tomatoes

Blender or food processor

1 Add the chickpeas, garlic, tahini, lemon juice, salt and pepper to a blender or food processor and purée on High until smooth, about 30 seconds. With the machine running, gradually add the olive oil and blend until well incorporated.

2 TO STORE: In each of six containers, add ¼ cup (60 mL) of hummus. In a separate compartment, add 4 carrots, 3 celery sticks and 3 cherry tomatoes to each. Cover and refrigerate for up to 5 days.

3 TO SERVE: Remove from the refrigerator and serve cold.

TOBY'S TIP | Tahini, or sesame seed paste, is usually found in the condiment aisle near the peanut butter. If you can't locate it, ask a store associate for assistance.

PER SERVING	TOTAL CALORIES	TOTAL FAT	SATURATED FAT	TRANS FAT
	168.40	9.82 g	1.36 g	0.0 g
	SODIUM	**CHOLESTEROL**	**TOTAL CARBOHYDRATES**	**FIBER**
	259.53 mg	0.0 mg	17.20 g	5.79 g
	SUGARS	**PROTEIN**	**POTASSIUM**	**PHOSPHORUS**
	5.95 g	4.96 g	439.34 mg	109.71 mg

ROASTED CHICKPEAS AND EDAMAME

SERVES	SERVING SIZE	TOTAL TIME	PREP TIME	COOK TIME
6	About 1/3 cup (75 mL)	45 minutes	15 minutes	30 minutes

Chickpeas, or garbanzo beans, are a legume that counts as either a vegetable or a protein. Edamame, or baby soybeans, are a protein. Combine the two and you have a protein and fiber–filled snack that will keep you feeling satisfied.

2 tbsp (30 mL) olive oil

1/2 tsp (2 mL) garlic powder

1/4 tsp (1 mL) plus 1/8 tsp (0.5 mL) sea salt

1/4 tsp (1 mL) ground black pepper

1 1/2 cups (375 mL) canned low-sodium chickpeas, drained, rinsed and dried well with a kitchen towel

1 1/2 cups (375 mL) shelled frozen edamame, thawed and dried with a kitchen towel

Rimmed baking sheet lined with parchment paper

Preheat the oven to 400°F (200°C)

1 In a medium bowl, whisk together the oil, garlic powder, salt and pepper. Add the chickpeas and edamame and toss to evenly coat.

2 Spread the mixture in a single layer on the prepared baking sheet. Bake, turning every 5 minutes, until browned and crisp, 25 to 30 minutes. Remove from the oven and let cool on the pan for at least 10 minutes.

3 TO STORE: In each of six sealable bags or containers, add about 1/3 cup (75 mL) of the roasted chickpea and edamame mixture. Store for up to 1 week at room temperature.

4 TO SERVE: Enjoy at room temperature.

TOBY'S TIP | You can play with adding various spices. Try flavoring with chili powder, Cajun spice mixture or Italian seasoning whisked together with the olive oil.

PER SERVING	TOTAL CALORIES	TOTAL FAT	SATURATED FAT	TRANS FAT
	138.76	7.55 g	1.12 g	0.0 g
	SODIUM	CHOLESTEROL	TOTAL CARBOHYDRATES	FIBER
	216.45 mg	0.0 mg	11.71 g	3.81 g
	SUGARS	PROTEIN	POTASSIUM	PHOSPHORUS
	2.31 g	6.76 g	90.69 mg	49.12 mg

HUMMUS-STUFFED DEVILED EGGS

SERVES	SERVING SIZE	TOTAL TIME	PREP TIME	COOK TIME
6	4 deviled eggs	23 minutes	20 minutes	3 minutes

This spin on deviled eggs uses hummus to fill the center of the egg instead of mayo and egg yolks. Top with a slice of your favorite non-starchy vegetables. I opted for tomatoes, but you can swap those for sliced radishes or cucumber.

12 large eggs

3/4 cup (175 mL) Homemade Hummus (page 148) or store-bought hummus

24 cherry tomatoes

1 In a medium pot, add the eggs and cover them with water. Bring the water to a boil over high heat. Boil the eggs for 3 minutes, then remove the pot from the heat, cover and let the eggs stand for 15 minutes. Drain the water from the pot and run cold water over the eggs or transfer to a bowl filled with cold water and ice until they are completely cool, about 10 minutes.

2 Peel the eggs and cut lengthwise. Remove the yolks and reserve for another purpose.

3 Spoon 1 1/2 tsp (7 mL) of the hummus in each of the twenty-four hard-cooked egg white halves. Top with a cherry tomato.

4 TO STORE: In each of six containers, add four hummus-filled deviled eggs. Cover and refrigerate for up to 1 week.

5 TO SERVE: Enjoy cold.

TOBY'S TIP | Uncut cherry tomatoes will last longer than those that are cut.

	TOTAL CALORIES	TOTAL FAT	SATURATED FAT	0.0 g
PER SERVING	130.76	5.16 g	0.70 g	
	SODIUM	CHOLESTEROL	TOTAL CARBOHYDRATES	FIBER
	242.72 mg	0.0 mg	11.73 g	3.17 g
	SUGARS	PROTEIN	POTASSIUM	PHOSPHORUS
	5.23 g	10.28 g	488.41 mg	81.08 mg

VEGETABLE CROQUETTES

SERVES	SERVING SIZE	TOTAL TIME	PREP TIME	COOK TIME
6	2 croquettes	36 minutes	20 minutes	15 minutes

Croquettes are vegetable patties that are pan-fried in a small amount of oil. This version uses potatoes, carrots, onion and celery and are mighty tasty.

1 large russet potato (unpeeled), shredded (1 lb/500 g)

⅓ cup (75 mL) plain bread crumbs

2 carrots, peeled and shredded

1 yellow onion, chopped

1 stalk celery, chopped

1 large egg, beaten

1 tsp (5 mL) dried parsley

¼ tsp (1 mL) plus ⅛ tsp (0.5 mL) salt

¼ tsp (1 mL) ground black pepper

¼ cup (60 mL) olive oil

1 In a medium bowl, add the potatoes, bread crumbs, carrots, onion, celery, egg, parsley, salt and pepper. Using clean hands, toss to combine.

2 Use your hands to form a ¼ cup (60 mL) patty. Place it on a large platter or plate and gently press with your palm to flatten it slightly. Repeat to make a total of 12 patties. Cover with plastic wrap and refrigerate for at least 20 minutes and up to 1 hour.

3 In a large sauté pan, heat the oil over medium heat. When the oil is shimmering, add the croquettes, leaving ½ inch (1 cm) around each. Cover the pan and sauté, flipping the croquettes halfway through, until golden brown, 15 minutes. Transfer to a paper towel–lined plate and let cool for at least 10 minutes.

4 TO STORE: In each of six containers, add two croquettes. Cover and refrigerate for up to 4 days or freeze for up to 2 months.

5 TO SERVE: If frozen, thaw in the refrigerator overnight. To reheat, microwave uncovered on High for 30 seconds. Allow 2 minutes for the heat to distribute before removing the container from the microwave. Serve warm.

TOBY'S TIP | Leaving the peel on the potatoes provides more fiber.

	TOTAL CALORIES	TOTAL FAT	SATURATED FAT	TRANS FAT
PER SERVING	187.01	10.26 g	2.86 g	0.0 g
	SODIUM 228.02 mg	**CHOLESTEROL** 31.0 mg	**TOTAL CARBOHYDRATES** 20.71 g	**FIBER** 2.86 g
	SUGARS 2.82 g	**PROTEIN** 3.75 g	**POTASSIUM** 434.19 mg	**PHOSPHORUS** 81.19 mg

ZUCCHINI MUFFINS

SERVES	SERVING SIZE	TOTAL TIME	PREP TIME	COOK TIME
12	1 muffin	38 minutes	20 minutes	18 minutes

These muffins, spiced with ginger, cinnamon and nutmeg, make your snack feel like a treat. Swap in a carrot for a zucchini for something extra special.

¾ cup (175 mL) unbleached all-purpose flour

¾ cup (175 mL) 100% whole wheat flour

2 tsp (10 mL) baking powder

1 tsp (5 mL) baking soda

1 tsp (5 mL) ground cinnamon

¼ tsp (1 mL) ground ginger

⅛ tsp (0.5 mL) ground nutmeg

¼ tsp (1 mL) salt

½ cup (125 mL) canola oil

¼ cup (60 mL) stevia brown sugar blend (such as Truvia or Splenda)

¾ cup (175 mL) nonfat plain Greek yogurt

2 large eggs, beaten

1 tsp (5 mL) vanilla extract

2 medium zucchini, shredded

½ cup (125 mL) raw walnuts, coarsely chopped

½ cup (125 mL) raisins

12-cup muffin pan coated with cooking spray

Preheat the oven to 375°F (190°C)

1 In a medium bowl, sift together the all-purpose flour, whole wheat flour, baking powder, baking soda, cinnamon, ginger, nutmeg and salt.

2 In a large bowl, whisk together the oil and brown sugar blend. Add the yogurt, eggs and vanilla and whisk until combined.

3 Gently fold the dry ingredients into the wet ingredients, being careful not to overmix the batter. Gently fold in the zucchini, walnuts and raisins, evenly distributing them throughout the batter.

4 Divide the batter equally among the cups in the prepared muffin pan. Tap the pan on the counter a few times to get rid of any bubbles in the batter.

5 Bake until the muffins are golden brown on top and a tester inserted in the center comes out clean, about 18 minutes. Remove the muffins from the oven and let cool in the pan for 10 minutes before transferring to a wire rack to finish cooling.

6 TO STORE: Package five muffins individually into sealable containers and keep at room temperature for up to 5 days. Freeze the remaining muffins in a sealable container for up to 2 months.

7 TO SERVE: If frozen, thaw at room temperature overnight. Serve at room temperature or warm in the toaster oven or microwave on High for 20 seconds.

PER SERVING			
TOTAL CALORIES	TOTAL FAT	SATURATED FAT	TRANS FAT
202.14	11.20 g	1.07 g	0.0 g
SODIUM	CHOLESTEROL	TOTAL CARBOHYDRATES	FIBER
254.58 mg	31.0 mg	21.56 g	1.63 g
SUGARS	PROTEIN	POTASSIUM	PHOSPHORUS
9.08 g	4.92 g	192.08 mg	83.42 mg

TOBY'S TIP | Swap your standard 12-cup muffin pan for a 36-cup mini muffin pan. Three mini muffins are equivalent to one standard-size muffin.

ORANGE CREAMSICLE CHIA PUDDING

SERVES	SERVING SIZE	TOTAL TIME	PREP TIME	COOK TIME
5	1 jar	20 minutes, plus overnight refrigeration	20 minutes	0 minutes

Chia seeds have a mild taste, so when you add bold flavors, like orange and vanilla, they really stand out. When mixed with milk or water, chia seeds swell (or gelatinize), and overnight that mixture transforms into pudding.

2½ cups (625 mL) nonfat milk

10 tbsp (185 mL) chia seeds

2½ tsp (7 mL) stevia honey blend (such as Truvia Nectar)

1¼ tsp (6 mL) vanilla extract

Zest of 1 orange

Juice of 2 oranges

Five 8-oz (250 mL) glass jars with lids

1 Into each of five glass jars, add ½ cup (125 mL) of the milk, 2 tbsp (30 mL) of the chia seeds, ½ tsp (2 mL) of the stevia honey blend and ¼ tsp (1 mL) of the vanilla. Stir to combine.

2 In a small bowl, mix the orange juice and zest. Divide the mixture evenly among the five jars and stir to combine.

3 TO STORE: Cover the jars and refrigerate overnight or up to 5 days.

4 TO SERVE: Enjoy cold.

TOBY'S TIP | To make this dairy-free, use unflavored soy milk instead of nonfat milk.

	TOTAL CALORIES	TOTAL FAT	SATURATED FAT	TRANS FAT
PER SERVING	153.83	6.29 g	0.73 g	0.03 g
	SODIUM 55.04 mg	**CHOLESTEROL** 2.45 mg	**TOTAL CARBOHYDRATES** 17.47 g	**FIBER** 7.30 g
	SUGARS 7.93 g	**PROTEIN** 7.62 g	**POTASSIUM** 318.94 mg	**PHOSPHORUS** 299.71 mg

SPICY CHICKEN MEATBALLS
WITH SRIRACHA YOGURT DIP

SERVES	SERVING SIZE	TOTAL TIME	PREP TIME	COOK TIME
6	2 meatballs, 2 tbsp (30 mL) dip	30 minutes	20 minutes	10 minutes

These warming chicken meatballs carry a satisfying kick. The meatballs are made with lots of fragrant spices, while the dip combines a spicy Thai chile sauce with cooling Greek yogurt.

MEATBALLS

8 oz (250 g) lean ground chicken

1 onion, chopped

¼ cup (60 mL) unseasoned bread crumbs

1 large egg, beaten

1 tsp (5 mL) garlic powder

½ tsp (2 mL) chili powder

½ tsp (2 mL) ground cumin

½ tsp (2 mL) paprika

¼ tsp (1 mL) salt

2 tbsp (30 mL) olive oil

DIP

¾ cup (175 mL) nonfat plain Greek yogurt

1 tbsp (15 mL) Thai chile sauce (such as Sriracha)

1 **TO MAKE THE MEATBALLS:** In a medium bowl, add the chicken, onion, bread crumbs, egg, garlic powder, chili powder, cumin, paprika and salt. Using clean hands, mix until well combined.

2 Roll 1 heaping tbsp (15 mL) of the chicken mixture into a 2-inch (5 cm) ball and place on a large plate. Repeat with the remaining chicken mixture to make a total of 12 meatballs.

3 Heat the olive oil in a large sauté pan over medium-high heat. Add the meatballs, cover and cook, turning once, until browned on all sides, 10 minutes.

4 **TO MAKE THE DIP:** In a small bowl, mix the yogurt and Thai chile sauce.

5 **TO STORE:** In each of six containers, add two meatballs and, in a separate compartment, 2 tbsp (30 mL) of the dip. Cover and refrigerate for up to 4 days. Freeze meatballs only for up to 2 months.

6 **TO SERVE:** If frozen, thaw in the refrigerator overnight. Microwave the meatballs only uncovered on High for 30 to 40 seconds. Allow 2 minutes for the heat to distribute before removing the container from the microwave. Serve warm with the dip.

TOBY'S TIP | If you prefer, swap the chicken for lean ground turkey breast or at least 90% lean ground beef.

	TOTAL CALORIES	TOTAL FAT	SATURATED FAT	TRANS FAT
PER SERVING	150.78	8.78 g	1.84 g	0.03 g
	SODIUM	CHOLESTEROL	TOTAL CARBOHYDRATES	FIBER
	219.19 mg	64.52 mg	6.54 g	0.72 g
	SUGARS	PROTEIN	POTASSIUM	PHOSPHORUS
	2.22 g	11.33 g	285.90 mg	132.03 mg

CHERRY PECAN GREEK YOGURT BARK

 · ·

SERVES	SERVING SIZE	TOTAL TIME	PREP TIME	COOK TIME
6	4 pieces	15 minutes, plus 4 hours freezer time	15 minutes	0 minutes

This no-cook, refreshing sweet treat uses Greek yogurt as the base. Spread out the ingredients on a baking sheet and pop the pan in the freezer. In a few hours you'll have a cooling snack that can be kept in the freezer for up to 1 month.

2 cups (500 mL) nonfat vanilla-flavored Greek yogurt

$\frac{1}{2}$ tsp (2 mL) ground cinnamon

$\frac{1}{2}$ cup (125 mL) coarsely chopped raw pecans

$\frac{1}{2}$ cup (125 mL) fresh or frozen pitted cherries, quartered

Rimmed baking sheet lined with parchment paper (see Note)

1 In a medium bowl, mix together the yogurt and cinnamon. Use a spatula to evenly spread the yogurt mixture onto the prepared baking sheet about $\frac{1}{2}$ inch (1 cm) thick.

2 Sprinkle the yogurt with the pecans and cherries.

3 Freeze the baking sheet for at least 4 hours or until the yogurt sets. Gently break the yogurt bark into 24 pieces.

4 TO STORE: Into each of six containers, add four pieces of the yogurt bark. Store in the freezer for up to 1 month.

5 TO SERVE: Enjoy cold, straight from the freezer.

   NOTE: Make sure the baking sheet fits into your freezer.

TOBY'S TIP | If you prefer, swap the pecans for the same amount of raw or unsalted dry-roasted peanuts, almonds, cashews or pistachios.

PER SERVING			
TOTAL CALORIES 120.90	**TOTAL FAT** 5.97 g	**SATURATED FAT** 0.52 g	**TRANS FAT** 0.0 g
SODIUM 30.21 mg	**CHOLESTEROL** 0.0 mg	**TOTAL CARBOHYDRATES** 9.39 g	**FIBER** 1.16 g
SUGARS 7.51 g	**PROTEIN** 8.45 g	**POTASSIUM** 173.82 mg	**PHOSPHORUS** 126.30 mg

LEMON RASPBERRY PROTEIN POPSICLES

	SERVES	SERVING SIZE	TOTAL TIME	PREP TIME	COOK TIME
	6	1 popsicle	15 minutes, plus 4 hours freezer time	15 minutes	0 minutes

These creamy, fruity popsicles have an added boost of protein from Greek yogurt and milk. The extra protein in the popsicles helps keep you feeling more satisfied for longer.

½ cup (125 mL) nonfat plain Greek yogurt

½ cup (125 mL) nonfat milk

1½ cups (375 mL) frozen raspberries

2 tbsp (30 mL) sugar-free maple syrup

1 tbsp (15 mL) fresh lemon juice

Blender

6 standard popsicle molds

1 In a blender, add the yogurt, milk, raspberries, maple syrup and lemon juice and purée on High until smooth.

2 Divide the yogurt mixture equally among six standard popsicle molds. Freeze the popsicles for at least 4 hours until solidly frozen.

3 TO STORE: Popsicles can be frozen for up to 2 months.

4 TO SERVE: Enjoy cold, straight from the freezer.

TOBY'S TIP | If you prefer, swap the raspberries for frozen strawberries, blueberries or mixed berries.

	TOTAL CALORIES	TOTAL FAT	SATURATED FAT	TRANS FAT
PER SERVING	38.23	0.01 g	0.03 g	0.0 g
	SODIUM	CHOLESTEROL	TOTAL CARBOHYDRATES	FIBER
	24.57 mg	1.35 mg	6.45 g	1.26 g
	SUGARS	PROTEIN	POTASSIUM	PHOSPHORUS
	3.47 g	2.87 g	61.12 mg	46.34 mg

CHAPTER 11

MAIN SOUPS AND SALADS

ITALIAN WEDDING SOUP

SERVES	SERVING SIZE	TOTAL TIME	PREP TIME	COOK TIME
6	1⅓ cups (325 mL)	1 hour, 10 minutes, plus refrigeration	30 minutes	40 minutes

This delicious soup is made with pork meatballs and cooked in a vegetable-based broth with spinach and orzo. It's a complete meal in one bowl!

MEATBALLS

8 oz (250 g) lean ground pork

¼ cup (60 mL) unseasoned bread crumbs

1 large egg, beaten

1 tbsp (15 mL) grated Parmesan

1 tsp (5 mL) garlic powder

1 tsp (5 mL) onion powder

1 tsp (5 mL) dried parsley flakes

½ tsp (2 mL) ground oregano

¼ tsp (1 mL) salt

⅛ tsp (0.5 mL) ground black pepper

2 tbsp (30 mL) olive oil

1 **TO MAKE THE MEATBALLS:** In a medium bowl, add the pork, bread crumbs, egg, Parmesan, garlic powder, onion powder, parsley, oregano, salt and pepper. Using clean hands, mix until well combined.

2 Roll 1 tsp (5 mL) of the pork mixture into a 1-inch (2.5 cm) ball and place on a large plate. Repeat with the remaining pork mixture to make a total of 18 small meatballs. Cover the plate and refrigerate for at least 30 minutes and up to 24 hours.

3 Heat 2 tbsp (30 mL) olive oil in a large soup pot over medium heat. Add the meatballs and cover. Cook, turning once, until browned on all sides, 8 minutes. Transfer the meatballs from the pot to a clean plate.

4 **TO MAKE THE SOUP:** In the same soup pot, heat 2 tbsp (30 mL) olive oil over medium heat. When the oil is shimmering, add the onion and cook until soft and translucent, about 3 minutes. Add the carrots, celery and garlic and continue cooking until the vegetables have softened, 3 minutes more.

5 Add the vegetable broth and water and bring to a boil over high heat. Add the orzo and meatballs and reduce the heat to medium-low. Cover and continue cooking until the orzo is cooked and the flavors have combined, 20 minutes. Add the spinach and stir until the spinach wilts, 2 to 3 minutes. Remove the pot from the heat and let cool for 15 minutes.

PER SERVING				
	TOTAL CALORIES 318.28	TOTAL FAT 14.77 g	SATURATED FAT 3.07 g	TRANS FAT 0.03 g
	SODIUM 316.65 mg	CHOLESTEROL 55.92 mg	TOTAL CARBOHYDRATES 32.48 g	FIBER 7.34 g
	SUGARS 3.36 g	PROTEIN 14.79 g	POTASSIUM 269.37 mg	PHOSPHORUS 112.99 mg

SOUP

2 tbsp (30 mL) olive oil

1 large onion, chopped

2 medium carrots, chopped

2 stalks celery, chopped

2 cloves garlic, minced

4 cups (1 L) low-sodium vegetable broth

2 cups (500 mL) water

1 cup (250 mL) whole wheat orzo pasta

3 cups (750 mL) baby spinach

COMPLETE YOUR PLATE

1 small whole wheat roll

6 **TO STORE:** Into each of six containers, add 1⅓ cups (325 mL) of the soup. Refrigerate for up to 4 days or freeze for up to 2 months.

7 **TO SERVE:** If frozen, thaw in the refrigerator overnight. Microwave uncovered on High for 1½ to 2 minutes. Allow 2 minutes for the heat to distribute before removing the container from the microwave. Alternatively, reheat in a saucepan on the stove by bringing the soup to a boil and then simmering over medium-low heat for about 10 minutes, until heated through. Serve warm.

TOBY'S TIP | If you prefer, swap the pork for ground chicken, turkey or at least 90% lean ground beef.

MINESTRONE SOUP
WITH CHICKPEAS AND SHRIMP

SERVES	SERVING SIZE	TOTAL TIME	PREP TIME	COOK TIME
8	1½ cups (375 mL)	55 minutes	20 minutes	35 minutes

The base of this soup — the Italian tomato-based classic minestrone — tastes fabulous on its own. Add protein-filled shrimp and chickpeas, and you've upped this everyday soup into one that will knock your socks off.

2 tbsp (30 mL) olive oil

1 large onion, chopped

2 cloves garlic, minced

2 medium carrots, chopped

2 stalks celery, chopped

1 large zucchini (8 oz/250 g), chopped

1 cup (250 mL) 100% whole wheat elbow macaroni

3½ cups (875 mL) no-salt-added canned diced tomatoes, with juice

1¾ cups (425 mL) canned low-sodium chickpeas, drained and rinsed

½ tsp (2 mL) dried oregano

½ tsp (2 mL) dried thyme

¼ tsp (1 mL) salt

1 In a large soup pot, heat the olive oil over medium heat. When the oil is shimmering, add the onion and cook until soft and translucent, about 3 minutes. Add the garlic, carrots, celery and zucchini and continue cooking until the vegetables have softened, 5 minutes more.

2 Add the pasta, tomatoes with juice, chickpeas, oregano, thyme, salt, hot pepper flakes and black pepper and stir to combine. Add the vegetable broth and water and bring to a boil over high heat. Reduce the heat to medium-low and cover. Cook until the flavors combine, about 20 minutes.

3 Add the shrimp and basil and bring back to a boil over high heat. Reduce the heat to medium-low and cook, uncovered, until the shrimp are opaque and the basil wilts, 3 minutes.

4 TO STORE: Into each of six containers, add 1½ cups (375 mL) of the soup. Cover and refrigerate for up to 4 days or freeze for up to 2 months.

	TOTAL CALORIES	TOTAL FAT	SATURATED FAT	TRANS FAT
PER SERVING	233.05	4.53 g	0.57 g	0.0 g
	SODIUM	CHOLESTEROL	TOTAL CARBOHYDRATES	FIBER
	243.63 mg	91.29 mg	30.51 g	6.96 g
	SUGARS	PROTEIN	POTASSIUM	PHOSPHORUS
	6.30 g	18.79 g	709.90 mg	190.49 mg

¼ tsp (1 mL) hot pepper flakes

¼ tsp (1 mL) ground black pepper

4 cups (1 L) low-sodium vegetable broth

2 cups (500 mL) water

1 lb (500 g) large shrimp, peeled and deveined

1 cup (250 mL) thinly sliced basil leaves

COMPLETE YOUR PLATE

A small vegetable salad with vinaigrette dressing

5 **TO SERVE:** If frozen, thaw in the refrigerator overnight. If the soup is too thick, add ¼ cup (60 mL) of water before reheating, if desired. To reheat, microwave uncovered on High for $1\frac{1}{2}$ to 2 minutes. Allow 2 minutes for the heat to distribute before removing the container from the microwave. Alternatively, reheat in a saucepan on the stove by bringing the soup to a boil and then simmering over medium-low heat until heated through, about 10 minutes. Serve warm.

TOBY'S TIP | If you prefer, swap the chickpeas for cannellini beans or great Northern beans.

EASY CHICKEN NOODLE SOUP

SERVES	SERVING SIZE	TOTAL TIME	PREP TIME	COOK TIME
6	1½ cups (375 mL)	45 minutes	20 minutes	25 minutes

What makes this chicken soup so easy? The rotisserie chicken used for the meat. Be sure to remove the skin of the chicken before shredding, as that's where most of the saturated fat is found. (For more information on saturated fat, see page 46.)

2 tbsp (30 mL) olive oil

1 yellow onion, chopped

2 stalks celery, chopped

1 turnip, chopped

2 cloves garlic, minced

8 oz (250 g) shredded rotisserie chicken, skin removed

3 carrots, peeled and cut into ½-inch (1 cm) rounds

4 oz (125 g) 100% whole wheat angel hair pasta, broken in half

1 tsp (5 mL) dried parsley flakes

½ tsp (2 mL) dried dillweed

⅛ tsp (0.5 mL) ground black pepper

4 cups (1 L) low-sodium chicken broth

3 cups (750 mL) water

1 In a large soup pot, heat the oil over medium heat. When the oil is shimmering, add the onion and cook until soft and translucent, about 3 minutes. Add the celery, turnip and garlic and cook until the vegetables soften, 3 minutes more.

2 Add the chicken, carrots, pasta, parsley, dillweed and pepper and stir to combine. Add the chicken broth and water and bring to a boil over high heat. Reduce the heat to medium-low and simmer, covered, until the flavors combine and the pasta is cooked, 15 minutes.

3 TO STORE: In each of six containers, add 1½ cups (375 mL) of the soup. Refrigerate for up to 4 days or freeze for up to 2 months.

4 TO SERVE: If frozen, thaw in the refrigerator overnight. To reheat, microwave uncovered on High for 1½ to 2 minutes. Allow 2 minutes for the heat to distribute before removing the container from the microwave. Alternatively, reheat in a saucepan on the stove by bringing the soup to a boil and then simmering over medium-low heat until heated through, about 10 minutes. Serve warm.

TOBY'S TIP | If you prefer, swap the rotisserie chicken for skinless grilled chicken or leftover cooked chicken.

COMPLETE YOUR PLATE
Small green salad with vinaigrette dressing.

	TOTAL CALORIES	TOTAL FAT	SATURATED FAT	TRANS FAT
PER SERVING	267.13	9.03 g	1.49 g	0.04 g
	SODIUM	CHOLESTEROL	TOTAL CARBOHYDRATES	FIBER
	427.54 mg	52.92 mg	31.63 g	5.48 g
	SUGARS	PROTEIN	POTASSIUM	PHOSPHORUS
	6.03 g	15.74 g	490.94 mg	133.98 mg

DECONSTRUCTED STUFFED CABBAGE SOUP

SERVES	SERVING SIZE	TOTAL TIME	PREP TIME	COOK TIME
8	1⅓ cups (325 mL)	1 hour, 20 minutes	20 minutes	1 hour

Although this soup takes an hour to cook, it's totally worth the wait. The balance of flavors between the cabbage, ground beef and brown rice makes it unbelievably delicious.

¼ cup (60 mL) olive oil, divided

1 lb (500 g) at least 90% lean ground beef

1 yellow onion, chopped

2 stalks celery, chopped

2 cloves garlic, minced

½ head green cabbage, coarsely chopped

2 carrots, peeled and cut into ½-inch (1 cm) rounds

½ cup (125 mL) long-grain brown rice

2 tbsp (30 mL) stevia brown sugar blend (such as Truvia or Splenda)

3 bay leaves

1 tsp (5 mL) apple cider vinegar

1 tsp (5 mL) ground oregano

¼ tsp (1 mL) ground black pepper

1 In a large soup pot, heat 2 tbsp (30 mL) of the oil over medium heat. When the oil is shimmering, add the ground beef and cook, breaking up the pieces with the back of a wooden spoon, until browned, about 8 minutes. Transfer the ground beef to a clean plate.

2 Using the same pot, heat the remaining 2 tbsp (30 mL) oil over medium heat. When the oil is shimmering, add the onion, celery and garlic and cook until the vegetables are soft and translucent, about 3 minutes. Add the cabbage and carrots, and cook until softened, about 5 minutes. Add the brown rice, brown sugar blend, bay leaves, apple cider vinegar, oregano and pepper and stir to combine.

3 Add the cooked beef, broth and tomato sauce and stir to combine. Bring the mixture to a boil over high heat. Reduce the heat to medium-low and simmer, covered, until the flavors combine and the rice is cooked, 45 minutes. Remove the bay leaves and discard.

4 TO STORE: In each of six containers, add 1⅓ cups (325 mL) of the soup. Cover and refrigerate for up to 4 days or freeze for up to 2 months.

PER SERVING			
TOTAL CALORIES	TOTAL FAT	SATURATED FAT	TRANS FAT
238.83	12.91 g	3.33 g	0.36 g
SODIUM	CHOLESTEROL	TOTAL CARBOHYDRATES	FIBER
132.63 mg	36.83 mg	16.13 g	2.36 g
SUGARS	PROTEIN	POTASSIUM	PHOSPHORUS
3.61 g	14.42 g	434.69 mg	171.53 mg

4 cups (1 L) low-sodium beef broth

2 cups (500 mL) low-sodium tomato sauce

COMPLETE YOUR PLATE

Small whole wheat roll with 1 tsp (5 mL) trans fat–free margarine

5 TO SERVE: If frozen, thaw in the refrigerator overnight. To reheat, microwave uncovered on High for $1\frac{1}{2}$ to 2 minutes. Allow 2 minutes for the heat to distribute before removing the container from the microwave. Alternatively, reheat in a saucepan on the stove by bringing the soup to a boil and then simmering over medium-low heat until heated through, about 10 minutes. Serve warm.

TOBY'S TIP | Use the remaining half cabbage head by adding shredded cabbage to a green salad or by sautéing it in 2 tbsp (30 mL) of olive oil for 10 to 15 minutes over medium heat. Add a sprinkle of salt and black pepper and serve warm.

BEANS AND GREENS SOUP
WITH FARRO

 · · · ·

SERVES	SERVING SIZE	TOTAL TIME	PREP TIME	COOK TIME
6	1⅓ cups (325 mL)	55 minutes	15 minutes	40 minutes

Farro is a whole grain that dates back to ancient Rome. Just like rice, it can be added to soups or cooked as a side dish.

2 tbsp (30 mL) olive oil

1 yellow onion, chopped

2 cloves garlic, minced

1¾ cups (425 mL) canned low-sodium great Northern beans

¾ cup (175 mL) farro

Zest, cut into four 1-inch (2.5 cm) strips, and juice of 1 lemon

1 tsp (5 mL) dried oregano

¼ tsp (1 mL) salt

¼ tsp (1 mL) hot pepper flakes

¼ tsp (1 mL) ground black pepper

4 cups (1 L) low-sodium vegetable broth

2 cups (500 mL) water

½ head escarole, chopped (about 4 cups/1 L)

1 In a large soup pot, heat the oil over medium heat. When the oil is shimmering, add the onion and garlic and cook until the onion is soft and translucent and the garlic is fragrant, about 3 minutes. Add the beans, farro, lemon zest and juice, oregano, salt, hot pepper flakes and black pepper and stir to combine.

2 Add the vegetable broth and water and bring to a boil over high heat. Reduce the heat to medium-low and simmer, covered, until the flavors combine and the farro is cooked, 30 minutes. Add the escarole and stir until cooked, 5 minutes. Remove the lemon zest strips.

3 TO STORE: In each of six containers, add 1⅓ cups (325 mL) of the soup. Cover and refrigerate for up to 4 days or freeze for up to 2 months.

4 TO SERVE: If frozen, thaw in the refrigerator overnight. To reheat, microwave uncovered on High for 1½ to 2 minutes. Allow 2 minutes for the heat to distribute before removing the container from the microwave. Alternatively, reheat in a saucepan on the stove by bringing the soup to a boil and then simmering over medium-low heat until heated through, about 10 minutes. If needed, add ¼ cup (60 mL) water to reach your preferred consistency. Serve warm.

COMPLETE YOUR PLATE

Small green salad with vinaigrette dressing

TOBY'S TIP | If you prefer, swap the great Northern beans for cannellini beans.

PER SERVING	TOTAL CALORIES	TOTAL FAT	SATURATED FAT	TRANS FAT
	217.26	5.97 g	0.83 g	0.0 g
	SODIUM	CHOLESTEROL	TOTAL CARBOHYDRATES	FIBER
	217.83 mg	0.0 mg	34.14 g	10.28 g
	SUGARS	PROTEIN	POTASSIUM	101.59 mg
	2.25 g	7.58 g	323.26 mg	

PASTA SALAD
WITH KALE AND PINTO BEANS

SERVES	SERVING SIZE	TOTAL TIME	PREP TIME	COOK TIME
4	1½ cups (375 mL)	30 minutes	15 minutes	15 minutes

When creating a pasta salad, it's all about portions. You'll notice this salad only uses 5 oz (140 g) of macaroni, but it also contains pinto beans, cherry tomatoes and kale, which not only add volume, but also delicious flavors and tons of nutrients.

5 oz (150 g) 100% whole wheat elbow macaroni

2 tbsp (30 mL) olive oil

2 cloves garlic, minced

4 cups (1 L) chopped kale, hard stems removed

¼ tsp (1 mL) salt

⅛ tsp (0.5 mL) hot pepper flakes

1 cup (250 mL) no-salt-added canned pinto beans, drained and rinsed

1 cup (250 mL) cherry tomatoes, halved

¼ cup (60 mL) shaved Parmesan cheese

½ cup (125 mL) Simple Lemon-Herb Vinaigrette (page 253)

1 Fill a large saucepan three-quarters with water and bring to a boil over high heat. Add the macaroni and return to a boil, then reduce the heat to low and simmer for 8 to 10 minutes until the pasta is al dente. Drain the pasta and let cool for 10 minutes.

2 In a large saucepan, heat the olive oil over medium heat. When the oil is shimmering, add the garlic and cook until fragrant, 30 seconds. Add the kale and cook until wilted, about 5 minutes. Add the salt and hot pepper flakes and toss to combine. Remove the saucepan from the heat and allow to cool for 10 minutes.

3 In a large bowl, add the macaroni, kale, beans, tomatoes and Parmesan cheese. Toss to combine. Add the Simple Lemon-Herb Vinaigrette and toss to evenly coat.

4 TO STORE: In each of four containers, add 1½ cups (375 mL) of the pasta salad. Cover and refrigerate for up to 4 days.

5 TO SERVE: Enjoy cold or at room temperature.

TOBY'S TIP | If you prefer, swap the kale for spinach or use a combination of spinach and kale.

PER SERVING			
TOTAL CALORIES	TOTAL FAT	SATURATED FAT	TRANS FAT
369.55	17.27 g	3.19 g	0.0 g
SODIUM	CHOLESTEROL	TOTAL CARBOHYDRATES	FIBER
379.41 mg	5.50 mg	44.51 g	8.96 g
SUGARS	PROTEIN	POTASSIUM	PHOSPHORUS
3.09 g	13.95 g	696.57 mg	261.07 mg

COUSCOUS SALAD
WITH CHICKPEAS AND FETA

SERVES	SERVING SIZE	TOTAL TIME	PREP TIME	COOK TIME
4	2 cups (500 mL) salad, 2 tbsp (30 mL) dressing, 2 tbsp (30 mL) cheese	25 minutes	20 minutes	5 minutes

Couscous is a Mediterranean grain made from semolina wheat. You can create a variety of dishes using Mediterranean ingredients, like in this salad that features chickpeas, lots of non-starchy vegetables and feta cheese.

1 cup (250 mL) low-sodium vegetable broth

1 cup (250 mL) chopped fresh parsley leaves, stems reserved

Zest of 1 lemon in 3 or 4 large slices

1 cup (250 mL) 100% whole wheat couscous

1¾ cups (425 mL) no-salt-added canned chickpeas, drained and rinsed

1½ cups (375 mL) shredded romaine lettuce

1 red bell pepper, chopped

1 cup cherry tomatoes, halved

½ English cucumber, chopped

¼ red onion, chopped

1 In small saucepan, bring the vegetable broth, parsley stems and lemon zest to a boil over high heat. When boiling, stir in the couscous, cover and remove the saucepan from the heat. Set aside for 5 minutes. Fluff the couscous with a fork and let cool for 5 to 10 minutes. Remove the parsley stems and lemon peel and discard.

2 In a large bowl, add the couscous, chickpeas, chopped parsley, lettuce, bell pepper, tomatoes, cucumber, onion, salt and black pepper. Toss to combine.

3 TO STORE: In each of four containers, add 2 cups (500 mL) of the salad and sprinkle with 2 tbsp (30 mL) of the feta cheese. Fill four small dressing containers each with 2 tbsp (30 mL) of the dressing and store with the salad. Cover and refrigerate for up to 4 days.

4 TO SERVE: Drizzle the salad with the dressing just before eating.

TOBY'S TIP | If you prefer, swap the romaine lettuce for red leaf lettuce or baby spinach.

	TOTAL CALORIES	TOTAL FAT	SATURATED FAT	TRANS FAT
PER SERVING	325.42	12.60 g	3.87 g	0.0 g
	SODIUM 399.44 mg	**CHOLESTEROL** 16.69 mg	**TOTAL CARBOHYDRATES** 43.94 g	**FIBER** 9.26 g
	SUGARS 5.14 g	**PROTEIN** 12.84 g	**POTASSIUM** 576.95 mg	**PHOSPHORUS** 188.51 mg

⅛ tsp (0.5 mL) salt

⅛ tsp (0.5 mL) ground black pepper

½ cup (125 mL) crumbled feta cheese, divided

½ cup (125 mL) Herbed Vinaigrette (page 250)

TUNA
WITH MIXED GREENS

SERVES	SERVING SIZE	TOTAL TIME	PREP TIME	COOK TIME
4	1 cup (250 mL) tuna, 1 cup (250 mL) mixed greens, 2 tbsp (30 mL) dressing	20 minutes	20 minutes	0 minutes

Some weeks you just want a simple salad that you can whip up in minutes. This tuna over greens is an easy dish to incorporate regularly in your weekly meal plans.

2 cans (5 oz/142 g) chunk light tuna packed in water, drained

1 cup (250 mL) cherry tomatoes

½ English cucumber, sliced into ½-inch (1 cm) rounds

½ small red onion, chopped

2 tbsp (30 mL) sliced Kalamata olives

4 cups (1 L) mixed spring greens

½ cup (125 mL) Walnut Basil Dressing (page 255)

COMPLETE YOUR PLATE

Half 8-inch (20 cm) 100% whole wheat pita or 1 slice 100% whole wheat bread

1 In a medium bowl, add the tuna, breaking up large pieces with the back of a wooden spoon. Add the cherry tomatoes, cucumber, onion and olives and toss to combine.

2 TO STORE: In each of four containers, add 1 cup (250 mL) of the mixed spring greens and top with 1 cup (250 mL) of the tuna mixture. Fill four small dressing containers each with 2 tbsp (30 mL) of the dressing and store with the salad. Cover and refrigerate for up to 4 days.

3 TO SERVE: Drizzle the salad with the dressing just before eating.

TOBY'S TIP | For variety, swap the tuna for canned salmon or chicken breast packed in water.

	TOTAL CALORIES	TOTAL FAT	SATURATED FAT	TRANS FAT
PER SERVING	279.14	19.06 g	2.63 g	0.0 g
	SODIUM	**CHOLESTEROL**	**TOTAL CARBOHYDRATES**	**FIBER**
	471.35 mg	29.75 mg	8.21 g	2.66 g
	SUGARS	**PROTEIN**	**POTASSIUM**	**PHOSPHORUS**
	3.71 g	20.05 g	596.19 mg	232.20 mg

GRILLED CHICKEN CAPRESE SALAD

SERVES	SERVING SIZE	TOTAL TIME	PREP TIME	COOK TIME
4	1⅓ cups (325 mL) salad, 2 tbsp (30 mL) dressing	40 minutes	15 minutes	25 minutes

Up your caprese salad — the classic Italian salad of tomato, basil and fresh mozzarella — by adding cooked chicken and quinoa to the mix. The extra protein and addition of whole grains balance this salad, plus make it that much more filling.

8 oz (250 g) boneless skinless chicken tenders

⅛ tsp (0.5 mL) salt

⅛ tsp (0.5 mL) ground black pepper

Cooking spray

¾ cup (175 mL) quinoa

1½ cups (375 mL) low-sodium chicken broth

3 oz (90 g) fresh mozzarella cheese, cubed

2 cups (500 mL) cherry tomatoes, halved

½ cup (125 mL) fresh basil leaves, thinly sliced

½ cup (125 mL) Balsamic Vinaigrette (page 252)

Grill pan or medium skillet

1 Sprinkle the chicken with the salt and pepper.

2 Coat a grill pan or medium skillet with cooking spray and place over medium heat. When the oil is shimmering, add the chicken tenders and grill, turning once, until an instant-read thermometer inserted into the thickest part of the chicken registers 165°F (74°C), 8 minutes. Transfer the chicken to a clean cutting board and let cool for 10 minutes. Cut into bite-size pieces.

3 In a medium saucepan, bring the quinoa and broth to a boil over high heat. Reduce the heat to low and simmer, covered, until the quinoa is cooked, 15 minutes. Fluff the quinoa with a fork and let cool for 10 to 15 minutes.

4 In a medium bowl, combine the quinoa, chicken, mozzarella cheese, tomatoes and basil.

5 TO STORE: In each of four containers, add 1⅓ cups (325 mL) of the salad. Fill four small dressing containers each with 2 tbsp (30 mL) of the Balsamic Vinaigrette. Cover all containers and refrigerate for up to 4 days.

6 TO SERVE: Drizzle the salad with the dressing just before eating and toss together to combine.

TOBY'S TIP | If you prefer, swap the low-sodium chicken broth for low-sodium vegetable broth or water.

	TOTAL CALORIES	TOTAL FAT	SATURATED FAT	TRANS FAT
PER SERVING	325.41	15.31 g	4.34 g	0.0 g
	SODIUM	CHOLESTEROL	TOTAL CARBOHYDRATES	FIBER
	300.86 mg	56.39 mg	26.50 g	3.03 g
	SUGARS	PROTEIN	POTASSIUM	PHOSPHORUS
	6.85 g	21.12 g	580.20 mg	257.04 mg

CHICKEN ORZO SALAD

SERVES	SERVING SIZE	TOTAL TIME	PREP TIME	COOK TIME
4	2 cups (500 mL) salad, 2 tbsp (30 mL) dressing, 1 tbsp (15 mL) cheese	27 minutes	15 minutes	12 minutes

Orzo pasta is typically made with semolina flour. Look for whole wheat orzo, which is made with whole wheat and provides some fiber.

4 oz (125 g) whole wheat orzo pasta

¼ cup (60 mL) pine nuts

4 cups (1 L) baby spinach, coarsely chopped

1 can (5 oz/150 g) chicken breast in water, drained

2 cups (500 mL) cherry tomatoes, halved

½ English cucumber, cut into ¾-inch (2 cm) rounds

½ small red onion, chopped

¼ cup (60 mL) crumbled feta cheese

½ cup (125 mL) Balsamic Vinaigrette (page 252)

1 Fill a medium saucepan three-quarters with water and bring to a boil over high heat. Add the orzo and cook until al dente, 7 to 8 minutes. Drain the orzo and let cool for 10 minutes.

2 In a small saucepan over low heat, toast the pine nuts until lightly browned, 3 to 4 minutes. Transfer the pine nuts to a clean bowl and let cool for 10 minutes.

3 In a large bowl, add the pasta, pine nuts, spinach, chicken, tomatoes, cucumber and onion. Gently toss to combine.

4 TO STORE: In each of four containers, add 2 cups (500 mL) of the orzo salad and top with 1 tbsp (15 mL) of the feta cheese. Fill four small dressing containers each with 2 tbsp (30 mL) of the vinaigrette. Cover all containers and refrigerate the salad and dressing for up to 4 days.

5 TO SERVE: Drizzle the salad with the dressing just before eating.

TOBY'S TIP | If you prefer, swap the pine nuts for chopped cashews or pistachios.

PER SERVING	TOTAL CALORIES	TOTAL FAT	SATURATED FAT	TRANS FAT
	336.13	16.10 g	3.17 g	0.0 g
	SODIUM	CHOLESTEROL	TOTAL CARBOHYDRATES	FIBER
	439.15 mg	20.84 mg	34.72 g	7.49 g
	SUGARS	PROTEIN	POTASSIUM	PHOSPHORUS
	8.92 g	14.77 g	337.69 mg	115.69 mg

LUNCH AND DINNER MAINS

BULGUR AND BLACK BEAN CHILI

SERVES	SERVING SIZE	TOTAL TIME	PREP TIME	COOK TIME
6	1⅓ cups (325 mL) chili, 2 tbsp (30 mL) cheese	45 minutes	15 minutes	30 minutes

A cozy favorite, this vegetarian chili is made with bulgur, which is a whole grain made from wheat.

1 tbsp (15 mL) olive oil or canola oil

1 yellow onion, chopped

2 cloves garlic, minced

1 red bell pepper, chopped

1 jalapeño pepper, seeds removed and chopped

1 tbsp (15 mL) chili powder

1 tsp (5 mL) ground cumin

1 tsp (5 mL) dried oregano

½ tsp (2 mL) salt

¼ tsp (1 mL) cayenne pepper

2 cups (500 mL) low-sodium vegetable broth

1 cup (250 mL) water

1 can (28 oz/796 mL) no-salt-added crushed tomatoes, with juice

1¾ cups (425 mL) no-salt-added canned black beans, drained and rinsed

1   In a large pot, heat the oil over medium heat. When the oil is shimmering, add the onion and garlic and cook until the onion is translucent and the garlic is fragrant, 3 minutes. Add the bell pepper and jalapeño pepper and cook until softened, about 3 minutes.

2   Add the chili powder, cumin, oregano, salt and cayenne pepper and stir to incorporate. Add the vegetable broth, water, crushed tomatoes, black beans, bulgur and lime juice and bring the mixture to a boil over high heat. Reduce the heat to medium-low and simmer, covered, until the bulgur is tender and the flavors combine, about 20 minutes. Remove the chili from the heat and let cool for 15 minutes.

3   TO STORE: In each of four containers, add 1⅓ cups (325 mL) of the chili. Fill six small containers each with 2 tbsp (30 mL) of the cheese and store with the chili. Cover all containers and refrigerate for up to 4 days or freeze for up to 2 months.

	TOTAL CALORIES	TOTAL FAT	SATURATED FAT	TRANS FAT
PER SERVING	252.91	6.0 g	2.03 g	0.0 g
	SODIUM	CHOLESTEROL	TOTAL CARBOHYDRATES	FIBER
	404.37 mg	7.91 mg	35.78 g	10.53 g
	SUGARS	PROTEIN	POTASSIUM	PHOSPHORUS
	6.67 g	13.21 g	724.84 mg	338.03 mg

¾ cup (175 mL) bulgur

Juice of 1 lime

¾ cup (175 mL) shredded
reduced-fat Cheddar cheese

COMPLETE YOUR PLATE

A small green salad with
2 tbsp (30 mL) vinaigrette

4 **TO SERVE:** If frozen, thaw in the refrigerator
overnight. To reheat, microwave uncovered on
High for 90 seconds. Allow 2 minutes for the heat
to distribute before removing the container from
the microwave. Alternatively, reheat in a saucepan
on the stove by bringing the chili to a boil and
then simmering over medium-low heat until
heated through, about 10 minutes. Serve warm
with cheese sprinkled over the top.

TOBY'S TIP | To make this dish vegan, leave out the
cheese or use non-dairy cheese instead.

RED LENTIL DAL

 · · · ·

SERVES	SERVING SIZE	TOTAL TIME	PREP TIME	COOK TIME
6	³⁄₄ cup (175 mL) dal, ¹⁄₂ cup (125 mL) rice	1 hour, 30 minutes	15 minutes	1 hour, 15 minutes

Dal is an Indian dish that is a thick purée, stew or soup made from lentils or peas. This recipe calls for colorful red lentils and is filled with aromatic spices. I've paired it with rice, but you can easily swap in another grain of your choice.

RICE

²⁄₃ cup (150 mL) brown basmati rice

1¹⁄₂ cups (375 mL) water

DAL

1¹⁄₂ cups (375 mL) red lentils, rinsed

4¹⁄₂ cups (1.125 L) water

1 tbsp (15 mL) coconut oil

1 yellow onion, chopped

2 cloves garlic, minced

1 tsp (5 mL) ground turmeric

¹⁄₂ tsp (2 mL) ground cumin

¹⁄₂ tsp (2 mL) ground ginger

¹⁄₂ tsp (2 mL) ground cardamom

¹⁄₂ tsp (2 mL) salt

¹⁄₈ tsp (0.5 mL) hot pepper flakes

1 **TO MAKE THE RICE:** In a medium saucepan, add the brown rice and 1¹⁄₂ cups (375 mL) water and bring to a boil over high heat. Reduce the heat to medium-low and simmer, covered, until the water is absorbed, about 40 minutes. Fluff with a fork and set aside to cool.

2 **TO MAKE THE DAL:** While the rice is cooking, in a medium saucepan, add the lentils and 4¹⁄₂ cups (1.125 L) water and bring to a boil over high heat. Reduce the heat to medium and cook, uncovered, until the lentils soften, 20 minutes. Drain the lentils and set aside.

3 In a large sauté pan, heat the coconut oil over medium heat. When the oil is shimmering, add the onion and garlic and cook until the onion is translucent and the garlic is fragrant, 3 minutes. Add the turmeric, cumin, ginger, cardamom, salt and hot pepper flakes and stir to combine.

4 Add the cooked lentils and stir to incorporate. Raise the heat to high to bring to a boil, then reduce the heat to medium-low and simmer for 5 minutes. Add the diced tomatoes with juice and lime juice and raise the heat to high to bring to a boil. Reduce the heat to medium-low and cook an additional 5 minutes. Remove the sauté pan from the heat and let cool for 15 minutes.

PER SERVING	TOTAL CALORIES	TOTAL FAT	SATURATED FAT	TRANS FAT
	268.30	3.91 g	2.15 g	0.0 g
	SODIUM	CHOLESTEROL	TOTAL CARBOHYDRATES	FIBER
	315.95 mg	0.0 mg	46.25 g	8.56 g
	SUGARS	PROTEIN	POTASSIUM	PHOSPHORUS
	4.11 g	13.54 g	477.68 mg	79.40 mg

1¾ cups (425 mL) no-salt-added canned diced tomatoes, with juice

Juice of 1 lime

COMPLETE YOUR PLATE

1 small salad with 2 tbsp (30 mL) vinaigrette dressing

5 **TO STORE:** In each of six containers, add ¾ cup (175 mL) of the red lentil dal alongside ½ cup (125 mL) of the rice. Cover and refrigerate for up to 4 days or freeze for up to 2 months.

6 **TO SERVE:** If frozen, thaw in the refrigerator overnight. To reheat, microwave uncovered on High for 90 seconds. Allow 2 minutes for the heat to distribute before removing the container from the microwave. Serve warm.

TOBY'S TIP | For lentils, I like Bob's Red Mill brand. If you use split red lentils, the cooking time is typically only 5 to 7 minutes, so be sure to check the package.

WHOLE WHEAT PASTA
WITH SPRING VEGETABLES AND EDAMAME

SERVES	SERVING SIZE	TOTAL TIME	PREP TIME	COOK TIME
6	2 cups (500 mL) pasta, 1 tbsp (15 mL) walnuts	45 minutes	20 minutes	25 minutes

This light and refreshing dish is perfect for a warm spring lunch or dinner. Use seasonal non-starchy vegetables that you have on hand to help reduce food waste in your kitchen.

¼ cup (60 mL) raw walnuts, coarsely chopped

10 oz (300 g) whole wheat rotini

1½ cups (375 mL) shelled edamame

Zest and juice of 1 lemon

¼ cup (60 mL) grated Parmesan cheese

¼ cup (60 mL) plus 1 tbsp (15 mL) olive oil, divided

2 tsp (10 mL) dried parsley flakes

½ tsp (2 mL) salt

¼ tsp (1 mL) ground black pepper

⅛ tsp (0.5 mL) hot pepper flakes

1 onion, chopped

2 cloves garlic, minced

1 red bell pepper, cut into 1-inch (2.5 cm) strips

1. Heat a small skillet over medium-low heat. When the skillet is hot, add the walnuts and toast until fragrant, being careful not to burn the nuts, about 3 minutes. Transfer the toasted nuts to a clean bowl and set aside.

2. Fill a large pot three-quarters with water and bring to a boil over high heat. Add the rotini and reduce the heat to medium. Boil gently until the pasta is al dente, 10 minutes. Add the edamame to a colander and drain the pasta by pouring it over the edamame. Reserve about ½ cup (125 mL) of the pasta water.

3. In a small bowl, make the sauce by whisking together the lemon juice and zest, Parmesan cheese, ¼ cup (60 mL) of the olive oil, parsley, salt, black pepper and hot pepper flakes.

4. In a large saucepan, heat the remaining 1 tbsp (15 mL) olive oil over medium heat. When the oil is shimmering, add the onion and garlic and cook until the onion is translucent and the garlic is fragrant, 3 minutes. Add the bell pepper, zucchini and carrots and cook until the vegetables soften slightly, about 5 minutes.

5. Add the tomatoes and toss for 1 minute more. Add the lemon sauce, pasta and edamame to the saucepan and toss to combine. If the pasta seems dry, add the reserved pasta water, a little bit at a time.

	TOTAL CALORIES	TOTAL FAT	SATURATED FAT	TRANS FAT
PER SERVING	371.93	16.63 g	2.78 g	0.0 g
	SODIUM	CHOLESTEROL	TOTAL CARBOHYDRATES	FIBER
	283.84 mg	3.67 mg	45.49 g	8.08 g
	SUGARS	PROTEIN	POTASSIUM	PHOSPHORUS
	6.68 g	12.67 g	299.12 mg	72.35 mg

1 zucchini, halved lengthwise and cut into ½-inch (1 cm) half-moons

2 carrots, peeled and shredded

1 cup (250 mL) cherry tomatoes

COMPLETE YOUR PLATE

This is a complete meal.

6 TO STORE: In each of four containers, add 2 cups (500 mL) of the pasta. Sprinkle each container with 1 tbsp (15 mL) of the toasted walnuts. Cover and refrigerate for up to 4 days or freeze for up to 2 months.

7 TO SERVE: If frozen, thaw in the refrigerator overnight. To reheat, microwave uncovered on High for 90 seconds. Allow 2 minutes for the heat to distribute before removing the container from the microwave. Serve warm.

TOBY'S TIP | If you prefer, swap the shelled edamame for lima beans.

GREENS AND GRAINS BOWLS

SERVES	SERVING SIZE	TOTAL TIME	PREP TIME	COOK TIME
4	1 cup (250 mL) chard mixture, $^1/_2$ cup (125 mL) brown rice, 1 tbsp (15 mL) cheese	1 hour, 5 minutes	15 minutes	50 minutes

Chard is a low-carbohydrate vegetable packed with nutrients and has a flavor similar to spinach. Remove the tough center stem before cooking.

$^2/_3$ cup (150 mL) long-grain brown rice

$1^1/_3$ cups (325 mL) low-sodium vegetable broth

2 tbsp (30 mL) olive oil

1 bunch rainbow chard, center stems removed and leaves coarsely chopped

$1^3/_4$ cups (425 mL) low-sodium canned chickpeas, drained and rinsed

1 cup (250 mL) cherry tomatoes

1 tsp (5 mL) dried oregano

$^1/_2$ tsp (2 mL) garlic powder

$^1/_8$ tsp (0.5 mL) salt

$^1/_8$ tsp (0.5 mL) ground black pepper

$^1/_4$ cup (60 mL) crumbled feta cheese

1 lemon, cut into 4 wedges

1 In a medium saucepan, add the brown rice and vegetable broth and bring to a boil over high heat. Reduce the heat to medium-low and simmer, covered, until the water is absorbed and the rice is tender, 40 minutes. Set aside and let cool for 10 minutes.

2 In a medium saucepan, heat the oil over medium heat. When the oil is shimmering, add the chard and cook until wilted, about 4 minutes. Add the chickpeas and cherry tomatoes and toss to combine. Add the oregano, garlic powder, salt and pepper and toss to evenly coat the vegetables. Cook for 5 minutes to allow the flavors to combine.

3 TO STORE: In each of four containers, add $^1/_2$ cup (125 mL) of the brown rice and top with 1 cup (250 mL) of the chard mixture. Sprinkle each container with 1 tbsp (15 mL) of the feta cheese. Add 1 lemon wedge to each container. Cover and refrigerate for up to 4 days.

4 TO SERVE: Remove the lemon and set aside. To reheat, microwave the container uncovered on High for 60 to 90 seconds. Allow 2 minutes for the heat to distribute before removing the container from the microwave. Squeeze the lemon wedge over the top before serving.

TOBY'S TIP | If you prefer, swap the chard for a bunch of fresh spinach.

PER SERVING	TOTAL CALORIES	TOTAL FAT	SATURATED FAT	TRANS FAT
	323.85	12.15 g	2.6 g	0.0 g
	SODIUM	**CHOLESTEROL**	**TOTAL CARBOHYDRATES**	**FIBER**
	439.0 mg	8.34 mg	44.78 g	7.01 g
	SUGARS	**PROTEIN**	**POTASSIUM**	**PHOSPHORUS**
	5.53 g	12.14 g	540.21 mg	164.07 mg

CHILE TOFU AND GREEN BEANS

SERVES	SERVING SIZE	TOTAL TIME	PREP TIME	COOK TIME
4	2 cups (500 mL)	50 minutes	20 minutes	30 minutes

You can easily switch up the non-starchy vegetables in this recipe to minimize food waste in your kitchen.

2 tbsp (30 mL) plus 2 tsp (10 mL) olive oil or canola oil, divided

1 lb (500 g) extra-firm tofu, cut into 1-inch (2.5 cm) cubes

12 oz (375 g) green beans, trimmed

¼ cup (60 mL) low-sodium vegetable broth

2 tbsp (30 mL) reduced-sodium soy sauce

1 tbsp (15 mL) cornstarch

2 tsp (10 mL) stevia brown sugar blend (such as Truvia or Splenda)

2 tsp (10 mL) unseasoned rice vinegar

2 tsp (10 mL) Thai chile sauce (such as Sriracha)

1 tsp (5 mL) garlic powder

1 green bell pepper, cut into 1-inch (2.5 cm) strips

1 red bell pepper, cut into 1-inch (2.5 cm) strips

1 tsp (5 mL) toasted sesame oil

1. In a large sauté pan, heat 2 tsp (10 mL) of the olive oil over medium heat. When the oil is shimmering, add the tofu and cook on all sides, about 12 minutes. Remove the tofu to a clean plate.

2. Fill a medium saucepan with 1 inch (2.5 cm) of water and fit with a steamer basket. Add the green beans, cover and bring to a boil over high heat. Steam until the green beans are cooked but crisp, 3 to 5 minutes. Transfer to a clean bowl.

3. In a small bowl, whisk together the vegetable broth, soy sauce, cornstarch, brown sugar blend, rice vinegar, Thai chile sauce and garlic powder.

4. In the pan used to cook the tofu, heat the remaining 2 tbsp (30 mL) olive oil over medium heat. When the oil is shimmering, add the red and green bell peppers and cook, tossing frequently, until slightly softened, about 8 minutes. Add the green beans and cooked tofu and toss to combine. Add the vegetable broth mixture and stir to evenly coat the vegetables. Reduce the heat to medium-low and simmer until the mixture thickens, 1 to 2 minutes. Add the toasted sesame oil and stir to combine.

5. TO STORE: In each of four containers, add 2 cups (500 mL) of the mixture. Cover and refrigerate for up to 4 days or freeze for up to 2 months.

6. TO SERVE: If frozen, thaw overnight in the refrigerator. To reheat, microwave uncovered on High for 90 seconds Allow the heat to distribute for 2 minutes before removing the container from the microwave. Serve warm.

PER SERVING			
TOTAL CALORIES 269.98	**TOTAL FAT** 16.38 g	**SATURATED FAT** 2.27 g	**TRANS FAT** 0.0 g
SODIUM 325.04 mg	**CHOLESTEROL** 0.0 mg	**TOTAL CARBOHYDRATES** 17.83 g	**FIBER** 5.12 g
SUGARS 7.91 g	**PROTEIN** 14.17 g	**POTASSIUM** 318.39 mg	**PHOSPHORUS** 58.36 mg

COMPLETE YOUR PLATE

1 cup (250 mL) cooked long-grain brown rice

TOBY'S TIP | This recipe calls for steaming the green beans, which keeps the vegetables crisp when cooked. Other firm vegetables that steam well include broccoli, cauliflower and carrots.

SHRIMP AND NOODLE BOWLS
WITH CUCUMBERS AND CARROTS

SERVES	SERVING SIZE	TOTAL TIME	PREP TIME	COOK TIME
4	4 oz (125 g) shrimp, ¾ cup (175 mL) vegetables, ¾ cup (175 mL) noodles, 2 tbsp (30 mL) sauce, 1 tbsp (15 mL) peanuts	40 minutes, plus marinating time (20 minutes to 2 hours)	25 minutes	15 minutes

Why order take-out when you can whip up this shrimp bowl with Vietnamese-inspired flavors? If you want to make this dish vegan, swap the shrimp for extra-firm tofu (cooking instructions below in Toby's Tip).

BOWL

5 oz (150 g) brown rice vermicelli noodles

1 shallot, coarsely chopped

1 lime, sliced, plus juice of 1 lime

1 tbsp (15 mL) canola oil or safflower oil

1 tsp (5 mL) reduced-sodium soy sauce

1 tsp (5 mL) stevia brown sugar blend (such as Truvia or Splenda)

⅛ tsp (0.5 mL) hot pepper flakes

1 lb (500 g) extra-large peeled and deveined shrimp

Blender or food processor

Grill pan or large skillet coated with cooking spray

1 TO MAKE THE BOWL: Bring 4 quarts (4 L) of water to a boil in a large pot over high heat. When the water is boiling, add the noodles and cook until tender, 5 minutes. Drain the noodles in a colander and rinse under cold water. Place in a large bowl and set aside to cool.

2 In a blender or food processor, add the shallot, lime juice, oil, soy sauce, brown sugar blend and hot pepper flakes. Blend on High until smooth.

3 In a large container, add the shrimp and the lime juice mixture. Toss to evenly coat. Cover the container and refrigerate for at least 20 minutes and up to 2 hours.

4 Heat the grill pan or large skillet over medium heat. When the oil is shimmering, remove the shrimp, shaking off excess marinade, and add to the skillet. Discard the marinade. Cook until an instant-read thermometer inserted into a few of the shrimp registers 145°F (63°C), about 3 minutes on each side. Transfer the shrimp to a clean plate.

5 In a medium bowl, add the cucumbers, carrots and cilantro and toss to combine.

	TOTAL CALORIES	TOTAL FAT	SATURATED FAT	TRANS FAT
PER SERVING	350.81	8.88 g	1.08 g	0.02 g
	SODIUM	**CHOLESTEROL**	**TOTAL CARBOHYDRATES**	**FIBER**
	270.51 mg	182.57 mg	41.81 g	2.93 g
	SUGARS	**PROTEIN**	**POTASSIUM**	**PHOSPHORUS**
	4.87 g	27.27 g	618.23 mg	364.08 mg

½ English cucumber, sliced lengthwise and then cut into half-moons

2 carrots, peeled and shredded

1 cup (250 mL) cilantro, chopped

¼ cup (60 mL) dry-roasted unsalted peanuts, coarsely chopped

SAUCE

¼ cup (60 mL) warm water

Juice of 2 limes

1 tsp (5 mL) stevia sugar (such as Truvia or Splenda)

¼ tsp (1 mL) garlic powder

⅛ tsp (0.5 mL) hot pepper flakes

6 **TO MAKE THE SAUCE:** In a small bowl, whisk together the warm water, lime juice, brown sugar blend, garlic powder and hot pepper flakes.

7 **TO STORE:** In each of four containers, place ⅔ cup (150 mL) of the noodles and ¾ cup (175 mL) of the vegetables next to each other and sprinkle with 1 tbsp (15 mL) of the peanuts. Top with 4 oz (125 g) of shrimp (six or seven pieces) and place a few slices of the lime on the side. In four small dressing containers, pack about 2 tbsp (30 mL) of the sauce. Cover all containers, pack the dressing with the bowls and refrigerate for up to 4 days.

8 **TO SERVE:** The shrimp can be eaten cold or reheated before serving. To reheat, transfer the shrimp to a separate container and microwave on High for 30 to 45 seconds. Return the shrimp to the bowl. Top with the dressing and a spritz of lime before eating.

TOBY'S TIP | To make this dish vegan, swap the shrimp for extra-firm tofu, cut into 1-inch (2.5 cm) cubes. Cook on the grill pan for a total of 12 minutes on all sides.

GRILLED COD
WITH ZESTY CABBAGE SLAW

 · ·

SERVES	SERVING SIZE	TOTAL TIME	PREP TIME	COOK TIME
4	1 fillet, ¹⁄₂ cup (125 mL) slaw, 2 tbsp (30 mL) salsa	30 minutes, plus marinating time	20 minutes	10 minutes

This take on Baja fish tacos is just as delicious as the fried version, with grilled or sautéed white fish and a sweet-yet-tart apple cider vinegar dressing for the slaw.

FISH

Juice and zest of 1 lime

¹⁄₂ tsp (2 mL) smoked paprika

5 tbsp (75 mL) canola oil or safflower oil, divided

¹⁄₄ tsp (1 mL) salt

1 lb (500 g) cod, cut into 4 equal fillets

SLAW

¹⁄₄ cup (60 mL) apple cider vinegar

3 tbsp (45 mL) canola oil or safflower oil

2 tsp (10 mL) stevia brown sugar blend (such as Truvia or Splenda)

¹⁄₄ tsp (1 mL) salt

¹⁄₈ tsp (0.5 mL) ground black pepper

Large grill pan or large skillet

1 TO MAKE THE FISH: In a medium bowl, whisk together the lime zest and juice, smoked paprika, ¹⁄₄ cup (60 mL) of the oil and salt. Add the cod pieces to the marinade and turn to coat evenly. Cover and refrigerate for at least 30 minutes and up to 2 hours.

2 Heat the remaining 1 tbsp (15 mL) oil in a large grill pan or skillet over medium heat. When the oil is shimmering, add the fish and discard the excess marinade. Cook until the fish is flaky and an instant-read thermometer inserted in the thickest part of a fillet registers 145°F (63°C), 4 minutes on each side.

3 TO MAKE THE SLAW: In a large bowl, whisk together the apple cider vinegar, oil, brown sugar blend, salt and black pepper. Add the cabbage, cilantro and jalapeño pepper and toss to evenly coat.

4 TO STORE: In each of four containers, add about ¹⁄₂ cup (125 mL) of the slaw and top with one fillet of the fish. In four small containers, pack 2 tbsp (30 mL) of the mango salsa. Cover all containers and refrigerate for up to 4 days.

5 TO SERVE: Reheat the fish in a separate container in the microwave on High for 30 to 45 seconds. Return the fish to the slaw and top with the mango salsa before eating.

	TOTAL CALORIES	TOTAL FAT	SATURATED FAT	TRANS FAT
PER SERVING	350.81	25.50 g	2.11 g	0.09 g
	SODIUM	CHOLESTEROL	TOTAL CARBOHYDRATES	FIBER
	379.50 mg	55.57 mg	7.82 g	1.22 g
	SUGARS	PROTEIN	POTASSIUM	PHOSPHORUS
	5.42 g	21.81 g	645.57 mg	285.22 mg

2 cups (500 mL) shredded red cabbage

1/2 cup (125 mL) fresh cilantro, coarsely chopped

1/2 jalapeño pepper, seeds and ribs removed and chopped

TO SERVE

1/2 cup (125 mL) Mango Salsa (page 256)

COMPLETE YOUR PLATE

Two 6-inch (15 cm) corn tortillas

TOBY'S TIPS | If you prefer, swap the cod for halibut.

When selecting fresh jalapeños, look for peppers with a nice green color with unwrinkled, unbroken skin and that are firm to the touch. Store whole jalapeños at room temperature for 2 to 3 days. If storing longer, store in the refrigerator for up to 1 week. Wash just before prepping.

SALMON "FRIED" BROWN RICE

SERVES	SERVING SIZE	TOTAL TIME	PREP TIME	COOK TIME
4	2 cups (500 mL)	1 hour, 35 minutes	20 minutes	1 hour, 15 minutes

We love salmon so much at my house that we are always looking for new ways to enjoy it. This lighter, nutrient-packed version of fried rice is now a regular part of our dinner meal repertoire.

10 oz (300 g) salmon fillet

1/8 tsp (0.5 mL) salt

1/8 tsp (0.5 mL) ground black pepper

1 cup (250 mL) brown rice

3 cups (750 mL) water

3/4 cup (275 mL) frozen shelled edamame

2 1/2 tbsp (37 mL) reduced-sodium soy sauce

1 tsp (5 mL) stevia brown sugar blend (such as Truvia or Splenda)

1/4 tsp (1 mL) ground ginger

1 tbsp (15 mL) canola oil or safflower oil

1 small yellow onion, chopped

1 red bell pepper, chopped

3 large eggs, beaten

2 green onions, white and green parts, sliced

Baking sheet coated with cooking spray

Large sauté pan

Preheat the oven to 400°F (200°C)

1. Place the salmon fillet skin-side down on the prepared baking sheet and sprinkle with the salt and black pepper. Bake until the fish is opaque and an instant-read thermometer inserted into the thickest part of the salmon registers 145°F (63°C), 18 to 20 minutes. Let cool for 10 minutes, then cut into bite-size pieces.

2. In a medium pot, bring the rice and water to a boil over high heat. Reduce the heat to medium-low, cover and simmer, stirring occasionally, until tender, about 40 minutes. Fluff with a fork.

3. Fill a small pot with water halfway and bring the water to a boil over high heat. Add the edamame, then reduce the heat to medium-low and simmer, uncovered, until cooked, about 5 minutes. Drain the water and set aside.

4. In a small bowl, whisk together the soy sauce, brown sugar blend and ginger.

5. In a large sauté pan, heat the oil over medium heat. When the oil is shimmering, add the yellow onion and bell pepper and cook until softened, 5 minutes. Add the beaten eggs and stir until the eggs are cooked, 2 to 3 minutes. Add the rice and stir to combine. Add the salmon, cooked edamame, soy sauce mixture and green onions and toss to combine. Continue cooking until warmed through, 1 to 2 minutes.

PER SERVING	TOTAL CALORIES	TOTAL FAT	SATURATED FAT	TRANS FAT
	383.33	13.89 g	2.55 g	0.01 g
	SODIUM	CHOLESTEROL	TOTAL CARBOHYDRATES	FIBER
	360.02 mg	31.17 mg	44.53 g	3.60 g
	SUGARS	PROTEIN	POTASSIUM	PHOSPHORUS
	5.37 g	19.31 g	418.76 mg	305.70 mg

COMPLETE YOUR PLATE

Side green salad with 1 tbsp (15 mL) vinaigrette dressing

6 **TO STORE:** In each of four containers, add 2 cups (500 mL) of the fried rice. Cover and refrigerate for up to 4 days or freeze for up to 2 months.

7 **TO SERVE:** If frozen, thaw in the refrigerator overnight. To reheat, microwave uncovered on High for about 1 minute until warmed through. Allow 2 minutes for the heat to distribute before removing the container from the microwave. Serve warm.

SHEET PAN CHILI-LIME SALMON

SERVES	SERVING SIZE	TOTAL TIME	PREP TIME	COOK TIME
4	1 fillet, ³⁄₄ cup (175 mL) bell peppers	35 minutes, plus marinating time (30 minutes to 2 hours)	15 minutes	20 minutes

The heat in this dish comes from the capsaicin, which is an antioxidant-rich plant compound found naturally in chile peppers. If you'd like your dish even spicier, increase the chili powder ¼ tsp (1 mL) at a time.

Juice of 2 limes

2 tbsp (30 mL) olive oil

1½ tsp (7 mL) chili powder

1 tsp (5 mL) ground cumin

1 tsp (5 mL) dried parsley flakes

½ tsp (2 mL) garlic powder

¼ tsp (1 mL) salt

1¼ lbs (625 g) salmon fillet, cut into 4 equal pieces

1 red bell pepper, cut into 1-inch (2.5 cm) strips

1 yellow bell pepper, cut into 1-inch (2.5 cm) strips

1 green bell pepper, cut into 1-inch (2.5 cm) strips

Rimmed baking sheet coated with cooking spray

1 In a large bowl, whisk together the lime juice, oil, chili powder, cumin, parsley, garlic powder and salt to make the marinade.

2 Divide the marinade evenly between two medium bowls. Add the salmon to one bowl and the red, yellow and green bell peppers to the other. Turn to coat evenly. Cover each bowl and refrigerate for at least 30 minutes and up to 2 hours.

3 Preheat the oven to 425°F (220°C).

4 Remove the salmon fillets from the marinade, shaking off the excess. Place the salmon in the center of the sheet pan, leaving ½ inch (1 cm) between pieces. Remove the bell peppers from the marinade, shaking off the excess. Add in a single layer around the salmon. Discard the remaining marinade from both containers.

5 Bake until the salmon is opaque and an instant-read thermometer inserted into the thickest part of the fillets registers 145°F (63°C), 15 to 18 minutes.

6 TO STORE: In each of four containers, add one salmon fillet and ³⁄₄ cup (175 mL) of the bell peppers. Cover and refrigerate for up to 4 days or freeze for up to 2 months.

7 TO SERVE: If frozen, thaw in the refrigerator overnight. To reheat, microwave uncovered on High for about 1 minute until heated through. Allow 2 minutes for the heat to distribute before removing the container from the microwave. Serve warm.

	TOTAL CALORIES	TOTAL FAT	SATURATED FAT	TRANS FAT
PER SERVING	389.51	26.24 g	5.31 g	0.0 g
	SODIUM 273.60 mg	**CHOLESTEROL** 77.92 mg	**TOTAL CARBOHYDRATES** 7.22 g	**FIBER** 2.38 g
	SUGARS 3.55 g	**PROTEIN** 30.13 g	**POTASSIUM** 743.98 mg	**PHOSPHORUS** 368.06 mg

COMPLETE YOUR PLATE

Small green salad with
1 tbsp (15 mL) vinaigrette
and ¾ cup (180 mL) cooked
brown rice or farro

TOBY'S TIP | When purchasing peppers, look
for shiny, wrinkle-free skin without any blemishes.
They should be firm to the touch. Store in the
refrigerator in a plastic bag in the crisper drawer
for 5 to 7 days. Wash just before using, as moisture
can cause them to spoil faster.

SHEET PAN TUNA
WITH BRUSSELS SPROUTS AND BABY POTATOES

SERVES	SERVING SIZE	TOTAL TIME	PREP TIME	COOK TIME
4	1 steak, 1½ cups (375 mL) vegetables	55 minutes, plus marinating time (30 minutes to 2 hours)	20 minutes	35 minutes

Sheet pan meals make meal prepping a snap. Once you have all your ingredients together, all you have to do is roast them up on one sheet pan. A delicious meal and fewer dishes — a total win-win!

MARINATED TUNA

1 tbsp (15 mL) olive oil

Zest of 1 lemon and juice of 2 lemons

¼ tsp (1 mL) salt

⅛ tsp (0.5 mL) ground black pepper

Four 5-oz (150 g) tuna steaks

SHEET PAN

Cooking spray

2 tbsp (30 mL) olive oil

1 tsp (5 mL) dried parsley flakes

1 tsp (5 mL) dried oregano

⅛ tsp (0.5 mL) hot pepper flakes

⅛ tsp (0.5 mL) salt

1 **TO MAKE THE MARINATED TUNA:** In a large bowl, whisk together the oil, lemon zest and juice, salt and black pepper. Add the tuna steaks and turn to coat. Cover and refrigerate for at least 30 minutes and up to 2 hours.

2 **TO MAKE THE SHEET PAN:** Preheat the oven to 425°F (220°C). Coat a rimmed baking sheet with cooking spray.

3 In a large bowl, whisk together the oil, parsley, oregano, hot pepper flakes, salt and black pepper. Add the potatoes to the bowl and toss to combine. Place the potatoes in a single layer on the prepared baking sheet. Add the Brussels sprouts to the bowl and toss in the remaining oil mixture.

4 Roast the potatoes for 10 minutes, then turn them and move them to the edges of the pan.

5 Remove the tuna steaks from the marinade, shaking off the excess. Place them in the center of the baking sheet, leaving ½ inch (1 cm) between the steaks, and top with the slices of lemon. Add the Brussels sprouts around the tuna steaks. Roast until an instant-read thermometer inserted into the thickest part of the tuna registers 145°F (63°C), 20 to 25 minutes.

PER SERVING			
TOTAL CALORIES 382.15	**TOTAL FAT** 11.40 g	**SATURATED FAT** 1.77 g	**TRANS FAT** 0.02 g
SODIUM 332.20 mg	**CHOLESTEROL** 55.25 mg	**TOTAL CARBOHYDRATES** 31.37 g	**FIBER** 7.89 g
SUGARS 4.73 g	**PROTEIN** 40.64 g	**POTASSIUM** 1,579.69 mg	**PHOSPHORUS** 547.84 mg

⅛ tsp (0.5 mL) ground black pepper

1 lb (500 g) baby potatoes, thoroughly dried

1 lemon, sliced into rounds

1 lb (500 g) Brussels sprouts, trimmed and halved

6 TO STORE: In each of four containers, add one tuna steak and 1½ cups (375 mL) of the potatoes and Brussels sprouts. Cover and refrigerate for up to 4 days or freeze for up to 2 months.

7 TO SERVE: If frozen, thaw in the refrigerator overnight. To reheat, microwave uncovered on High for 60 to 90 seconds. Allow 2 minutes for the heat to distribute before removing the container from the microwave. Serve warm.

TOBY'S TIP | Brussels sprouts are sold either on or off the stalk. Choose small, firm sprouts that are tightly closed. Look for bright green color without any yellow or brown spots. Avoid those with tears to the leaves. If the sprouts are attached to the stalk, pluck them off and trim any remaining stem before cooking. Store unwashed sprouts off the stalk in a plastic bag in the refrigerator for up to 3 days.

ONE-POT GROUND TURKEY
WITH VEGETABLES AND PASTA

SERVES	SERVING SIZE	TOTAL TIME	PREP TIME	COOK TIME
6	1³⁄₄ cups (425 mL) turkey-pasta mixture, 1 tbsp (15 mL) cheese	1 hour	20 minutes	40 minutes

This all-in-one family-friendly dish provides lean protein, non-starchy vegetables and whole grains. Fill up with every food group on your plate! Freeze extra portions for a busy weeknight when you don't have time to cook.

6 oz (175 g) 100% whole wheat elbow macaroni

1¹⁄₂ cups (375 mL) broccoli florets, cut into bite-size pieces

1¹⁄₂ cups (375 mL) cauliflower florets, cut into bite-size pieces

¹⁄₂ cup (125 mL) low-sodium chicken broth

1 tbsp (15 mL) cornstarch

1 tsp (5 mL) dried parsley flakes

1 tsp (5 mL) dried oregano

1 tsp (5 mL) dried basil

¹⁄₄ tsp (1 mL) salt

¹⁄₄ tsp (1 mL) ground black pepper

¹⁄₈ tsp (0.5 mL) hot pepper flakes

1 Fill a medium saucepan three-quarters with water and bring to a boil over high heat. Add the macaroni and cook until al dente, 10 minutes. Drain, reserving ¹⁄₂ cup (125 mL) of the pasta water, and set aside.

2 Fill a large saucepan with 1 inch (2.5 cm) of water and fit with a steamer basket. Add the broccoli and cauliflower and cook, covered, until the vegetables are cooked but crisp, 5 minutes. Transfer the broccoli and cauliflower to a medium bowl.

3 In a small bowl, whisk together the chicken broth, cornstarch, parsley, oregano, basil, salt, black pepper and hot pepper flakes.

4 In a large sauté pan, heat the oil over medium heat. When the oil is shimmering, add the turkey and cook, breaking up the larger pieces with a spoon, until browned on all sides, 7 minutes. Add the onion and garlic and cook until the onion is translucent and the garlic is fragrant, 3 minutes. Add the mushrooms and cook until softened, 5 minutes.

5 Add the pasta, broccoli and cauliflower and toss to combine. Add the broth mixture and mix until the sauce thickens, 1 minute. Add the ¹⁄₂ cup (125 mL) reserved pasta water and stir to combine. Cover and cook over low heat to allow the flavors to combine, 5 minutes.

PER SERVING	TOTAL CALORIES	TOTAL FAT	SATURATED FAT	TRANS FAT
	325.80	14.88 g	3.94 g	0.11 g
	SODIUM	CHOLESTEROL	TOTAL CARBOHYDRATES	FIBER
	406.62 mg	62.69 mg	28.43 g	3.64 g
	SUGARS	PROTEIN	POTASSIUM	PHOSPHORUS
	2.15 g	22.74 g	514.83 mg	321.15 mg

2 tbsp (30 mL) olive oil or
canola oil

1 lb (500 g) at least 90% lean
ground turkey

1 yellow onion, chopped

1 clove garlic, minced

8 oz (250 g) button mushrooms,
sliced

6 tbsp (90 mL) grated Parmesan
cheese

6 **TO STORE:** In each of six containers, add 1¾ cups
(425 mL) of the turkey and pasta mixture and
sprinkle with 1 tbsp (15 mL) of the Parmesan
cheese. Cover and refrigerate for up to 4 days
or freeze for up to 2 months.

7 **TO SERVE:** If frozen, thaw in the refrigerator
overnight. To reheat, microwave uncovered on High
for 1½ to 2 minutes. Allow 2 minutes for the heat
to distribute before removing the container from
the microwave. Serve warm.

TOBY'S TIPS | If you prefer, swap the ground
turkey for lean ground chicken breast or at least
90% lean ground beef.

To make the dish dairy-free, omit the Parmesan
cheese or substitute nutritional yeast.

PENNE
WITH TURKEY-CARROT MEATBALLS

	SERVES	SERVING SIZE	TOTAL TIME	PREP TIME	COOK TIME
	4	¾ cup (175 mL) pasta, ⅔ cup (150 mL) meatballs with sauce	40 minutes	15 minutes	25 minutes

Veggie up your meatballs with delicious carrots! It's a fun way to ramp up the flavor of mild turkey and get more non-starchy vegetables in your meal prep.

6 oz (175 g) whole wheat penne

8 oz (250 g) at least 90% lean ground turkey

2 carrots, peeled and shredded

¼ cup (60 mL) plain bread crumbs

1 large egg, beaten

1 tsp (5 mL) dried parsley flakes

¼ tsp (1 mL) salt

⅛ tsp (0.5 mL) ground black pepper

2 tbsp (30 mL) olive oil

1 cup (250 mL) Homemade Tomato Sauce (page 262) or low-sodium pasta sauce

COMPLETE YOUR PLATE

Small tossed salad with 1 tbsp (15 mL) vinaigrette

1 Fill a large pot three-quarters with water and bring to a boil over high heat. Add the penne and reduce the heat to medium. Boil gently until the pasta is al dente, 10 minutes. Drain and set aside to cool.

2 In a medium bowl, add the ground turkey, carrots, bread crumbs, egg, parsley, salt and pepper. Using clean hands, mix until combined. Form 1 tbsp (15 mL) of the mixture into a 2-inch (5 cm) ball and place on a large plate. Repeat with the remaining mixture to make about 14 meatballs. Cover and refrigerate for 30 minutes and up to 3 hours.

3 In a large skillet or sauté pan, heat the oil over medium-high heat. Add the meatballs and cook, covered, turning once, until browned on all sides, 8 minutes. Add the tomato sauce and bring to a boil over high heat. Reduce the heat to medium-low and cook, covered, until the flavors combine and an instant-read thermometer inserted into a few meatballs registers 165°F (74°C), 5 minutes.

4 TO STORE: In each of four containers, add ¾ cup (175 mL) of the pasta and top with ⅔ cup (150 mL) of the meatballs and sauce. Cover and refrigerate for up to 4 days or freeze for up to 2 months.

5 TO SERVE: If frozen, thaw in the refrigerator overnight. To reheat, microwave uncovered on High for 1½ to 2 minutes. Alternatively, reheat in a saucepan by bringing the pasta and sauce to a boil and then simmering over medium-low heat until heated through, about 10 minutes. Serve warm.

PER SERVING	TOTAL CALORIES	TOTAL FAT	SATURATED FAT	TRANS FAT
	396.77	16.65 g	3.26 g	0.09 g
	SODIUM	CHOLESTEROL	TOTAL CARBOHYDRATES	FIBER
	402.55 mg	89.59 mg	43.58 g	6.32 g
	SUGARS	PROTEIN	POTASSIUM	PHOSPHORUS
	5.15 g	19.21 g	462.92 mg	193.02 mg

CHICKEN CACCIATORE

SERVES	SERVING SIZE	TOTAL TIME	PREP TIME	COOK TIME
4	4 oz (125 g) chicken, 1 cup (250 mL) sauce	1 hour, 5 minutes	20 minutes	45 minutes

You can make your own diabetes-friendly Italian food. If you want to save time, then opt for a tomato-based low-sodium pasta sauce from the grocery.

2 tbsp (30 mL) olive oil, divided

1 lb (500 g) boneless skinless chicken tenders

2 cloves garlic, minced

1 yellow onion, thinly sliced

2 red bell peppers, cut into 1-inch (2.5 cm) strips

8 oz (250 g) mushrooms, thinly sliced

1/2 cup (125 mL) white cooking wine or dry white wine

1 1/2 cups (375 mL) Homemade Tomato Sauce (page 262) or low-sodium pasta sauce

1/4 cup (60 mL) Kalamata olives (1 1/2 oz/45 g), halved lengthwise

1/4 tsp (1 mL) ground black pepper

COMPLETE YOUR PLATE

3/4 cup (175 mL) cooked 100% whole wheat spaghetti

1 In a large sauté pan, heat 1 tbsp (15 mL) of the oil over medium heat. When the oil is shimmering, add the chicken and cook until browned, 5 minutes on each side. Transfer the chicken to a clean plate.

2 In the same sauté pan, heat the remaining 1 tbsp (15 mL) oil over medium heat. When the oil is shimmering, add the garlic and cook until fragrant, 30 seconds. Add the onion, red bell peppers and mushrooms and cook until the vegetables have softened slightly, 8 minutes. Add the white wine and bring the mixture to a boil over high heat. Lower the heat to medium-low and simmer until the wine is reduced by half, about 4 minutes.

3 Add the tomato sauce, olives and black pepper and stir to combine. Add the chicken and turn to coat. Raise the heat and bring to a boil, then reduce the heat to medium-low and cook, covered, until the flavors combine and an instant-read thermometer inserted into the center of a chicken tender registers 165°F (74°C), 20 minutes.

4 TO STORE: Divide the chicken equally among four containers and top with 1 cup (250 mL) of the sauce. Cover and refrigerate for up to 4 days or freeze for up to 2 months.

5 TO SERVE: If frozen, thaw in the refrigerator overnight. To reheat, microwave uncovered on High for 60 to 90 seconds. Allow 2 minutes for the heat to distribute before removing the container from the microwave. Serve warm.

	TOTAL CALORIES	TOTAL FAT	SATURATED FAT	TRANS FAT
PER SERVING	315.65;	14.38 g	1.89 g	0.01 g
	SODIUM	**CHOLESTEROL**	**TOTAL CARBOHYDRATES**	**FIBER**
	476.89 mg	72.58 mg	16.98 g	4.38 g
	SUGARS	**PROTEIN**	**POTASSIUM**	**PHOSPHORUS**
	9.79 g	27.39 g	1,058.55 mg	362.36 mg

PARMESAN-CRUSTED CHICKEN BREASTS

SERVES	SERVING SIZE	TOTAL TIME	PREP TIME	COOK TIME
4	1 chicken breast	30 minutes	20 minutes	10 minutes

I find the best taste testers to be my own children, especially since they are rather picky. After I served this dish to my teenage son, he loved it so much that it now makes a regular appearance on our dinner table.

Four 5-oz (150 g) boneless skinless chicken breasts, trimmed

1/2 cup (125 mL) white whole wheat flour

1 large egg

2 large egg whites

3/4 cup (175 mL) unseasoned bread crumbs

1/4 cup (60 mL) grated Parmesan cheese

1 tsp (5 mL) dried parsley flakes

1 tsp (5 mL) dried oregano

1 tsp (5 mL) dried basil

1 tsp (5 mL) garlic powder

1/4 tsp (1 mL) salt

1/4 tsp (1 mL) ground black pepper

3 tbsp (45 mL) canola oil

1 Place one chicken breast in a sealable plastic bag, pressing out as much air as possible before sealing. Pound with a rolling pin or the flat side of a meat mallet until it is evenly 1/2 inch (1 cm) thick. Repeat with the remaining 3 chicken breasts.

2 In a medium bowl, add the flour.

3 In a separate medium bowl, add the egg and egg whites and whisk together.

4 In a third medium bowl, add the bread crumbs, Parmesan cheese, parsley, oregano, basil, garlic powder, salt and pepper. Mix to combine.

5 Dredge each chicken breast first in the flour, next in the eggs, allowing the excess eggs to drip off, and lastly in the bread crumb mixture and place on a clean plate.

6 In a large sauté pan, heat the oil over medium heat. When the oil is shimmering, add the chicken breasts and cook until browned and an instant-read thermometer inserted into the thickest part of a breast registers 165°F (74°C), 5 minutes on each side.

7 TO STORE: In each of four containers, add one chicken breast. Cover and refrigerate for up to 4 days or freeze for up to 2 months.

8 TO SERVE: If frozen, thaw in the refrigerator overnight. To reheat, microwave uncovered on High for 60 to 90 seconds. Allow 2 minutes for the heat to distribute before removing the container from the microwave. Serve warm.

	TOTAL CALORIES	TOTAL FAT	SATURATED FAT	TRANS FAT
PER SERVING	400.31	17.21 g	2.84 g	0.05 g
	SODIUM	CHOLESTEROL	TOTAL CARBOHYDRATES	FIBER
	391.74 mg	142.48 mg	19.54 g	1.96 g
	SUGARS	PROTEIN	POTASSIUM	PHOSPHORUS
	1.30 g	39.90 g	590.99 mg	381.98 mg

COMPLETE YOUR PLATE

Spicy Steamed Broccoli
(page 240) and ¾ cup
(175 mL) whole-grain pasta

TOBY'S TIP | White whole wheat flour is made
from hard white spring or winter wheat, which has
the same nutrition as whole wheat flour but with
a milder flavor and whiter color. If you don't have it
on hand, you can swap in 100% whole wheat flour.

CHICKEN FAJITA SKILLET

SERVES	SERVING SIZE	TOTAL TIME	PREP TIME	COOK TIME
4	2 cups (500 mL)	1 hour, 35 minutes, plus marinating time (30 minutes to overnight)	20 minutes	1 hour, 15 minutes

This all-in-one dish has the flavors you love in fajitas but in a one-pot meal! What could be better than that?

MARINATED CHICKEN

2 tbsp (30 mL) olive oil or canola oil

1 clove garlic, minced

1½ tsp (7 mL) ground paprika

½ tsp (2 mL) ground cumin

⅛ tsp (0.5 mL) salt

⅛ tsp (0.5 mL) ground black pepper

12 oz (375 g) boneless skinless chicken breasts, cut into 1-inch (2.5 cm) strips

SKILLET

2 cups (500 mL) low-sodium chicken broth, divided

½ cup (125 mL) long-grain brown rice

Cooking spray

1 TO MAKE THE MARINATED CHICKEN: In a large bowl, whisk the oil, garlic, smoked paprika, cumin, salt and black pepper. Add the chicken and turn to evenly coat. Cover the bowl and refrigerate for at least 30 minutes and up to overnight.

2 TO MAKE THE SKILLET: In a medium saucepan, add 1 cup (250 mL) of the chicken broth and the rice and bring to a boil over high heat. Reduce the heat to low and simmer, covered, until the rice is tender and the broth is absorbed, 40 minutes. Fluff with a fork.

3 Coat a large skillet or sauté pan with cooking spray and heat over medium heat. When the oil is shimmering, add the chicken strips, shaking off excess marinade, and cook, turning occasionally, until an instant-read thermometer inserted in several pieces of chicken registers 165°F (74°C), about 8 minutes. Discard the excess marinade. Transfer the chicken to a clean plate.

4 In the same skillet or sauté pan, add the oil and heat over medium heat. When the oil is shimmering, add the garlic and cook until fragrant, 30 seconds. Add the onion and red and yellow bell peppers and cook until the vegetables begin to soften, 3 minutes.

PER SERVING			
TOTAL CALORIES	TOTAL FAT	SATURATED FAT	TRANS FAT
386.10	12.63 g	1.70 g	0.0 g
SODIUM	CHOLESTEROL	TOTAL CARBOHYDRATES	FIBER
419.53 mg	0.0 mg	40.79 g	7.3 g
SUGARS	PROTEIN	POTASSIUM	PHOSPHORUS
7.75 g	27.23 g	636.27 mg	260.70 mg

LUNCH AND DINNER MAINS

1 tbsp (15 mL) olive oil or canola oil

1 clove garlic, minced

1 yellow onion, thinly sliced

1 red bell pepper, cut into 1-inch (2.5 cm) strips

1 yellow bell pepper, cut into 1-inch (2.5 cm) strips

1¾ cups (425 mL) no-salt-added canned diced tomatoes, with juice

1 cup (250 mL) no-salt-added canned black beans, drained and rinsed

1 tsp (5 mL) ground paprika

½ tsp (2 mL) ground cumin

Juice of 1 lime

5 Add the remaining 1 cup (250 mL) chicken broth, diced tomatoes, black beans, paprika and cumin. Stir to combine. Raise the heat to high and bring the mixture to a boil. Reduce the heat to medium-low and cook, covered, until the flavors combine, about 10 minutes.

6 Add the chicken, rice and lime juice and toss to evenly coat. Continue cooking, uncovered, over medium-low heat, until the liquid is mostly absorbed, 10 minutes.

7 TO STORE: In each of four containers add 2 cups (500 mL) of the chicken fajita mixture. Cover and refrigerate for up to 4 days or freeze for up to 2 months.

8 TO SERVE: If frozen, thaw in the refrigerator overnight. To reheat, microwave uncovered on High for 1½ to 2 minutes. Allow 2 minutes for the heat to distribute before removing the container from the microwave. Serve warm.

BLACK BEAN–CHICKEN CASSEROLE
WITH SALSA AND GREEN CHILES

SERVES	SERVING SIZE	TOTAL TIME	PREP TIME	COOK TIME
4	1 cup (250 mL)	1 hour, 40 minutes	20 minutes	1 hour, 20 minutes

A creamy casserole can be heart healthy with a few simple swaps, like choosing reduced-fat cheese and creating a creamy sauce with reduced-fat sour cream and nonfat plain Greek yogurt. The end result is filled with a fiesta of flavors!

$\frac{1}{2}$ cup (125 mL) long-grain brown rice

1 cup (250 mL) water

1 lb (500 g) boneless skinless chicken breasts, cut into 1-inch (2.5 cm) cubes

$\frac{1}{4}$ tsp (1 mL) salt, divided

$\frac{1}{8}$ tsp (0.5 mL) ground black pepper

1 tbsp (15 mL) olive oil

Cooking spray

1 cup (250 mL) shredded reduced-fat Monterey Jack cheese, divided

$1\frac{1}{4}$ cups (300 mL) canned mild chopped green chiles, with juice

1   In a medium saucepan, add the rice and water and bring to a boil over high heat. Reduce the heat to low and simmer, covered, until the rice is tender and the water is absorbed, 40 minutes. Fluff with a fork.

2   Sprinkle both sides of the chicken with $\frac{1}{8}$ tsp (0.5 mL) of the salt and the black pepper.

3   In a medium skillet, heat the oil over medium heat. When the oil is shimmering, add the chicken and cook until browned on all sides, 8 minutes. Let cool for about 10 minutes.

4   Preheat the oven to 375°F (190°C). Coat an 8-inch (20 cm) square glass baking dish with cooking spray.

5   In a large bowl, mix together $\frac{1}{2}$ cup (125 mL) of the shredded cheese, green chiles, salsa, sour cream, yogurt, chili powder, garlic powder, onion powder, cumin and the remaining $\frac{1}{8}$ tsp (0.5 mL) salt. Add the rice, chicken, black beans and corn and toss to combine.

6   Add the mixture to the prepared baking dish and top with the remaining $\frac{1}{2}$ cup (125 mL) shredded cheese. Cover with aluminum foil and bake until the top is brown and casserole is bubbling, 20 minutes. Remove the aluminum foil and bake for an additional 10 minutes.

	TOTAL CALORIES	TOTAL FAT	SATURATED FAT	TRANS FAT
PER SERVING	349.19	10.86 g	3.71 g	0.0 g
	SODIUM	CHOLESTEROL	TOTAL CARBOHYDRATES	FIBER
	428.13 mg	70.66 mg	33.25 g	5.98 g
	SUGARS	PROTEIN	POTASSIUM	PHOSPHORUS
	2.87 g	29.06 g	476.76 mg	237.44 mg

½ cup (125 mL) Tomato Salsa (page 258) or store-bought tomato salsa

¼ cup (60 mL) reduced-fat sour cream

¼ cup (60 mL) nonfat plain Greek yogurt

1 tsp (5 mL) chili powder

1 tsp (5 mL) garlic powder

1 tsp (5 mL) onion powder

1 tsp (5 mL) ground cumin

1¾ cups (425 mL) no-salt-added canned black beans, drained and rinsed

1½ cups (375 mL) frozen corn, thawed

7 TO STORE: In each of six containers, add 1 cup (250 mL) of the casserole. Cover and refrigerate for up to 4 days or freeze for up to 2 months.

8 TO SERVE: If frozen, thaw in the refrigerator overnight. To reheat, microwave uncovered on High for 1½ to 2 minutes. Allow 2 minutes for the heat to distribute before removing the container from the microwave. Serve warm.

TOBY'S TIP | Look for canned chopped green chiles in the international aisle at your supermarket. They are typically with Latin foods.

SESAME-GINGER PORK MEATBALLS

SERVES	SERVING SIZE	TOTAL TIME	PREP TIME	COOK TIME
4	4 meatballs with sauce	30 minutes, plus refrigeration (30 minutes to 3 hours)	20 minutes	10 minutes

There are lots of ways to enjoy these flavorful meatballs. Try them over whole wheat pasta or brown rice, on a salad or citrus-y slaw or in a whole wheat hot dog bun.

MEATBALLS

1 lb (500 g) lean ground pork

3 green onions, white and green parts, chopped

1 carrot, peeled and grated

2 cloves garlic, minced

2 tbsp (30 mL) reduced-sodium soy sauce

¼ tsp (1 mL) ground ginger

2 tbsp (30 mL) olive oil or canola oil

SAUCE

1 tbsp (15 mL) sesame oil

1 tbsp (15 mL) unseasoned rice vinegar

2 tsp (10 mL) cornstarch

1 tsp (5 mL) garlic powder

1. **TO MAKE THE MEATBALLS:** In a medium bowl, add the pork, green onions, carrot, garlic, soy sauce and ground ginger. Using clean hands, mix until combined.

2. Roll 1 tbsp (15 mL) of the pork mixture into a 2-inch (5 cm) ball. Place on a large plate and repeat with the remaining pork mixture to make about 16 meatballs. Loosely cover the plate and place in the refrigerator for at least 30 minutes and up to 3 hours.

3. In a large skillet or sauté pan, heat the olive oil over medium-high heat. When the oil is shimmering, add the meatballs and cover. Cook, turning once, until browned on all sides, 8 minutes. Using a slotted spoon, transfer the meatballs to a clean plate and set the pan aside.

4. **TO MAKE THE SAUCE:** In a small bowl, whisk together the sesame oil, rice vinegar, cornstarch, garlic powder, brown sugar blend, salt, ginger and hot pepper flakes.

5. In the same skillet or sauté pan used to cook the meatballs, add the sauce and bring to a boil over high heat, whisking frequently and scraping the browned bits at the bottom of the pan. Reduce the heat to low and simmer, whisking constantly, until the sauce thickens, 1 to 2 minutes. Add the meatballs to the sauce and turn to evenly coat.

	TOTAL CALORIES	TOTAL FAT	SATURATED FAT	TRANS FAT
PER SERVING	309.79	21.67 g	5.23 g	0.07 g
	SODIUM	CHOLESTEROL	TOTAL CARBOHYDRATES	FIBER
	432.27 mg	72.01 mg	6.58 g	0.86 g
	SUGARS	PROTEIN	POTASSIUM	PHOSPHORUS
	2.53 g	23.26 g	411.99 mg	214.62 mg

½ tsp (2 mL) stevia brown sugar blend (such as Truvia or Splenda)

¼ tsp (1 mL) salt

⅛ tsp (0.5 mL) ground ginger

⅛ tsp (0.5 mL) hot pepper flakes

COMPLETE YOUR PLATE

¾ cup (175 mL) steamed broccoli and ¾ cup (175 mL) cooked whole wheat spaghetti

6 **TO STORE:** In each of four containers, add four meatballs and evenly divide any additional sauce among the containers. Cover and refrigerate for up to 4 days or freeze for up to 2 months.

7 **TO SERVE:** If frozen, thaw in the refrigerator overnight. To reheat, microwave uncovered on High for 90 seconds. Allow 2 minutes for the heat to distribute before removing the container from the microwave. Serve warm.

TOBY'S TIP | If you prefer, swap the pork for lean ground chicken or turkey.

PORK GOULASH

 · ·

SERVES	SERVING SIZE	TOTAL TIME	PREP TIME	COOK TIME
6	1¼ cups (300 mL) goulash, ¾ cup (175 mL) noodles	1 hour, 50 minutes	20 minutes	1 hour, 30 minutes

Goulash is a Hungarian dish that is popular throughout Europe. This rustic stew is seasoned with paprika and can be made with vegetables and beef, chicken, lamb or pork. This version uses carrots, bell peppers and peas, but if you want to swap the non-starchy vegetables for leftover ones in your kitchen, don't be shy!

6 oz (175 g) wide egg noodles

1¼ lbs (625 g) pork tenderloin, cut into 2-inch (5 cm) cubes

¼ tsp (1 mL) salt

⅛ tsp (0.5 mL) ground black pepper

⅓ cup (75 mL) unbleached all-purpose flour

3 tbsp (45 mL) olive oil or canola oil, divided

1 yellow onion, chopped

2 cloves garlic, minced

1 red bell pepper, chopped

1 green bell pepper, chopped

3 carrots, peeled and diced

1 Fill a medium saucepan three-quarters with water and bring to a boil over high heat. Add the egg noodles and reduce the heat to medium. Boil gently until the noodles are al dente, 8 minutes. Drain the noodles and set aside.

2 In a large bowl, add the pork tenderloin pieces and sprinkle with the salt, black pepper and flour. Toss to evenly coat.

3 In a large sauté pan, heat 2 tbsp (30 mL) of the oil over medium heat. When the oil is shimmering, add the pork and, turning two or three times, brown on all sides, 8 minutes. Transfer the pork to a clean plate.

4 In the same pan, heat the remaining 1 tbsp (15 mL) oil over medium heat. When the oil is shimmering, add the onion and garlic and cook until the onion is translucent and the garlic is fragrant, 3 minutes. Add the red and green bell peppers and the carrots and cook, stirring occasionally, until slightly softened, 5 minutes. Add the pork, beef broth, green peas, diced tomatoes with juice, paprika and tomato paste and stir to combine. Raise the heat to high and bring the mixture to a boil. Reduce the heat to medium-low and simmer, covered, for 1 hour, stirring occasionally, until the internal temperature of the pork pieces reaches 145°F (63°C). Remove the cover and continue to simmer for an additional 10 minutes, stirring occasionally.

PER SERVING			
TOTAL CALORIES 379.14	TOTAL FAT 11.53 g	SATURATED FAT 2.45 g	TRANS FAT 0.05 g
SODIUM 430.54 mg	CHOLESTEROL 70.12 mg	TOTAL CARBOHYDRATES 41.84 g	FIBER 6.54 g
SUGARS 8.49 g	PROTEIN 26.95 g	POTASSIUM 825.04 mg	PHOSPHORUS 379.96 mg

1 cup (250 mL) low-sodium beef broth

1 cup (250 mL) frozen green peas, thawed

1¾ cups (425 mL) no-salt-added canned diced tomatoes, with juice

2 tbsp (30 mL) sweet paprika

2 tbsp (30 mL) no-salt-added tomato paste

5 TO STORE: In each of six containers, add ¾ cup (175 mL) of the egg noodles and top with 1¼ cups (300 mL) of the goulash. Cover and refrigerate for up to 4 days or freeze for up to 2 months.

6 TO SERVE: If frozen, thaw in the refrigerator overnight. To reheat, microwave uncovered on High for 1½ to 2 minutes. Allow 2 minutes for the heat to distribute before removing the container from the microwave. Alternatively, reheat in a small saucepan on the stove by bringing the goulash to a boil and then simmering over medium heat until heated through, 10 minutes. Serve warm.

TOBY'S TIP | Although goulash is traditionally served with egg noodles, you can also serve it with brown rice, quinoa or whole wheat rotini in order to increase your whole grains and fiber.

HERBED GARLIC BUTTER PORK CHOPS

SERVES	SERVING SIZE	TOTAL TIME	PREP TIME	COOK TIME
6	1 pork chop, 1 tbsp (15 mL) sauce	40 minutes	15 minutes	25 minutes

Who says butter can't fit into your diabetes-friendly meal plan? Using a small amount lends yummy buttery flavor without much saturated fat.

3 tbsp (45 mL) unsalted butter, softened

2 cloves garlic, minced

1 tsp (5 mL) dried parsley flakes

$\frac{1}{2}$ tsp (2 mL) dried rosemary

Six 5-oz (150 g) boneless pork chops

$\frac{1}{4}$ tsp (1 mL) salt

$\frac{1}{4}$ tsp (1 mL) ground black pepper

$\frac{1}{3}$ cup (75 mL) unbleached all-purpose flour

2 tbsp (30 mL) olive oil

2 shallots, chopped

1 In a small bowl, whisk together the butter, garlic, parsley and rosemary.

2 In a large bowl, add the pork chops. Sprinkle both sides of the pork chops with the salt, pepper and flour. Turn to evenly coat.

3 In a large sauté pan, heat the oil over medium heat. When the oil is shimmering, add the shallots and cook until translucent, 3 minutes. Add the pork chops and cook until an instant-read thermometer inserted into the thickest part of a pork chop registers 145°F (63°C), 4 minutes on each side. Add the butter sauce and simmer, covered, until combined, 15 minutes.

4 TO STORE: In each of six containers, add one pork chop plus 1 tbsp (15 mL) of the sauce. Cover and refrigerate for up to 4 days or freeze for up to 2 months.

5 TO SERVE: If frozen, thaw in the refrigerator overnight. To reheat, microwave uncovered on High for 60 to 90 seconds. Allow 2 minutes for the heat to distribute before removing the container from the microwave. Serve warm.

COMPLETE YOUR PLATE

$\frac{1}{2}$ cup (125 mL) Easy Herbed Quinoa (page 230) and $\frac{3}{4}$ cup (175 mL) Sheet Pan Vegetable Medley (page 237)

TOBY'S TIP | For a citrus spin, add 1 to 2 tbsp (15 to 30 mL) of lemon juice to the sauce, if you would like.

	TOTAL CALORIES	TOTAL FAT	SATURATED FAT	TRANS FAT
PER SERVING	220.03	12.19 g	4.79 g	0.21 g
	SODIUM	CHOLESTEROL	TOTAL CARBOHYDRATES	FIBER
	297.82 mg	62.47 mg	4.73 g	0.44 g
	SUGARS	PROTEIN	POTASSIUM	PHOSPHORUS
	0.86 g	23.43 g	554.24 mg	317.05 mg

LAMB BOLOGNESE

SERVES	SERVING SIZE	TOTAL TIME	PREP TIME	COOK TIME
6	¾ cup (175 mL) pasta, ¾ cup (175 mL) sauce	1 hour, 15 minutes	20 minutes	55 minutes

Lamb can absolutely fit into a diabetes-friendly meal plan. Ground lamb is sold in many markets or ask your butcher.

8 oz (250 g) 100% whole wheat angel hair spaghetti

1 tbsp (15 mL) olive oil

1 yellow onion, chopped

2 cloves garlic, minced

2 carrots, peeled and shredded

1 lb (500 g) lean ground lamb

3¼ cups (810 mL) no-salt-added canned crushed tomatoes, with juice

¼ cup (60 mL) red cooking wine

1 tsp (5 mL) stevia brown sugar blend (such as Truvia or Splenda)

1 tsp (5 mL) dried parsley flakes

1 tsp (5 mL) dried oregano

1 tsp (5 mL) dried basil

3 bay leaves

½ tsp (2 mL) salt

¼ tsp (1 mL) ground black pepper

1 Fill a medium saucepan three-quarters with water and bring to a boil over high heat. Add the spaghetti and reduce the heat to medium. Boil gently until the pasta is al dente, 7 minutes. Drain the spaghetti and set aside to cool.

2 In a large sauté pan, heat the oil over medium heat. When the oil is shimmering, add the onion and garlic and cook, stirring occasionally, until the onion is translucent and the garlic is fragrant, 3 minutes. Add the carrots and cook until softened, 3 to 4 minutes. Add the ground lamb and cook, breaking up the chunks of meat with the back of the spoon, until the meat is browned, 8 minutes.

3 Add the tomatoes with juice, wine, brown sugar blend, parsley, oregano, basil, bay leaves, salt and pepper and bring to a boil. Reduce the heat to medium-low and simmer, covered, until the flavors combine, 30 minutes. Discard the bay leaves.

4 TO STORE: In each of six containers, add ¾ cup (175 mL) of the spaghetti and top with about ¾ cup (175 mL) of the sauce. Cover and refrigerate for up to 4 days or freeze for up to 2 months.

5 TO SERVE: If frozen, thaw in the refrigerator overnight. To reheat, microwave uncovered on High for 90 seconds. Allow 2 minutes for the heat to distribute before removing the container from the microwave. Serve warm.

COMPLETE YOUR PLATE

1 small tossed salad with 1 tbsp (15 mL) vinaigrette

PER SERVING	TOTAL CALORIES	TOTAL FAT	SATURATED FAT	TRANS FAT
	384.14	14.02 g	5.19 g	0.54 g
	SODIUM	CHOLESTEROL	TOTAL CARBOHYDRATES	FIBER
	278.42 mg	49.39 mg	39.62 g	6.54 g
	SUGARS	PROTEIN	POTASSIUM	PHOSPHORUS
	8.12 g	20.33 g	831.87 mg	264.27 mg

VEGETABLE-LOADED MEATLOAF

SERVES	SERVING SIZE	TOTAL TIME	PREP TIME	COOK TIME
8	1 slice	2 hours, 25 minutes	25 minutes	2 hours

How do you boost the flavor of meatloaf? Add a boatload of vegetables: carrots, zucchini, mushrooms, bell pepper and sweet potato! You can always swap the non-starchy vegetables for others like summer squash or even shredded Brussels sprouts.

1 large sweet potato
(14 oz/400 g)

1 tbsp (15 mL) olive oil

1 yellow onion, chopped

2 cloves garlic, minced

8 oz (250 g) cremini mushrooms, chopped

2 carrots, chopped

1 red bell pepper, chopped

1 medium zucchini, shredded

1 lb (500 g) at least 90% lean ground beef

1 cup (250 mL) Easy Barbecue Sauce (page 263), divided

1 cup (250 mL) quick-cooking rolled oats

1 large egg, beaten

$\frac{1}{2}$ tsp (2 mL) salt

$\frac{1}{4}$ tsp (1 mL) ground black pepper

Baking sheet coated with cooking spray

Large skillet

9- by 5-inch (23 cm by 12.5 cm) glass loaf pan coated with cooking spray

Preheat the oven to 400°F (200°C)

1 Pierce the sweet potato several times with a fork. Place on the prepared baking sheet and bake until tender, about 40 minutes. Remove from the oven and let cool for at least 10 minutes before halving lengthwise. Reduce the oven temperature to 350°F (180°C).

2 In a large skillet, heat the oil over medium heat. When the oil is shimmering, add the onion and garlic and cook until the onion is translucent and the garlic is fragrant, 3 minutes. Add the mushrooms, carrots, red bell pepper and zucchini and toss to combine. Cook until the vegetables have softened, 7 minutes. Remove the pan from the heat and let the vegetables cool for 10 minutes.

3 In a large bowl, add the flesh of the sweet potato and mash with a fork. Add the vegetable mixture, ground beef, $\frac{1}{2}$ cup (125 mL) of the barbecue sauce, oats, egg, salt and black pepper. Using clean hands, mix until well combined.

4 Press the mixture into the prepared loaf pan, making sure the top is even. Pour the remaining $\frac{1}{2}$ cup (125 mL) barbecue sauce over the top of the meatloaf and, using a spatula or the back of a wooden spoon, spread the sauce evenly over the meatloaf.

PER SERVING	TOTAL CALORIES 287.76	TOTAL FAT 8.97 g	SATURATED FAT 2.89 g	TRANS FAT 0.36 g
	SODIUM 336.88 mg	CHOLESTEROL 60.08 mg	TOTAL CARBOHYDRATES 36.12 g	FIBER 4.03 g
	SUGARS 16.0 g	PROTEIN 15.91 g	POTASSIUM 702.40 mg	PHOSPHORUS 244.16 mg

LUNCH AND DINNER MAINS

COMPLETE YOUR PLATE

1 small tossed salad with
1 tbsp (15 mL) vinaigrette
dressing

5   Bake until an instant-read thermometer inserted into the center of the meatloaf registers 155°F (68°C), about 1 hour.

6   Remove the meatloaf from the oven and let cool for 10 minutes. Cut into 8 equal portions.

7   TO STORE: In each of eight containers, add one slice of meatloaf. Cover and refrigerate for up to 4 days or freeze for up to 2 months.

8   TO SERVE: If frozen, thaw in the refrigerator overnight. To reheat, microwave uncovered on High for 1 minute. Allow 2 minutes for the heat to distribute before removing the container from the microwave. Serve warm.

TOBY'S TIP | If you prefer, swap the ground beef for lean ground chicken, turkey or lamb.

BEEF AND VEGETABLE STIR-FRY

SERVES	SERVING SIZE	TOTAL TIME	PREP TIME	COOK TIME
4	1 cup (250 mL) stir-fry, 1 tbsp (15 mL) sauce	40 minutes	20 minutes	20 minutes

Stir-fries are easy, adaptable weeknight dishes. It's a snap to swap out the protein and use whatever non-starchy vegetables you have.

¾ cup (175 mL) low-sodium beef broth

3 tbsp (45 mL) reduced-sodium soy sauce

1 tbsp (15 mL) cornstarch

1 tsp (5 mL) garlic powder

1 tsp (5 mL) onion powder

½ tsp (2 mL) stevia brown sugar blend (such as Truvia or Splenda)

⅛ tsp (0.5 mL) hot pepper flakes

12 oz (375 g) top sirloin, cut into 1½-inch (4 cm) strips

⅛ tsp (0.5 mL) salt

⅛ tsp (0.5 mL) ground black pepper

1 tbsp (15 mL) canola oil

8 oz (250 g) cremini mushrooms, thinly sliced

1 red bell pepper, sliced into 1-inch (2.5 cm) strips

2 cups (500 mL) broccoli florets

2 tbsp (30 mL) sesame seeds

Large wok or large sauté pan

1 In a small bowl, whisk together the beef broth, soy sauce, cornstarch, garlic powder, onion powder, brown sugar blend and hot pepper flakes.

2 Sprinkle both sides of the sirloin strips with the salt and black pepper.

3 In a large wok or large sauté pan, heat the oil over high heat. When the oil is shimmering, add the beef and cook until browned on all sides, 8 minutes. Transfer the beef to a clean plate.

4 With the wok still over high heat, add the mushrooms, bell pepper and broccoli and cook until slightly softened, 5 minutes, tossing occasionally. Add the beef back to the wok and pour in the broth mixture. Cook until the sauce thickens slightly, 5 minutes. Remove the stir-fry from the heat and sprinkle with the sesame seeds.

5 TO STORE: In each of four containers, add 1 cup (250 mL) of the stir-fry mixture and 1 tbsp (15 mL) of the sauce from the wok. Cover and refrigerate for up to 4 days or freeze for up to 2 months.

6 TO SERVE: If frozen, thaw in the refrigerator overnight. To reheat, microwave uncovered on High for 90 seconds. Alternatively, reheat in a small saucepan on the stove by adding about ¼ cup (60 mL) of water or low-sodium chicken broth, bringing the stir-fry to a boil over high heat and simmering over medium-low heat until heated through, 10 minutes. Serve warm.

PER SERVING			
TOTAL CALORIES	TOTAL FAT	SATURATED FAT	TRANS FAT
287.48	17.46 g	5.07 g	0.0 g
SODIUM	CHOLESTEROL	TOTAL CARBOHYDRATES	FIBER
450.37 mg	63.79 mg	12.07 g	1.87 g
SUGARS	PROTEIN	POTASSIUM	PHOSPHORUS
4.49 g	22.13 g	732.79 mg	294.97 mg

COMPLETE YOUR PLATE

Small green salad with 1 tbsp (15 mL) vinaigrette dressing and ¾ cup (175 mL) cooked brown rice

TOBY'S TIP | You can swap the vegetables for whatever non-starchy vegetables you have left over in your refrigerator, such as cauliflower, green beans, asparagus or cabbage.

HERBED BEEF FILLETS

SERVES	SERVING SIZE	TOTAL TIME	PREP TIME	COOK TIME
4	1 (4 oz/125 g) fillet	18 minutes, plus marinating time (30 minutes to 24 hours)	10 minutes	8 minutes

Sticking to your portion sizes of meat and poultry can be tricky, as they can vary. Your best bet is to stop by the butcher counter. They'll be happy to cut the fillets the size you wish.

Four 4-oz (125 g) beef tenderloin fillets

½ cup (125 mL) Herbed Vinaigrette (page 250)

Cooking spray or 1 tbsp (15 mL) olive oil

COMPLETE YOUR PLATE

Red Potatoes with Chives (page 236) and Sheet Pan Vegetable Medley (page 237)

Grill pan or grill

1 Place the beef tenderloin fillets in a medium bowl. Add the vinaigrette and turn the fillets to evenly coat. Cover and refrigerate for at least 30 minutes and up to 24 hours.

2 Coat a grill pan with cooking spray or brush the grates of a grill with olive oil and preheat over medium heat. Remove the fillets, shaking off the excess marinade, and place on the grill pan or grill. Discard the marinade. Grill, turning once, until an instant-read thermometer inserted into the thickest part of the fillets registers 145°F (63°C), 8 minutes.

3 Transfer the fillets to a cutting board and let rest for 10 minutes to allow the heat to evenly distribute.

4 TO STORE: In each of four containers, add one beef tenderloin fillet. Cover and refrigerate for up to 4 days or freeze for up to 2 months.

5 TO SERVE: If frozen, thaw in the refrigerator overnight. To reheat, microwave uncovered on High for 1 minute. Allow 2 minutes for the heat to distribute before removing the container from the microwave. Serve warm.

TOBY'S TIP | For a different flavor, try the Soy-Garlic Marinade (page 260) in place of the Herbed Vinaigrette.

	TOTAL CALORIES	TOTAL FAT	SATURATED FAT	TRANS FAT
PER SERVING	218.9	13.14 g	3.57 g	0.40 g
	SODIUM 174.41 mg	**CHOLESTEROL** 69.17 mg	**TOTAL CARBOHYDRATES** 1.12 g	**FIBER** 0.19 g
	SUGARS 0.38 g	**PROTEIN** 24.75 g	**POTASSIUM** 348.13 mg	**PHOSPHORUS** 243.31 mg

GRAIN AND VEGETABLE SIDES

EASY HERBED QUINOA

SERVES	SERVING SIZE	TOTAL TIME	PREP TIME	COOK TIME
4	$\frac{1}{2}$ cup (125 mL)	25 minutes	10 minutes	15 minutes

Quinoa, pronounced "KEEN-wah," is actually a seed (not a grain), but it has similar characteristics and prep methods to most grains. People have been cultivating it for 5,000 years! The color can be beige, red or black. No matter what color you choose, quinoa has a mild, nutty flavor and pleasingly chewy-yet-firm texture.

$\frac{2}{3}$ cup (150 mL) quinoa

$1\frac{1}{3}$ cups (325 mL) low-sodium vegetable broth

$\frac{1}{4}$ cup (60 mL) olive oil

1 tsp (5 mL) dried parsley flakes

1 tsp (5 mL) dried basil

$\frac{1}{4}$ tsp (1 mL) dried thyme

$\frac{1}{4}$ tsp (1 mL salt

$\frac{1}{8}$ tsp (0.5 mL) ground black pepper

COMPLETE YOUR PLATE

Herbed Garlic Butter Pork Chops (page 220) and Roasted Carrots with Dill (page 242)

1 In a medium saucepan, add the quinoa and vegetable broth and bring to a boil over high heat. Reduce the heat to low, cover and cook until the quinoa is tender and the liquid is absorbed, 15 minutes. Remove the saucepan from the heat and let cool for 10 minutes.

2 In a small bowl, whisk together the oil, parsley, basil, thyme, salt and pepper.

3 Pour the dressing over the quinoa and toss to evenly coat.

4 TO STORE: In each of four containers, add $\frac{1}{2}$ cup (125 mL) of the quinoa. Cover and refrigerate for up to 4 days or freeze for up to 2 months.

5 TO SERVE: If frozen, thaw in the refrigerator overnight. Serve warm or cold. To reheat, microwave uncovered on High for 45 to 60 seconds. Allow 2 minutes for the heat to distribute before removing the container from the microwave.

TOBY'S TIP | For another twist on this dish, add the juice of $\frac{1}{2}$ lemon to the dressing.

	TOTAL CALORIES	TOTAL FAT	SATURATED FAT	TRANS FAT
PER SERVING	230.96	15.24 g	2.07 g	0.0 g
	SODIUM	CHOLESTEROL	TOTAL CARBOHYDRATES	FIBER
	189.27 mg	0.0 mg	19.45 g	2.50 g
	SUGARS	PROTEIN	POTASSIUM	PHOSPHORUS
	0.34 g	4.43 g	171.18 mg	130.62 mg

BROWN RICE
WITH CHOPPED BROCCOLI

SERVES	SERVING SIZE	TOTAL TIME	PREP TIME	COOK TIME
4	$2/3$ cup (150 mL)	1 hour	15 minutes	45 minutes

This dish is made with long-grain rice, which has a long, slender kernel with a chewy texture and slightly nutty flavor. Opt for brown rice or whole grains whenever possible because they have more fiber compared to white rice or pasta.

1 tbsp (15 mL) olive oil or canola oil

1 small onion, chopped

1 clove garlic, minced

2 cups (500 mL) finely chopped broccoli

$2/3$ cup (150 mL) long-grain brown rice

$1\frac{1}{2}$ cups (375 mL) low-sodium vegetable broth

$\frac{1}{4}$ tsp (1 mL) salt

$\frac{1}{8}$ tsp (0.5 mL) ground black pepper

1 in a medium saucepan, heat the oil over medium heat. When the oil is shimmering, add the onion and garlic and cook until the onion softens and the garlic is fragrant, about 3 minutes. Add the broccoli and cook until slightly softened, 5 minutes.

2 Add the rice, broth, salt and black pepper and bring to a boil over high heat. Reduce the heat to low and simmer, covered, until the rice is tender and the broth is absorbed, 40 minutes. Fluff with a fork.

3 TO STORE: In each of four containers, add $2/3$ cup (150 mL) of the rice. Cover and refrigerate for up to 4 days or freeze for up to 2 months.

4 TO SERVE: If frozen, thaw in the refrigerator overnight. To reheat, microwave uncovered on High for 45 to 60 seconds. Allow 2 minutes for the heat to distribute before removing the container from the microwave. Serve warm.

TOBY'S TIP | If you prefer, swap the broccoli for the same amount of cauliflower.

COMPLETE YOUR PLATE

3 oz (90 g) cooked boneless skinless chicken breast and Roasted Carrots with Dill (page 242)

	TOTAL CALORIES	TOTAL FAT	SATURATED FAT	TRANS FAT
PER SERVING	173.30	4.47 g	0.67 g	0.0 g
	SODIUM 210.44 mg	**CHOLESTEROL** 0.0 mg	**TOTAL CARBOHYDRATES** 29.89 g	**FIBER** 2.97 g
	SUGARS 2.16 g	**PROTEIN** 4.35 g	**POTASSIUM** 242.05 mg	**PHOSPHORUS** 139.03 mg

ISRAELI COUSCOUS
WITH MUSHROOMS AND THYME

 · · · · ·

SERVES	SERVING SIZE	TOTAL TIME	PREP TIME	COOK TIME
4	¾ cup (175 mL)	45 minutes	15 minutes	30 minutes

Mushrooms add a depth of flavor known as umami. Plus, they add volume to your dish for few calories and carbs. See what varieties of mushrooms are available at your grocery, and switch up the type you add to this recipe to find your favorites.

1 tbsp (15 mL) olive oil

1 small onion, chopped

1 clove garlic, minced

8 oz (250 g) cremini mushrooms, chopped

²/₃ cup (150 mL) whole wheat Israeli (pearled) couscous

1¼ cups (300 mL) low-sodium vegetable broth

½ tsp (2 mL) dried thyme

¼ tsp (1 mL) salt

⅛ tsp (0.5 mL) ground black pepper

1 In a medium saucepan, heat the oil over medium heat. When the oil is shimmering, add the onion and garlic and cook until the onion softens and the garlic is fragrant, about 3 minutes. Add the mushrooms and cook until softened, 5 minutes.

2 Add the couscous, broth, thyme, salt and pepper and bring to a boil over high heat. Reduce the heat to low and simmer, covered, until the couscous is tender, 15 to 20 minutes. Fluff with a fork.

3 TO STORE: In each of four containers, add ¾ cup (175 mL) of the couscous. Cover and refrigerate for up to 4 days or freeze for up to 2 months.

4 TO SERVE: If frozen, thaw in the refrigerator overnight. To reheat, microwave uncovered on High for 45 to 60 seconds. Allow 2 minutes for the heat to distribute before removing the container from the microwave. Serve warm.

TOBY'S TIP | Choose mushrooms that are firm with a fresh, smooth appearance. The surface of the mushrooms should be plump and dry but not dried out. Store fresh mushrooms in their original packaging or in a paper bag in the refrigerator for up to 1 week.

COMPLETE YOUR PLATE

5 oz (150 g) cooked salmon and Sheet Pan Vegetable Medley (page 237)

	TOTAL CALORIES	TOTAL FAT	SATURATED FAT	TRANS FAT
PER SERVING	165.52	3.96 g	0.48 g	0.0 g
	SODIUM	**CHOLESTEROL**	**TOTAL CARBOHYDRATES**	**FIBER**
	196.77 mg	0.0 mg	29.19 g	3.65 g
	SUGARS	**PROTEIN**	**POTASSIUM**	**PHOSPHORUS**
	2.6 g	6.04 g	286.52 mg	74.37 mg

FARRO
WITH SPINACH

SERVES	SERVING SIZE	TOTAL TIME	PREP TIME	COOK TIME
6	½ cup (125 mL)	55 minutes	10 minutes	45 minutes

This Italian-born grain dates back to ancient Rome. It has a similar taste to brown rice, but with a slightly nuttier flavor and chewier texture.

1 tbsp (15 mL) olive oil

6 cups (1.5 L) baby spinach

2½ cups (625 mL) low-sodium vegetable broth

1 cup (250 mL) farro

¼ tsp (1 mL) salt

¼ tsp (1 mL) ground black pepper

COMPLETE YOUR PLATE

3 oz (90 g) cooked boneless skinless chicken breast and Sheet Pan Vegetable Medley (page 237)

1 In a large sauté pan, heat the oil over medium heat. When the oil is shimmering, add the spinach and cook until wilted, 3 minutes. Remove the pan from the heat and let cool slightly.

2 In a medium saucepan, add the vegetable broth, farro, salt and pepper and bring to a boil over high heat. Reduce the heat to low and simmer, covered, until the water is absorbed and the farro is tender, 40 minutes. Add the spinach to the farro and toss to combine.

3 TO STORE: In each of six containers, add ½ cup (125 mL) of the farro and spinach. Cover and refrigerate for up to 4 days or freeze for up to 2 months.

4 TO SERVE: If frozen, thaw in the refrigerator overnight. To reheat, microwave uncovered on High for 45 to 60 seconds. Allow 2 minutes for the heat to distribute before removing the container from the microwave. Serve warm.

TOBY'S TIP | Be sure to remove the spinach from the heat after 3 minutes, as leaving it to cook longer can destroy some of the vitamins.

PER SERVING	TOTAL CALORIES	TOTAL FAT	SATURATED FAT	TRANS FAT
	135.11	309 g	0.49 g	0.0 g
	SODIUM	CHOLESTEROL	TOTAL CARBOHYDRATES	FIBER
	193.91 mg	0.0 mg	21.61 g	5.43 g
	SUGARS	PROTEIN	POTASSIUM	PHOSPHORUS
	0.42 g	5.33 g	1.08 mg	0.0 mg

WHOLE WHEAT SPAGHETTI
WITH GARLIC AND OLIVE OIL

SERVES	SERVING SIZE	TOTAL TIME	PREP TIME	COOK TIME
6	$\frac{1}{2}$ cup (125 mL)	17 minutes	10 minutes	7 minutes

This simple pasta dish is a versatile side and easily adjustable. Change up the flavors by adding a handful of chopped fresh herbs or a squeeze of lemon. If you're worried about garlic breath at work, just leave the garlic out.

6 oz (175 g) 100% whole wheat spaghetti

3 tbsp (45 mL) olive oil

2 cloves garlic, minced

$\frac{1}{4}$ tsp (1 mL) salt

$\frac{1}{8}$ tsp (0.5 mL) ground black pepper

COMPLETE YOUR PLATE

3 oz (90 g) cooked boneless skinless chicken breast and Spicy Steamed Broccoli (page 240)

1 Fill a medium saucepan three-quarters with water and bring to a boil over high heat. Add the spaghetti and gently boil until it is al dente, 7 minutes. Using a colander, drain the water and return the pasta to the pot.

2 In a small bowl whisk together the oil, garlic, salt and pepper. Add the mixture to the pasta and toss to combine.

3 TO STORE: In each of six containers, add $\frac{1}{2}$ cup (125 mL) of the spaghetti. Cover and refrigerate for up to 4 days or freeze for up to 2 months.

4 TO SERVE: If frozen, thaw in the refrigerator overnight. To reheat, microwave uncovered on High for 60 to 90 seconds. Allow 2 minutes for the heat to distribute before removing the container from the microwave. Serve warm.

TOBY'S TIP | If you prefer, swap in another 100% whole wheat pasta, such as rotini, penne or macaroni.

	TOTAL CALORIES	TOTAL FAT	SATURATED FAT	TRANS FAT
PER SERVING	166.33	7.25 g	0.93 g	0.0 g
	SODIUM	CHOLESTEROL	TOTAL CARBOHYDRATES	FIBER
	98.55 mg	0.0 mg	21.33 g	1.02 g
	SUGARS	PROTEIN	POTASSIUM	PHOSPHORUS
	1.01 g	3.56 g	4.10 mg	1.53 mg

RED POTATOES
WITH CHIVES

SERVES	SERVING SIZE	TOTAL TIME	PREP TIME	COOK TIME
10	½ cup (125 mL)	50 minutes	20 minutes	30 minutes

Red potatoes are small to medium in size and have thin red skin and white flesh. The texture of these spuds is creamy and smooth with a subtly sweet flavor. These potatoes work well roasted (like in this recipe) or mashed, or try them in soups, stews and salads.

2 tbsp (30 mL) olive oil

2 cloves garlic, minced

1 tsp (5 mL) dried chives

¼ tsp (1 mL) salt

¼ tsp (1 mL) ground black pepper

2 lbs (1 kg) small red potatoes, thoroughly cleaned and dried

COMPLETE YOUR PLATE

Herbed Beef Fillets (page 226) and Spicy Steamed Broccoli (page 240)

Rimmed baking sheet lined with parchment paper
Preheat the oven to 425°F (220°C)

1. In a large bowl, whisk together the oil, garlic, chives, salt and pepper. Add the potatoes and toss to combine.

2. Place the potatoes in a single layer on the prepared baking sheet and bake, tossing halfway through, until tender, 30 minutes. Remove from the oven and let cool for 10 minutes.

3. TO STORE: In each of ten containers, add ½ cup (125 mL) of the potatoes. Cover and refrigerate for up to 4 days or freeze for up to 2 months.

4. TO SERVE: If frozen, thaw in the refrigerator overnight. To reheat, microwave uncovered on High for 90 seconds. Allow 2 minutes for the heat to distribute before removing the container from the microwave. Serve warm.

TOBY'S TIP | Store uncooked potatoes in a cool, dry place ideally at temperatures between 45 and 50°F (7 and 10°C). If stored properly, they can last for up to 5 months. If you find your potatoes are sprouting, cut off the offshoots before cooking. Storing potatoes in a well-ventilated area helps reduce sprouting.

PER SERVING	TOTAL CALORIES	TOTAL FAT	SATURATED FAT	
	82.20	2.15 g	0.31 g	0.0 g
	SODIUM	CHOLESTEROL	TOTAL CARBOHYDRATES	FIBER
	60.65 mg	0.0 mg	14.58 g	1.56 g
	SUGARS	PROTEIN	POTASSIUM	PHOSPHORUS
	1.17 g	1.75 g	415.50 mg	56.03 mg

SHEET PAN VEGETABLE MEDLEY

SERVES	SERVING SIZE	TOTAL TIME	PREP TIME	COOK TIME
6	¾ cup (175 mL)	40 minutes	20 minutes	20 minutes

A rainbow of vegetables means you're taking in more of the nutrients your body needs. This colorful array will brighten up any protein and starch you pair it with.

2 tbsp (30 mL) olive oil

2 tbsp (30 mL) balsamic vinegar

2 cloves garlic, minced

2 tsp (10 mL) Dijon mustard

1 tsp (5 mL) dried oregano

1 tsp (5 mL) dried basil

½ tsp (2 mL) dried rosemary

½ tsp (2 mL) dried thyme

¼ tsp (1 mL) salt

3 cups (750 mL) baby carrots
(12 oz/375 g)

3 cups (750 mL) broccoli florets
(8 oz/250 g)

2 yellow bell peppers, cut into
1-inch (2.5 cm) strips

Rimmed baking sheet lined with parchment paper
Preheat the oven to 425°F (220°C)

1 In a large bowl, whisk together the oil, vinegar, garlic, Dijon mustard, oregano, basil, rosemary, thyme and salt. Add the carrots, broccoli and bell peppers and toss to evenly coat.

2 Place the vegetables in a single layer on the prepared baking sheet. Roast, turning once halfway through, until the vegetables are browned, 18 to 20 minutes.

3 TO STORE: In each of six containers, add ¾ cup (175 mL) of the vegetables. Cover and refrigerate for up to 4 days or freeze for up to 2 months.

4 TO SERVE: If frozen, thaw in the refrigerator overnight. To reheat, microwave uncovered on High for 1 minute. Allow 2 minutes for the heat to distribute before removing the container from the microwave. Serve warm.

TOBY'S TIP | To change things up, swap out one of the vegetables in this recipe for halved Brussels sprouts or 2-inch (5 cm) slices of zucchini or summer squash.

COMPLETE YOUR PLATE

Roasted Salmon in Barbecue Sauce (page 102) and Whole Wheat Spaghetti with Garlic and Olive Oil (page 235)

	TOTAL CALORIES	TOTAL FAT	SATURATED FAT	TRANS FAT
PER SERVING	79.60	3.73 g	0.52 g	0.0 g
	SODIUM 147.25 mg	**CHOLESTEROL** 0.0 mg	**TOTAL CARBOHYDRATES** 10.53 g	**FIBER** 2.43 g
	SUGARS 4.98 g	**PROTEIN** 2.03 g	**POTASSIUM** 356.01 mg	**PHOSPHORUS** 53.60 mg

ROASTED SWEET POTATOES

 · · ·   ·

SERVES	SERVING SIZE	TOTAL TIME	PREP TIME	COOK TIME
8	½ cup (125 mL)	40 minutes	15 minutes	25 minutes

These lightly seasoned oven-roasted sweet potatoes are so scrumptious that you'll forget they are heart healthy. This side dish is sure to become part of your regular meal prepping repertoire.

2 tbsp (30 mL) olive oil

1 tsp (5 mL) ground cumin

½ tsp (2 mL) chili powder

¼ tsp (1 mL) salt

3 sweet potatoes (2 lbs/1 kg), peeled and cut into 1-inch (2.5 cm) dice

COMPLETE YOUR PLATE

Sheet Pan Chili-Lime Salmon with Peppers (page 202)

Rimmed baking sheet lined with parchment paper
Preheat the oven to 400°F (200°C)

1 In a large bowl, whisk together the oil, cumin, chili powder and salt. Add the potatoes and toss to evenly coat.

2 Place the sweet potatoes in a single layer on the prepared baking sheet. Roast, tossing halfway through, until the potatoes are fork-tender, 20 to 25 minutes.

3 TO STORE: In each of eight containers, add ½ cup (125 mL) of the sweet potatoes. Cover and refrigerate for up to 4 days or freeze for up to 2 months.

4 TO SERVE: If frozen, thaw in the refrigerator overnight. To reheat, microwave uncovered on High for 60 to 90 seconds. Allow 2 minutes for the heat to distribute before removing the container from the microwave. Serve warm.

TOBY'S TIP | If you prefer, swap the sweet potatoes for russet potatoes.

	TOTAL CALORIES	TOTAL FAT	SATURATED FAT	TRANS FAT
PER SERVING	106.05	2.64 g	0.37 g	0.0 g
	SODIUM	**CHOLESTEROL**	**TOTAL CARBOHYDRATES**	**FIBER**
	109.56 mg	0.0 mg	19.39 g	2.97 g
	SUGARS	**PROTEIN**	**POTASSIUM**	**PHOSPHORUS**
	4.0 g	1.55 g	326.56 mg	44.97 mg

SPICY STEAMED BROCCOLI

 · · · ·

SERVES	SERVING SIZE	TOTAL TIME	PREP TIME	COOK TIME
6	¾ cup (175 mL)	20 minutes	15 minutes	5 minutes

Broccoli is one of the most beloved vegetables by both kids and adults. Dress it up with a touch of garlic and chile — simple, easy and delicious.

2 tbsp (30 mL) olive oil

1 tsp (5 mL) garlic powder

¼ tsp (1 mL) salt

⅛ tsp (0.5 mL) hot pepper flakes

6 cups (1.5 L) broccoli florets

COMPLETE YOUR PLATE

Herbed Garlic Butter Pork Chops (page 220) and Red Potatoes with Chives (page 236)

1 In a small bowl, whisk together the oil, garlic powder, salt and hot pepper flakes.

2 Fill a large saucepan with 1 inch (2.5 cm) of water and fit it with a steamer basket. Add the broccoli, then cover and bring the water to a boil over high heat. Steam until the broccoli is cooked yet firm, 5 minutes.

3 Immediately transfer the broccoli to a large bowl. Drizzle with the olive oil mixture and toss to evenly coat.

4 TO STORE: In each of six containers, add ¾ cup (175 mL) of the broccoli. Cover and refrigerate for up to 4 days or freeze for up to 2 months.

5 TO SERVE: If frozen, thaw in the refrigerator overnight. To reheat, microwave uncovered on High for 45 seconds. Allow 2 minutes for the heat to distribute before removing the container from the microwave. Serve warm.

TOBY'S TIP | Choose broccoli heads with tight, bluish-green florets. They should be odorless and have firm stalks. Store fresh broccoli unwashed in an unsealed plastic bag. Alternatively, wrap the broccoli in a damp paper towel. Use within 5 days.

	TOTAL CALORIES	TOTAL FAT	SATURATED FAT	TRANS FAT
PER SERVING	61.20	4.75 g	0.66 g	0.0 g
	SODIUM	CHOLESTEROL	TOTAL CARBOHYDRATES	FIBER
	117.78 mg	0.0 mg	4.06 g	0.04 g
	SUGARS	PROTEIN	POTASSIUM	PHOSPHORUS
	0.01 g	2.19 g	236.37 mg	48.79 mg

ROASTED CARROTS
WITH DILL

SERVES	SERVING SIZE	TOTAL TIME	PREP TIME	COOK TIME
6	½ cup (125 mL)	40 minutes	15 minutes	25 minutes

Who says meal prep can't be simple and flavorful? In this dish, carrots are tossed in a quick and easy mixture where fresh dill is the star — and the flavor is out of this world!

¼ cup (60 mL) fresh dill, chopped

2 tbsp (30 mL) olive oil

¼ tsp (1 mL) salt

⅛ tsp (0.5 mL) ground black pepper

1½ lbs (750 g) baby carrots

COMPLETE YOUR PLATE

3 oz (90 g) cooked boneless skinless chicken breast and Easy Herbed Quinoa (page 230)

Rimmed baking sheet lined with parchment paper

Preheat the oven to 400°F (200°C)

1 In a large bowl, whisk together the dill, oil, salt and pepper. Add the carrots and toss to evenly coat.

2 Spread the carrots in a single layer on the prepared baking sheet. Roast, tossing halfway through, until the carrots are slightly browned, 25 minutes.

3 TO STORE: In each of six containers, add ½ cup (125 mL) of the carrots. Cover and refrigerate for up to 4 days or freeze for up to 2 months.

4 TO SERVE: If frozen, thaw in the refrigerator overnight. To reheat, microwave uncovered on High for 45 seconds. Allow 2 minutes for the heat to distribute before removing the container from the microwave. Serve warm.

TOBY'S TIP | If you prefer, swap the baby carrots for 1½ lbs (750 g) peeled carrots cut into 3-inch (7.5 cm) sticks.

	TOTAL CALORIES	TOTAL FAT	SATURATED FAT	TRANS FAT
PER SERVING	79.80	4.65 g	0.64 g	0.0 g
	SODIUM	CHOLESTEROL	TOTAL CARBOHYDRATES	FIBER
	187.01 mg	0.0 mg	9.37 g	3.30 g
	SUGARS	PROTEIN	POTASSIUM	PHOSPHORUS
	5.40 g	0.74 g	271.56 mg	32.0 mg

BRUSSELS SPROUTS
WITH TURKEY BACON

	SERVES	SERVING SIZE	TOTAL TIME	PREP TIME	COOK TIME
	6	1 cup (250 mL)	45 minutes	15 minutes	30 minutes

Brussels sprouts are part of the cabbage family and are packed with flavor and nutrition. A $\frac{1}{2}$ cup (125 mL) of cooked Brussels sprouts is an excellent source of vitamins A, C and K and a good source of folate. Plus, they're also packed with vitamin B6, thiamin, potassium and manganese — so dig in!

$1\frac{1}{2}$ lbs (750 g) Brussels sprouts, trimmed and halved

2 tbsp (30 mL) olive oil

$\frac{1}{4}$ tsp (1 mL) salt

$\frac{1}{8}$ tsp (0.5 mL) ground black pepper

Cooking spray

2 oz (60 g) turkey bacon (2 slices)

COMPLETE YOUR PLATE

Parmesan-Crusted Chicken Breasts (page 210) and Whole Wheat Spaghetti with Garlic and Olive Oil (page 235)

Rimmed baking sheet lined with parchment paper
Preheat the oven to 425°F (220°C)

1 In a large bowl, add the Brussels sprouts, oil, salt and pepper and toss to coat evenly.

2 Spread the Brussels sprouts in a single layer on the prepared baking sheet. Bake, turning halfway through, until the Brussels sprouts are slightly browned, about 20 minutes. Remove from the oven and transfer the Brussels sprouts to a clean large bowl.

3 Coat a large skillet with cooking spray and place over medium heat. When the oil is shimmering, add the bacon and cook, turning occasionally, until crisp, 8 minutes. Remove the bacon to a cutting board and let cool for 8 minutes.

4 Coarsely chop the bacon and add it to the Brussels sprouts. Toss to combine.

5 TO STORE: In each of six containers, add 1 cup (250 mL) of the Brussels sprouts. Cover and refrigerate for up to 4 days or freeze for up to 2 months.

6 TO SERVE: If frozen, thaw in the refrigerator overnight. To reheat, microwave uncovered on High for 45 seconds. Allow 2 minutes for the heat to distribute before removing the container from the microwave. Serve warm.

	TOTAL CALORIES	TOTAL FAT	SATURATED FAT	TRANS FAT
PER SERVING	112.28	6.53 g	1.37 g	0.0 g
	SODIUM	CHOLESTEROL	TOTAL CARBOHYDRATES	FIBER
	248.19 mg	10.12 mg	10.18 g	4.32 g
	SUGARS	PROTEIN	POTASSIUM	PHOSPHORUS
	2.50 g	5.19 g	441.78 mg	78.32 mg

EGGPLANT
WITH TOMATOES AND CUMIN

 · · · · ·

SERVES	SERVING SIZE	TOTAL TIME	PREP TIME	COOK TIME
6	2/3 cup (150 mL)	36 minutes	15 minutes	21 minutes

My family is from the Mediterranean region, where my mom learned to make lots of vegetable dishes with cumin and tomatoes. This dish is perfect for meal prepping and reheating, especially with the tomato-based sauce.

2 tbsp (30 mL) olive oil

2 cloves garlic, minced

1 eggplant, diced into 2-inch (5 cm) cubes

1¾ cups (425 mL) no-salt-added canned diced tomatoes, with juice

1 tsp (5 mL) ground cumin

1 tsp (5 mL) smoked paprika

¼ tsp (1 mL) salt

⅛ tsp (0.5 mL) ground black pepper

COMPLETE YOUR PLATE

Herbed Beef Fillets (page 226) and Red Potatoes with Chives (page 236)

1 In a large sauté pan, heat the olive oil over medium heat. When the oil is shimmering, add the garlic and cook until fragrant, 30 seconds. Add the eggplant and cook until softened, 10 minutes, turning occasionally.

2 Add the diced tomatoes with juice, cumin, smoked paprika, salt and pepper and toss to combine. Raise the heat to high and bring the mixture to a boil. Reduce the heat to medium-low and simmer, covered, until the flavors combine, 10 minutes.

3 TO STORE: In each of six containers, add 2/3 cup (150 mL) of the eggplant mixture. Cover and refrigerate for up to 4 days or freeze for up to 2 months.

4 TO SERVE: If frozen, thaw in the refrigerator overnight. To reheat, microwave uncovered on High for 1 minute. Allow 2 minutes for the heat to distribute before removing the container from the microwave. Serve warm.

TOBY'S TIP | When choosing eggplants, pick them up. They should feel heavy in your hand. The skin should be smooth and shiny, and when you press your fingers, it should feel slightly firm. Choose small- to medium-size eggplant, as the larger sizes tend to be bitter.

	TOTAL CALORIES	TOTAL FAT	SATURATED FAT	TRANS FAT
PER SERVING	87.99	4.79 g	0.65 g	0.0 g
	SODIUM	CHOLESTEROL	TOTAL CARBOHYDRATES	FIBER
	101.31 mg	0.0 mg	8.84 g	4.22 g
	SUGARS	PROTEIN	POTASSIUM	PHOSPHORUS
	4.30 g	2.21 g	409.39 mg	93.65 mg

CHAPTER 14

DRESSINGS, CONDIMENTS AND SAUCES

HERBED VINAIGRETTE

 · · · ·

MAKES	SERVING SIZE	TOTAL TIME	PREP TIME	COOK TIME
1 cup (250 mL)	2 tbsp (30 mL)	15 minutes	15 minutes	0 minutes

There's nothing better than making your own vinaigrette. The bottled versions tend to be higher sodium and added sugar. This easy-to-make vinaigrette purées all the ingredients in a blender, so you press a button and it's done!

1 shallot, coarsely chopped

1 clove garlic, crushed

3 tbsp (45 mL) white wine vinegar

Juice of 1 lemon

¼ cup (60 mL) fresh parsley, coarsely chopped

¼ cup (60 mL) fresh basil, coarsely chopped

2 tsp (10 mL) Dijon mustard

½ tsp (2 mL) salt

¼ tsp (1 mL) ground black pepper

¼ cup (60 mL) extra virgin olive oil

Blender

1 Add the shallot, garlic, vinegar, lemon juice, parsley, basil, mustard, salt and pepper to a blender and blend on High until smooth. Slowly add the olive oil and blend until incorporated.

2 TO STORE: Transfer the vinaigrette to a sealable container. Cover and refrigerate for up to 5 days.

TOBY'S TIP | You can swap the herbs for whatever you have available, like cilantro, rosemary or thyme.

	TOTAL CALORIES	TOTAL FAT	SATURATED FAT	TRANS FAT
PER SERVING	66.59	7.04 g	1.01 g	0.0 g
	SODIUM	CHOLESTEROL	TOTAL CARBOHYDRATES	FIBER
	166.02 mg	0.0 mg	1.49 g	0.25 g
	SUGARS	PROTEIN	POTASSIUM	PHOSPHORUS
	0.51 g	0.24 g	34.76 mg	5.39 mg

BALSAMIC VINAIGRETTE

MAKES	SERVING SIZE	TOTAL TIME	PREP TIME	COOK TIME
¾ cup (175 mL)	2 tbsp (30 mL)	10 minutes	10 minutes	0 minutes

This dressing goes with almost any salad you choose to make. It just might become your go-to dressing for meal prepping.

½ cup (125 mL) balsamic vinegar

¼ cup (60 mL) water

2 tsp (10 mL) stevia brown sugar blend (such as Truvia or Splenda)

1 tbsp (15 mL) Dijon mustard

¼ tsp (1 mL) salt

⅛ tsp (0.5 mL) ground black pepper

3 tbsp (45 mL) extra virgin olive oil

1 In a small bowl, whisk together the vinegar, water, brown sugar blend, mustard, salt and pepper. Slowly drizzle in the olive oil while whisking continuously until incorporated.

2 TO STORE: Transfer the vinaigrette to a sealable container. Cover and refrigerate for up to 1 week.

TOBY'S TIP | Store oils, including extra virgin olive oil, in a cool, dark place away from the light. Do not store oils next to your stove, as the heat will spoil them faster.

PER SERVING	TOTAL CALORIES	TOTAL FAT	SATURATED FAT	TRANS FAT
	87.48	7.0 g	1.0 g	0.0 g
	SODIUM	CHOLESTEROL	TOTAL CARBOHYDRATES	FIBER
	135.93 mg	0.0 mg	5.49 g	0.01 g
	SUGARS	PROTEIN	POTASSIUM	PHOSPHORUS
	4.51 g	0.11 g	24.51 mg	4.11 mg

SIMPLE LEMON-HERB VINAIGRETTE

 · · · · ·

MAKES 1/2 cup (125 mL)	SERVING SIZE 2 tbsp (30 mL)	TOTAL TIME 15 minutes	PREP TIME 15 minutes	COOK TIME 0 minutes

Every time I head to the grocery, I pick up a few lemons and stash them in a basket on my countertop so I always have them on hand. Their versatility and clean flavor is perfect for so many dishes, from grain salads to vegetables to chicken and fish.

1/4 cup (60 mL) fresh lemon juice (juice of 2 lemons)

2 tbsp (30 mL) apple cider vinegar

1 tsp (5 mL) lemon zest

1/4 tsp (1 mL) ground oregano

1/4 tsp (1 mL) dried basil

1/4 tsp (1 mL) salt

1/8 tsp (0.5 mL) ground black pepper

3 tbsp (45 mL) extra virgin olive oil

1 In a small bowl, whisk together the lemon juice, vinegar, lemon zest, oregano, basil, salt and pepper. Slowly drizzle in the olive oil while whisking continuously until incorporated.

2 TO STORE: Transfer the vinaigrette to a sealable container. Cover and refrigerate for up to 1 week.

TOBY'S TIP | Choose lemons that are bright yellow, firm and plump. They should be heavy for their size. Store for up to 7 days at room temperature or in the refrigerator drawer for up to 3 weeks.

PER SERVING	TOTAL CALORIES 62.85	TOTAL FAT 7.03 g	SATURATED FAT 1.01 g	TRANS FAT 0.0 g
	SODIUM 98.44 mg	CHOLESTEROL 0.0 mg	TOTAL CARBOHYDRATES 0.86 g	FIBER x g
	SUGARS 0.27 g	PROTEIN 0.07 g	POTASSIUM 14.20 mg	PHOSPHORUS 1.21 mg

LIGHTER PARMESAN DRESSING

MAKES	SERVING SIZE	TOTAL TIME	PREP TIME	COOK TIME
¾ cup (175 mL)	2 tbsp (30 mL)	10 minutes	10 minutes	0 minutes

Parmesan cheese has a potent flavor, which means that a little bit goes a long way!

¼ cup (60 mL) light mayonnaise

¼ cup (60 mL) nonfat plain Greek yogurt

½ cup (125 mL) low-fat buttermilk

1½ tbsp (22 mL) grated Parmesan cheese

2 cloves garlic, crushed

2 tsp (10 mL) Worcestershire sauce

1 tsp (5 mL) white wine vinegar

¼ tsp (1 mL) dried parsley flakes

⅛ tsp (0.5 mL) salt

⅛ tsp (0.5 mL) ground black pepper

Blender

1 In a blender, add the mayonnaise, yogurt, buttermilk, Parmesan cheese, garlic, Worcestershire sauce, vinegar, parsley, salt and pepper. Blend on High until smooth.

2 TO STORE: Store the dressing in a sealable container in the refrigerator for up to 5 days.

TOBY'S TIP | Try this flavorful dressing on a Caesar salad or on the Tuna with Mixed Greens (page 178).

	TOTAL CALORIES	TOTAL FAT	SATURATED FAT	TRANS FAT
PER SERVING	60.46	3.9 g	0.71 g	0.02 g
	SODIUM	CHOLESTEROL	TOTAL CARBOHYDRATES	FIBER
	219.97 mg	6.22 mg	3.3 g	0.06 g
	SUGARS	PROTEIN	POTASSIUM	PHOSPHORUS
	2.45 g	3.42 g	70.48 mg	59.29 mg

WALNUT BASIL DRESSING

MAKES	SERVING SIZE	TOTAL TIME	PREP TIME	COOK TIME
1/2 cup (125 mL)	2 tbsp (30 mL)	15 minutes	15 minutes	0 minutes

How do you get nuts into a dressing? Blend them in! Walnuts add a nutty flavor to this dressing, along with nutrients like copper, manganese, magnesium, phosphorus and omega-3 fats.

1 cup (250 mL) fresh basil leaves

1/3 cup (75 mL) raw or unsalted roasted walnuts, coarsely chopped

1/4 cup (60 mL) water

3 tbsp (45 mL) red wine vinegar

1 clove garlic, crushed

1 tsp (5 mL) stevia brown sugar blend (such as Truvia or Splenda)

1/4 tsp (1 mL) salt

1/8 tsp (0.5 mL) ground black pepper

3 tbsp (45 mL) extra virgin olive oil

Blender

1 Place the basil, walnuts, water, vinegar, garlic, brown sugar blend, salt and pepper in a blender and blend on High until smooth. Slowly drizzle in the olive oil and blend until incorporated.

2 TO STORE: Transfer the dressing to a sealable container. Cover and refrigerate for up to 1 week.

TOBY'S TIP | Choose fresh basil with bright green leaves without yellow or brown spots. Place the cut stems in a container of water and store on the windowsill for up to 1 week, changing the water every other day. You can also store basil in the refrigerator wrapped in a damp paper towel for up to 4 days.

	TOTAL CALORIES	TOTAL FAT	SATURATED FAT	TRANS FAT
PER SERVING	154.29	15.98 g	2.02 g	0.0 g
	SODIUM	CHOLESTEROL	TOTAL CARBOHYDRATES	FIBER
	149.25 mg	0.0 mg	2.62 g	0.69 g
	SUGARS	PROTEIN	POTASSIUM	PHOSPHORUS
	1.24 g	1.52 g	62.89 mg	34.34 mg

MANGO SALSA

MAKES	SERVING SIZE	TOTAL TIME	PREP TIME	COOK TIME
2¼ cups (560 mL)	2 tbsp (30 mL)	15 minutes	15 minutes	0 minutes

Mango salsa has a sweet and spicy flavor that complements many dishes. Try it over white fish or chicken, or use it as a dip for tortilla chips or vegetables.

1 mango, peeled, pitted and finely diced

½ red bell pepper, finely diced

¼ small red onion, chopped

½ jalapeño pepper, seeds removed and chopped

¼ cup (60 mL) chopped cilantro

Juice of 2 limes

¼ tsp (1 mL) salt

1. In a medium bowl, add the mango, bell pepper, red onion, jalapeño, cilantro, lime juice and salt. Toss to combine. Refrigerate for at least 20 minutes to allow the flavors to blend.

2. **TO STORE:** Transfer the salsa to a sealable container. Cover and refrigerate for up to 4 days.

TOBY'S TIP | Change up the flavors of this salsa by swapping the mango for papaya.

	TOTAL CALORIES	TOTAL FAT	SATURATED FAT	TRANS FAT
PER SERVING	9.33	0.06 g	0.01 g	0.0 g
	SODIUM 33.22 mg	**CHOLESTEROL** 0.0 mg	**TOTAL CARBOHYDRATES** 2.33 g	**FIBER** 0.3 g
	SUGARS 1.83 g	**PROTEIN** 0.16 g	**POTASSIUM** 33.85 mg	**PHOSPHORUS** 3.44 mg

TOMATO SALSA

 · · · ·

MAKES	SERVING SIZE	TOTAL TIME	PREP TIME	COOK TIME
4 cups (1 L)	2 tbsp (30 mL)	20 minutes	20 minutes	0 minutes

There's nothing more satisfying than making your own salsa. During the summer months when tomatoes are in season, choose different varieties and colors to jazz up your salsa.

1 lb (500 g) plum (Roma) tomatoes

1 green bell pepper, cored, seeded and chopped

1/4 red onion, chopped

1 jalapeño, seeds and ribs removed, chopped

1/4 cup (60 mL) chopped cilantro

Juice of 2 limes

2 tbsp (30 mL) extra virgin olive oil

1 clove garlic, minced

1/2 tsp (2 mL) salt

1/8 tsp (0.5 mL) ground black pepper

1. In a medium bowl, mix together the tomatoes, bell pepper, red onion, jalapeño and cilantro.

2. Add the lime juice, olive oil, garlic, salt and black pepper and toss to evenly coat.

3. TO STORE: Transfer to a sealable container. Cover and refrigerate for up to 5 days.

TOBY'S TIP | Use leftover salsa paired with tortilla chips for a snack throughout the week.

	TOTAL CALORIES	TOTAL FAT	SATURATED FAT	TRANS FAT
PER SERVING	12.08	0.92 g	0.13 g	0.0 g
	SODIUM	CHOLESTEROL	TOTAL CARBOHYDRATES	FIBER
	38.19 mg	0.0 mg	0.99 g	0.29 g
	SUGARS	PROTEIN	POTASSIUM	PHOSPHORUS
	0.53 g	0.23 g	52.95 mg	5.78 mg

TERIYAKI MARINADE

MAKES	SERVING SIZE	TOTAL TIME	PREP TIME	COOK TIME
¾ cup (175 mL)	1 tbsp (15 mL)	10 minutes	10 minutes	0 minutes

This teriyaki marinade pairs well with chicken, pork, fish, tofu and even vegetables. It only takes a few moments to whisk up and can be used to marinate chicken, fish, beef, tofu or pork, like in Teriyaki Pork Tenderloin (page 117).

¼ cup (60 mL) low-sodium vegetable broth

¼ cup (60 mL) water

3 tbsp (45 mL) reduced-sodium soy sauce

5 tsp (25 mL) stevia brown sugar blend (such as Truvia or Splenda)

2 cloves garlic, minced

¼ tsp (1 mL) ground ginger

1 In a medium bowl, whisk together the broth, water, soy sauce, brown sugar blend, garlic and ginger.

2 TO STORE: Transfer to a sealable container. Cover and refrigerate for up to 1 week.

TOBY'S TIP | After marinating your food, shake off excess marinade before placing your food to cook and discard any leftover marinade.

	TOTAL CALORIES	TOTAL FAT	SATURATED FAT	TRANS FAT
PER SERVING	Total Calories: 13.27	0.0 g	0.0 g	0.0 g
	SODIUM	CHOLESTEROL	TOTAL CARBOHYDRATES	FIBER
	142.74 mg	0.0 mg	2.42 g	0.04 g
	SUGARS	PROTEIN	POTASSIUM	PHOSPHORUS
	2.19 g	0.56 g	2.55 mg	0.83 mg

SOY-GARLIC MARINADE

MAKES	SERVING SIZE	TOTAL TIME	PREP TIME	COOK TIME
¾ cup (175 mL)	1 tbsp (15 mL)	10 minutes	10 minutes	0 minutes

Having easy, tasty marinade recipes on hand helps make meal prepping easier. This marinade pairs nicely on beef, chicken, fish, tofu and cooked vegetables.

6 tbsp (90 mL) olive oil

¼ cup (60 mL) water

3 tbsp (45 mL) reduced-sodium soy sauce

4 cloves garlic, minced

Juice of 1 lemon

½ tsp (2 mL) stevia brown sugar blend (such as Truvia or Splenda)

⅛ tsp (0.5 mL) hot pepper flakes

1 In a small bowl, whisk together the olive oil, water, soy sauce, garlic, lemon juice, brown sugar blend and hot pepper flakes.

2 TO STORE: Transfer to a sealable container. Cover and refrigerate for up to 1 week.

TOBY'S TIP | If you prefer, substitute the garlic cloves with 1½ tsp (7 mL) garlic powder.

	TOTAL CALORIES	TOTAL FAT	SATURATED FAT	TRANS FAT
PER SERVING	65.05	6.76 g	0.93 g	0.0 g
	SODIUM	CHOLESTEROL	TOTAL CARBOHYDRATES	FIBER
	97.98 mg	0.0 mg	1.17 g	0.03 g
	SUGARS	PROTEIN	POTASSIUM	PHOSPHORUS
	0.74 g	0.32 g	6.74 mg	1.73 mg

LEMON TAHINI SAUCE

MAKES	SERVING SIZE	TOTAL TIME	PREP TIME	COOK TIME
³/₄ cup (175 mL)	2 tbsp (30 mL)	10 minutes	10 minutes	0 minutes

Tahini is a paste made from sesame seeds and is commonly used in Mediterranean cuisine. You can use it as a dip for fresh vegetables or drizzle it over grains like couscous and brown rice.

¹/₃ cup (75 mL) tahini

¹/₄ cup (60 mL) warm water

Juice of 1 lemon

1 tbsp (15 mL) olive oil

1 clove garlic, minced

¹/₄ tsp (1 mL) stevia brown sugar blend (such as Truvia or Splenda)

¹/₄ tsp (1 mL) salt

¹/₈ tsp (0.5 mL) ground black pepper

1 In a small bowl, whisk together the tahini with the warm water. Add the lemon juice, oil, garlic, brown sugar blend, salt and pepper and whisk to combine.

2 TO STORE: Transfer to a sealable container. Cover and refrigerate for up to 1 week.

TOBY'S TIP | You can find tahini in your supermarket in the condiment aisle or in the international food aisle.

	TOTAL CALORIES	TOTAL FAT	SATURATED FAT	TRANS FAT
PER SERVING	99.53	8.67 g	1.21	0.0 g
	SODIUM	CHOLESTEROL	TOTAL CARBOHYDRATES	FIBER
	108.59 mg	0.0 mg	4.37 g	1.28 g
	SUGARS	PROTEIN	POTASSIUM	PHOSPHORUS
	0.47 g	2.43 g	63.17 mg	101.51 mg

HOMEMADE TOMATO SAUCE

MAKES	SERVING SIZE	TOTAL TIME	PREP TIME	COOK TIME
5 cups (1.25 L)	¼ cup (60 mL)	35 minutes	10 minutes	25 minutes

Those jars of low-sodium pasta sauce can cost a pretty penny! Luckily, you can make your own using easy to find ingredients at your local market. You can even make a double batch and store half in the freezer for another week.

2 tbsp (30 mL) olive oil

5 cloves garlic, minced

3½ cups (875 mL) no-salt-added canned whole peeled plum tomatoes, with juice

3¼ cups (810 mL)) no-salt-added canned crushed tomatoes, with juice

1 tsp (5 mL) dried basil

1 tsp (5 mL) dried parsley

1 tsp (5 mL) dried oregano

1 tsp (5 mL) salt

½ tsp (2 mL) ground black pepper

Blender

1 In a medium pot, heat the oil over medium heat. When the oil is shimmering, add the garlic and cook until fragrant, about 30 seconds. Add the plum tomatoes with juice, crushed tomatoes with juice, basil, parsley, oregano, salt and pepper and stir to combine.

2 Cover and bring to a boil over high heat. Reduce the heat to low and simmer, covered, breaking up the tomatoes as they cook. Cook until the tomatoes have softened, 20 minutes. Remove the pot from the heat and let cool for 10 to 15 minutes.

3 Transfer the sauce to a blender and blend on High until smooth.

4 **TO STORE:** Transfer the tomato sauce to a sealable container. Cover and refrigerate for up to 5 days or freeze for up to 2 months.

5 **TO SERVE:** If frozen, thaw in the refrigerator overnight. Reheat individual portions in the microwave uncovered on High for 60 seconds. Alternatively, reheat in a saucepan on the stove by bringing the sauce to a boil and simmering over low heat until heated through, about 10 minutes. Serve warm.

TOBY'S TIP | Like your tomato sauce very garlicky? Add 1 or 2 more cloves of garlic.

PER SERVING			
TOTAL CALORIES 39.35	**TOTAL FAT** 1.36 g	**SATURATED FAT** 0.19 g	**TRANS FAT** 0.0 g
SODIUM 127.80 mg	**CHOLESTEROL** 0.0 mg	**TOTAL CARBOHYDRATES** 4.86 g	**FIBER** 1.37 g
SUGARS 3.23 g	**PROTEIN** 1.06 g	**POTASSIUM** 213.03 mg	**PHOSPHORUS** 40.45 mg

EASY BARBECUE SAUCE

MAKES	SERVING SIZE	TOTAL TIME	PREP TIME	COOK TIME
1 cup (250 mL)	2 tbsp (30 mL)	10 minutes	10 minutes	0 minutes

Many store-bought barbecue sauces contain too much added sugar. By making your own, you take control over the ingredients.

1 cup (250 mL) plus 2 tbsp (30 mL) no-salt-added ketchup

2 tbsp (30 mL) apple cider vinegar

2 tbsp (30 mL) Worcestershire sauce

2 tsp (10 mL) stevia brown sugar blend (such as Truvia or Splenda)

2 tsp (10 mL) smoked paprika

2 cloves garlic, minced

1/4 tsp (1 mL) salt

1. In a small bowl, whisk together the ketchup, vinegar, Worcestershire sauce, brown sugar blend, smoked paprika, garlic and salt.

2. TO STORE: Transfer the sauce to a sealable container. Cover and refrigerate for up to 1 week.

TOBY'S TIP | Try this as a marinade for steak, chicken, tofu or salmon.

	TOTAL CALORIES	TOTAL FAT	SATURATED FAT	TRANS FAT
PER SERVING	57.07	0.10 g	0.0 g	0.0 g
	SODIUM	CHOLESTEROL	TOTAL CARBOHYDRATES	FIBER
	100.66 mg	0.0 mg	13.55 g	0.22 g
	SUGARS	PROTEIN	POTASSIUM	PHOSPHORUS
	10.76 g	0.15 g	16.82 mg	1.15 mg

SIMPLE PESTO SAUCE

MAKES	SERVING SIZE	TOTAL TIME	PREP TIME	COOK TIME
½ cup (125 mL)	1 tbsp (15 mL)	10 minutes	10 minutes	0 minutes

Of course you can buy pesto at the store, but it is also incredibly easy to whip up your own. Give this recipe a whirl and you'll be making your own fresh pesto from now on. The flavor is beyond compare, and you'll know exactly what goes into the recipe.

1½ cups (375 mL) fresh basil leaves

¼ cup (60 mL) grated Parmesan cheese

¼ cup (60 mL) pine nuts

3 cloves garlic, crushed

¼ tsp (1 mL) salt

⅓ cup (75 mL) extra virgin olive oil

1 Place the basil, Parmesan cheese, pine nuts, garlic and salt in a blender and blend until smooth. While the machine is running, drizzle in the olive oil until incorporated.

2 TO STORE: Transfer the pesto to a sealable container. Cover and refrigerate for up to 1 week.

TOBY'S TIP | If you prefer, swap the pine nuts for walnuts.

	TOTAL CALORIES	TOTAL FAT	SATURATED FAT	TRANS FAT
PER SERVING	124.13	12.81 g	1.99 g	0.0 g
	SODIUM	**CHOLESTEROL**	**TOTAL CARBOHYDRATES**	**FIBER**
	122.10 mg	2.75 mg	1.17 g	0.25 g
	SUGARS	**PROTEIN**	**POTASSIUM**	**PHOSPHORUS**
	0.20 g	1.99 g	46.98 mg	51.28 mg

SPICY PEANUT DRESSING

MAKES	SERVING SIZE	TOTAL TIME	PREP TIME	COOK TIME
¾ cup (175 mL)	2 tbsp (30 mL)	10 minutes	10 minutes	0 minutes

This Thai-inspired, peanut butter–based dressing combines the tart flavor of lime juice with the umami flavor of soy sauce. Add garlic and ginger and you've got a delicious salad dressing that can also be used as a marinade for chicken, pork, fish and tofu.

¼ cup (60 mL) creamy peanut butter

1½ tbsp (22 mL) reduced-sodium soy sauce

2 tbsp (30 mL) warm water

Juice of 2 limes

1 tbsp (15 mL) unseasoned rice vinegar

2 cloves garlic, minced

2 tsp (10 mL) Thai chile sauce (such as Sriracha)

1 tsp (5 mL) stevia brown sugar blend (such as Truvia or Splenda)

¼ tsp (1 mL) ground ginger

1 In a medium bowl, whisk together the peanut butter, soy sauce, water, lime juice, rice vinegar, garlic, Thai chile sauce, brown sugar blend and ginger.

2 TO STORE: Transfer to a sealable container and refrigerate for up to 1 week.

TOBY'S TIP | If you would like the dressing thinner, after whisking all your ingredients add more warm water — 1 tbsp (15 mL) at a time — until the desired consistency is reached.

	TOTAL CALORIES	TOTAL FAT	SATURATED FAT	TRANS FAT
PER SERVING	74.50	5.68 g	1.17 g	0.0 g
	SODIUM	**CHOLESTEROL**	**TOTAL CARBOHYDRATES**	**FIBER**
	225.08 mg	0.0 mg	4.28 g	0.73 g
	SUGARS	**PROTEIN**	**POTASSIUM**	**PHOSPHORUS**
	2.14 g	2.69 g	14.06 mg	2.73 mg

ACKNOWLEDGMENTS

Every cookbook I write takes a team effort. There are many people I want to thank for making this amazing cookbook possible. First and foremost, I want to thank my three children, Schoen, Ellena and Micah, for supporting me through this long process and all the recipes you taste tested. All three of you are the forces that drive everything I do and I love you very much. Micah, thank you for being my assistant when testing recipes. You are always the best kitchen assistant a mom could ask for and your kitchen skills have tremendously improved!

A huge thank you to my literary agent, Sally Ekus, from the Lisa Ekus Group, who always believed in me. Thanks to Jaimee Constantine and Sara Pokorny from The Lisa Ekus Group for your kindness and support throughout the process. Many thanks to Robert Dees from Robert Rose Inc. for teaming up with me on this project and believing in me. To my fabulous editor, Kate Bolen, thank you for your continued support, guidance and patience throughout this project. I cannot think of a better editor to work with than you! Thanks to Kevin Cockburn for the design of this book. Lastly, thank you to Ashley Lima for continuing to work on the photography for my cookbooks and for being the best food photographer a gal could ask for!

INDEX